Standing on Principle

Standing on Principle

Lessons Learned in Public Life

JAMES J. FLORIO

Foreword by Senator Bill Bradley

RUTGERS UNIVERSITY PRESS
NEW BRUNSWICK, CAMDEN, AND NEWARK,
NEW JERSEY, AND LONDON

EAGLETON
INSTITUTE
of POLITICS

Published in cooperation with the Center on the American Governor, Eagleton Institute of Politics, Rutgers University

A Cataloging-in-Publication record for this book is available from the Library of Congress.

A British Cataloging-in-Publication record for this book is available from the British Library.

978-0-8135-9430-9
978-0-8135-9429-3
978-0-8135-9431-6
978-0-8135-9433-0

♾ The paper used in this publication meets the requirements of the American National Standard for Information Sciences—Permanence of Paper for Printed Library Materials, ANSI Z39.48-1992.

www.rutgersuniversitypress.org

Manufactured in the United States of America

This book is dedicated to my grandchildren—Matthew, Chelsea, Alexandra, Elizabeth, Peter, Victoria, Stephanie, Jack, Bret, and Troy—so they will know what their "Pop Pop" did.

Contents

Foreword

Senator Bill Bradley

Jim Florio has always been his own man. He was a politician whose strength was rooted in substance. He cared about ideas. He cared even more about policy and good government, from his work on the initial Superfund Bill to clean up toxic wastes, to economic development strategies during his time as governor. He always thought of the long term, a very rare political trait.

In my first campaign for the Senate, he was part of a very small—very small!—group of New Jersey political leaders who endorsed me in the primary. For that, I am forever grateful.

He built a strong organization in South Jersey—one that was independent of the county organization. He had a loyal following among young people, who admired his idealism; among the business community, who appreciated his openness; and among the public, who felt his compassion. He led by example. No one was going to outwork him and all knew that as a former boxer he could take a punch—and give one.

While his service in the Congress was admirable, being governor is where he left his biggest mark. New Jersey has had a continuing fiscal crisis for many decades, with the issue of taxes and spending at the core of any state politician's career.

Most politicians get state money in three ways: they either raise taxes to fund commitments, especially in transportation, education, pensions, and health; they borrow money so they can keep those commitments; or in the case of pensions, they make rosy assumptions about pension fund investment performance, thereby freeing up money to spend that should be going to shore up our solemn commitments to working people.

Jim Florio was different. He saw that he had a budget problem. He cut spending and found it did not close the budget gap enough. He then raised taxes, which outraged the public, which ignored the benefits it derived from government. He was castigated and demonized by political opponents and even the press. But those who opposed him offered no alternative, and post-Florio the New Jersey financial circumstance has only gone downhill. It is always easier to pass the problem on to the next governor. Jim Florio and Harry Truman agreed—the buck stopped with the leader. Many politicians run away from that thought. Jim faced it.

The gauge of fiscally responsible government in this regard is found in the state's bond rating. If there are giant gaps in funding for pensions and health care and other spending, bond ratings drop. If bond ratings drop, the state will have to pay more in interest. It's a very simple proposition: pay now or pay more later. One of the most telling details about Jim is that he had the highest bond rating of any governor of New Jersey in the last thirty years. But then, he had raised taxes, paying the price that real leaders are prepared to pay to secure the future of their state.

I think history will be very kind to Jim Florio. He's a man who made the tough choices and lived to take pride in them. I hope when people finish this book that they'll see the full dimension of his leadership and come to admire the man even more.

Prologue

Maybe the best way to explain what I want this book to be about is to first describe what it isn't about.

This book is not a compendium or recitation of facts about my public career. That information can be found in the 600+ cases of documents in the State Archives in Trenton that contain the exhaustive details of my four-year gubernatorial term; in references in the Library of Congress to the 400+ pieces of major legislation in which I was intimately involved during my fifteen years in the House of Representatives; and in the Eagleton Institute of Politics' remarkable Center on the American Governor series, which has compiled more facts and information about me than could ever be condensed into a single book.

This is also not a "tell-all" book. I met many fascinating political characters, both good and bad, during my decades in public office. Many life-changing issues and events occurred between my first campaign for the New Jersey General Assembly in 1969 and my last campaign for the U.S. Senate in 2000. But there are no political scandals or secrets to tell of in my own life—although there are, up front, two facts in my private life that even some of my closest friends and associates may not be aware of: (1) my younger brother Bill was gay, and he died of AIDS in 1991; and (2) my father Vincenzo, after being diagnosed with a terminal illness and fearful that the enormous monthly out-of-pocket pharmaceutical expenses he was bearing would leave my mother penniless, committed suicide.

Both of these events hit me hard. I've never talked openly about them—I felt they were intensely private matters—but I've thought a lot about how my brother had to live in the shadows for so much of his life and how society's slowness to accept the LGBTQ lifestyle allowed the AIDS epidemic to spread unchecked for so many years before researchers developed effective treatment. And I've thought about how unfair it is that the richest country on earth still thinks of health care as a privilege rather than a right, forcing people like my father to choose between a life of poverty or self-inflicted death.

This book is about the major public issues and battles of my life, first as an elected public officeholder for nearly a quarter-century, and subsequently as a teacher for nearly the same length of time at the college level. If there is a confession to make, it is that I am a dedicated policy wonk. And the issues that were important to me at the beginning of my public life are just as relevant and challenging today as they were nearly fifty years ago.

This book is also about the people who were dedicated and committed to my ideas and supported me in the causes I have fought for—many from the beginning to the end of my career, and many who urged me for years to tell "my side of the story." None is more important than my wife Lucinda, who literally changed my life.

For as much as I have taught and been involved in politics and public policy, I have also learned a great many important and valuable lessons from the many political campaigns and policy fights in which I have engaged over the years—probably as much, if not more, from the losing campaigns and fights than the winning ones.

If my philosophy of achieving political success can be summed up in a single phrase, it is to "engage and inform" on the issues—to make sure that combatants and constituencies, the voters and the public, are engaged and informed in the decision-making process and that they are provided with the information they need to make sound, rational decisions.

That is why I have chosen to begin my story not in chronological order but with the fight for a ban on assault weapons in New Jersey, which I proudly signed into law on May 30, 1990, four months after taking office as governor. This ban, still in effect today, led to one of the greatest honors of my life: receiving the "Profile in Courage" award from the John F. Kennedy Presidential Library and Museum three years later.

I hope this book also serves as a lesson, not only for my grandchildren but also for the many students who passed through my classrooms and seminars over the years. If public service was my vocation, teaching has always been my passion.

To sum up the lessons I have learned and what I would want most to impart to others, let me quote the final line in John Steinbeck's *In Dubious Battle*, which I first read as a freshman in college. It is a book that had a profound effect on me as a young man trying to choose a career path, and it is a quote that has sustained me in my drive to combat unfairness throughout my public life.

Those final words, uttered as a eulogy over the dead body of Steinbeck's hero, Jim—a labor organizer killed in a Depression-era strike that turned violent—are simply this: "This guy didn't want nothing for himself—he didn't want nothing for himself."

Standing on Principle

CHAPTER 1

The Assault Weapons Ban

"One person of courage can make a majority."

—Sen. Edward M. Kennedy

I begin my story with this fight because it captures and represents my belief that any issue, even the thorniest and most emotional, can be won if the people are engaged and informed. It is also a case study of how representative democracy is supposed to work, with the broad public interest prevailing over a narrow special interest.

On January 17, 1989, a young man dressed in military fatigues walked onto the playground at Cleveland Elementary School in Stockton, California, and went on a three-minute shooting rampage with a semiautomatic, Chinese-made AK-47 rifle.

The gunman, twenty-four-year-old Patrick Edward Purdy, fired 105 rounds into the crowd of at least 300 pupils from the first through third grades who were playing during the noontime recess. Five children between the ages of six and nine, all of them refugees from Southeast Asia, were killed, and more than thirty teachers and students were wounded, before Purdy pulled out a 9 mm pistol and shot himself in the head.

According to a report by the California attorney general's office, Purdy had a lengthy history of mental illness, several brushes with the law, and a well-documented hatred of minorities and immigrants—in particular the Vietnamese, who were in his view receiving unwarranted compensation from the U.S. government.

Two weeks before the shooting, Purdy, clad in camouflage clothing and a fatigue jacket, told a bartender in Stockton that he had an AK-47 and was ready to use it. The bartender told him a gun like that wouldn't do him much good if he was going to go deer hunting. Purdy, holding out his arms and demonstrating how he would fire the weapon in a spraying motion, back and forth from side to side, replied, "You're going to read about me in the papers."

All of America read about—and was shocked by—the Stockton school-yard massacre. Long before towns like Columbine, Colorado, and New-town, Connecticut, became household names, Stockton, California, was the site of the first mass shooting of schoolchildren in America.

The gunman, it turned out, had purchased the AK-47 legally in Oregon in the summer of 1988. Some months later, he bought a seventy-five-round drum magazine, an additional thirty-round magazine, and ten boxes of ammunition for the AK-47 legally in Connecticut. Although he was under a condition of probation that prohibited him from possessing firearms, and had been committed to a mental health facility for treatment because he was deemed dangerous to himself and others, he bought the handgun he used to kill himself legally in California.

The California legislature responded promptly to the mass murder, approving a law in May 1989 (to take effect on January 1, 1990) that made it a crime, punishable by a term of four to eight years in prison, for any civilian to "import, manufacture, distribute, sell, give or lend" any assault weapon—defined as a weapon that has "such a high rate of fire and capacity for firepower that its function as a legitimate sports or recreational firearm is substantially outweighed by the danger that it can be used to kill and injure human beings."

Sarah Brady, chairwoman of Handgun Control, Inc., the advocacy group she and her husband James founded after he was shot and permanently disabled in the assassination attempt on President Ronald Reagan in 1981, said California's action should send a "strong signal to Congress that Americans want to take back our streets." She urged President George H. W. Bush and Congress to "follow California's lead."

President Bush, a life member of the National Rifle Association and an avowed opponent of gun control, was not inclined to do so. Instead, he resisted calls in Congress—and across the country—for federal legislation similar to California's. Only after concerned law-enforcement officials and his director of national drug policy, William J. Bennett, prevailed on him to take action did the president declare a ban on the import (but not the manufacture, distribution, or sale) of semiautomatic assault rifles.

The ban did not affect virtually identical weapons manufactured in the United States, which made it not only palatable but also economically favorable to domestic weapons manufacturers. Nor did it affect an estimated 750,000 foreign-made semiautomatic weapons already in the hands of American gun owners.

And that, as 1989 came to a close, is as far as federal action on this issue went.

I have never owned a gun. I have never in my life fired a gun. In my four years in the navy, I never used a gun. When I worked as a night watchman while going to law school, I never carried a gun.

In my three terms in the New Jersey General Assembly and my eight terms in the U.S. Congress, however, I represented a great many people who owned, fired, used, and carried guns. A substantial number of my constituents in Camden, Gloucester, and Burlington Counties were hunters—or, as they preferred to call themselves, sportsmen.

I generally enjoyed support from them and from organized South Jersey gun groups, because they liked my stand on the environment. They appreciated the fact that I worked to preserve open space, which expanded their ability to hunt.

There was, for example, a very active organization in Gibbsboro called the Square Circle Sportsmen of Camden County. It was a genuinely friendly, down-to-earth group of responsible, law-abiding gun owners. They would invite me regularly to join them for events like family picnics, and I would attend and have a really nice time.

Yet the assassination attempt on President Reagan, and the subsequent emergence of Sarah and James Brady's organization as a forceful advocate for gun control, had sensitized me to the importance of this issue. The only significant piece of gun-related legislation that came before Congress during my tenure was the Firearms Owners' Protection Act of 1986, a bill that actually eased rather than toughened restrictions on the sale of guns. But I supported an important amendment, introduced by my colleague, Bill Hughes, of the neighboring 2nd Congressional District, that would forbid the sale to civilians of all automatic weapons made after the law took effect. Much to President Reagan's credit, he signed the bill, with the Hughes Amendment attached.

The Stockton shooting brought this issue back into the public eye in 1989 and turned the focus of attention from automatic to semiautomatic weapons. As California was crafting its response to Stockton and the Bush administration was taking steps to ban the import of semiautomatic weapons, I was running for governor of New Jersey.

Issues related to "law and order" arose regularly during the campaign, but mostly they revolved around the question of whether my opponent, Congressman Jim Courter, or I was taking the more forceful stance on the death penalty. Although I have since concluded that the death penalty serves neither as an effective deterrent to crime nor as an appropriate punishment, at the time I favored it in very specific, limited circumstances. Congressman Courter, in contrast, said he wanted to shorten the time from conviction to execution by eliminating some of the avenues of appeal.

Guns and gun control did not seem to be a prominent concern among voters, and although I let it be known that I felt something needed to be done at the state level about semiautomatic weapons, this did not arise as a significant campaign issue.

Still, I was deeply moved by the events in Stockton, and I couldn't get a nagging question out of the back of my mind: Why should anyone in New Jersey be allowed to carry around an assault rifle? Intuitively, I just sensed there was overwhelming public sentiment in agreement, that there's something fundamentally wrong when people are shot in their communities with weapons of war.

So I was determined, soon after taking office as governor in January 1990, to push for legislation that would ban the sale, and severely limit ownership, of assault weapons in New Jersey.

From the very start, I knew that getting a tough assault weapons bill through both houses of the New Jersey legislature would not be easy. Although the size of my victory in the gubernatorial race had generated some coattails, leading to Democratic majorities of 23–17 in the New Jersey Senate and 44–36 in the General Assembly, there were plenty of legislators, both Democrat and Republican, whose districts, like my former legislative and congressional districts, contained substantial numbers of gun owners.

Not that New Jersey was ever home to a large gun-toting constituency. The combination of the state's small size and dense population severely limits the amount of land available for hunting, trap shooting, target practice, or other recreational activities that involve firearms. In 1989, 46 percent of American households had at least one firearm; in the decade from 1981 to 1990, the corresponding figure in New Jersey was 36.3 percent. In the decade that followed, that proportion dropped to 33.3 percent.

Nevertheless, the State Police estimated that the number of semiautomatic weapons in the hands of New Jersey residents in 1990 was somewhere between 200,000 and 300,000. And there were plenty of vocal members of active gun-owner groups, like my friends from the Square

Circle Sportsmen, all across New Jersey, especially in the rural parts of the state: Sussex, Warren, and Hunterdon Counties in the north and Cape May, Cumberland, and Salem Counties in the south.

There was also a very active statewide lobbying group—the Coalition of New Jersey Sportsmen—that had a large and influential membership. And, of course, the National Rifle Association (NRA) was not going to sit idly by while New Jersey debated a bill that would take certain weapons out of its members' hands. In fact, between 1990, when I called on the legislature to ban assault weapons, and 1993, NRA membership in New Jersey jumped from 4,000 to 12,000.

We did have a couple of factors working in our favor. For one thing, opinion polls showed that a clear majority of New Jerseyans supported an assault weapons ban. Second, leaders in both houses of the legislature were working tirelessly to round up the votes necessary to pass the bill and send it to my desk for signature.

One of these leaders, Assembly Speaker Joe Doria, was very supportive and undertook this task with enthusiasm. The other, Senate President John Lynch, was more apprehensive. He agreed to shepherd the bill through the upper house, and he ended up doing so masterfully, but he warned me early on that there would be political consequences. In fact, he told me point-blank, "This will kill you. You don't want to do this."

John had good political insights. He knew how the gun lobby and the sportsmen's clubs would respond. He knew there would be pushback in his own caucus from members who were either gun owners themselves or represented districts where gun ownership was an important issue.

He was absolutely right in the sense that, politically, pushing what we knew would be a controversial bill to ban assault weapons didn't make a lot of sense. But to me, it did make sense as a matter of public policy. I told John I appreciated the political difficulties this would cause, but it was something I felt strongly about. And he was fine with that. He was loyal. He went out and fought for it and got it passed, even though he knew there would be serious repercussions.

In retrospect, the scene that unfolded in the assembly chamber on May 17, 1990, should have given us an inkling of what was to come. That was the day the assembly, after four-and-a-half hours of intense debate, voted 43–33 to give final approval to the assault weapons ban. It was also a day that people who were there still say, more than a quarter-century later, was one of the scariest they've ever lived through.

An estimated 400 demonstrators, many of them wearing bright-orange hunting vests, jammed the hallway outside the assembly chamber, which was temporarily housed in the State House Annex while the old chamber was undergoing renovations. Armed with walkie-talkies and loudspeakers, the demonstrators chanted, "Florio must go." They banged on the windows. They raised their hands in a salute, with thumb and forefinger extended in the shape of a pistol. One carried a Nazi flag with the words "Florio's New Jersey" written on it. State troopers had to be called in to keep the mob scene from turning violent.

The demonstrations weren't limited to the State House. Protesters turned up outside Drumthwacket, the governor's residence in Princeton, shouting insults and holding up posters depicting me with a Hitler moustache. Inside, my wife Lucinda was horrified; she said she had never in her life witnessed the level of incivility unleashed by passage of the assault weapons bill.

The law I signed less than two weeks later banned the purchase of all assault weapons in New Jersey. Unlike the California law that had taken effect earlier in the year, our law did not exempt current owners; instead, it severely restricted possession of any assault weapon not used for legitimate collecting or target-shooting purposes. Current owners were given one year to either sell their weapon or render it inoperable by certifying that the parts necessary to fire it had been removed from their immediate possession, making the gun purely a collector's piece.

"I am proud to sign this bill into law today," I said as I put my signature to it. "It's the toughest law in the nation. It's right. It's fair, and it will make New Jersey a better place."

Little did I know that, after we had fought such a bitter fight to get this law enacted, an even tougher fight lay ahead—to save it.

⋘⋙

Despite the commotion they had caused outside the assembly chamber, the NRA and the Coalition of New Jersey Sportsmen knew that public sentiment was not on their side. They saw the same surveys we saw, indicating that 80 percent of New Jersey voters supported the assault weapons ban. So instead of pushing for outright repeal of the law, they sought to weaken it—and they found the legislature receptive.

By the spring of 1991, legislators in both houses were in full election mode. Because of redistricting following the 1990 census, every seat in both the senate and assembly would be on the ballot in November, and the gun lobby was already putting a target on legislators who had voted for the assault weapons ban.

On May 23, hundreds of gun advocates returned to the State House, clamoring for the assembly to pass an amendment, already approved by the senate, that would allow current owners to keep and register their assault weapons. That evening, the same assembly that had voted 43–33 for the assault weapons ban a year earlier voted 48–25 to weaken it.

I understood why certain legislators believed their vote for a complete ban on assault weapons made them vulnerable in their bid for re-election and why they felt compelled to support the amendment that would weaken the law. Neither party loyalty nor statewide polls could necessarily compete with the loud voices of local constituents. One South Jersey Democrat in particular, Senator Ray Zane, represented mostly rural parts of Cumberland, Gloucester, and Salem Counties where gun ownership was practically a way of life, and there was no way a vote in favor of any form of gun control would be welcomed in his district.

But I also knew—and the legislators did too—that voting for the amendment to weaken the assault weapons ban was largely a symbolic exercise. There was never any doubt that I would veto it. Nor was there any doubt that the legislature, still in the hands of Democrats, would fail to override the veto. Yet by voting for the amendment, legislators who might be targeted by the NRA and the Coalition of New Jersey Sportsmen could tell them, "Don't blame me, blame Florio."

Those groups did blame me, of course. But they didn't spare the legislators, and neither did the voters, who were angry about a lot of other things in November 1991. A powerful anti-tax movement, spurred by a grassroots organization calling itself Hands Across New Jersey (and enthusiastically supported by a fledgling FM radio station, New Jersey 101.5, that was looking to make a statewide name for itself), swept Democratic lawmakers out of office in record numbers.

The NRA and the Coalition of New Jersey Sportsmen contributed $25,000 to the assembly Republican majority and more than $250,000 to the campaigns of candidates they knew to be hostile to gun control. We were to learn later that the NRA was also a silent but significant financial benefactor to Hands Across New Jersey.

When the dust settled after the November 1991 election, Republicans had won veto-proof majorities in both houses: 27–13 in the senate and 58–22 in the assembly. That set the stage for the *real* battle over assault weapons.

It was readily apparent from the moment the 205th New Jersey legislature convened in January 1992 that repeal of the assault weapons ban would be among its highest priorities. The new assembly Speaker, Garabed "Chuck" Haytaian, declared early on that his constituents in rural Warren County, together with many senior law-enforcement officers, were urging his GOP colleagues and him to repeal the ban.

As contentious as this issue was, and as aggressively as the new Republican majority pressed for repeal, it's important to note that the battle inside the State House never descended to the level of personal attacks that were being hurled by the NRA and its supporters outside the legislative chambers. Chuck Haytaian was a tough opponent; he and I had decidedly different views on this issue, as well as on many others. But we always treated each other cordially and respectfully.

Another illustration of the difference between disagreeing and being disagreeable is my relationship with Don Sico, who served as Haytaian's chief of staff after Republicans captured the majority. He worked as hard in that capacity to repeal the assault weapons ban in 1992 as he had worked as former congressman Jim Courter's communication director to defeat me in the 1989 election. But these battles were always political, never personal. In the years since we both left public office, Don and I have worked closely on a number of projects of mutual interest. Today, I count him as a close personal friend.

⟨⟨⟨⟩

In May 1992, repeal legislation sailed through the assembly by a 55–18 vote. The senate later approved a slightly different version. When the two houses reconciled the two bills in August, the final vote was 28–10 in the senate and 47–16 in the assembly. Once again, everyone knew I would veto the bill—but this time, with the vote for repeal in both houses having surpassed the two-thirds majority necessary to override a veto, it was widely assumed that the assault weapons law was headed for the dustbin of history.

I had forty-five days to veto the bill. I decided to use that time to launch a campaign to engage and inform the public, to encourage the voices of citizens to prevail over the influence of a powerful special interest.

I brought my staff together and said, "We're going to do this. We have the time. We're going to mobilize everyone." And that's what we did.

The engage-and-inform strategy began on the very day the legislature voted to repeal the assault weapons ban. I happened to be hosting a meeting of the National Governors Association in Princeton, and I asked two of my fellow governors, William Donald Schaefer of Maryland and John Waihee III of Hawaii, to join me at the Mercer County Detention Center for a demonstration of the firepower of military-style weapons.

With the media looking on, a State Police sergeant laid down a barrage of fire with three assault weapons—an AK-47, Uzi, and Intratec 9 pistol—at the rate of five or six shots per second. The reporters witnessed, and the cameras captured, a vivid display of one-gallon plastic milk jugs filled with red liquid being blown to bits. Governor Schaefer, who had been trying for years to get an assault weapons ban passed in Maryland, said the demonstration gave vivid testimony to his belief that assault weapons "have only one purpose—to kill people."

In our public campaign, we had the help of a Methodist minister in Cape May, the Rev. Jack Johnson, who offered to rally the clergy, encouraging ministers and priests to talk about their experiences presiding at the funerals of gunshot victims. We engaged the health care community—doctors and nurses who had treated gunshot wounds in emergency rooms, including a physician at the University of Medicine and Dentistry, Dr. Eric Muñoz, who testified that the Department of Defense came to Newark to train their medical staff on gunshot wounds because they were so common in our state's largest city. We got teachers to talk about their experiences with children who had been exposed to gun violence.

Attorney General Bob DelTufo and State Police Superintendent Justin Dintino led the long list of prominent law-enforcement professionals who supported the ban. In Camden County, law-enforcement officials lamented that they were hesitant to send police into North Camden because the neighborhood criminals, armed with semiautomatic weapons, had more firepower than the police had. After a fifteen-year-old girl was shot and killed in Paterson, I spoke at the scene of the shooting and held up a weapon like the one that killed her as tearful family members and friends looked on.

I even took my campaign into the belly of the beast, getting a not-so-friendly reception from the Square Circle Sportsmen in Gibbsboro. I wanted to know why the people who had supported me for so many years were so bitterly opposed to a ban on assault weapons. "Does anybody here have an assault weapon?" I asked. "No," they answered. "Does anybody here hunt with one?" I asked. "No," they replied. So, I said, "Well, what's your problem?" One of the members volunteered, "Well, we learned from the NRA that once these things start, you have that slippery slope. The next thing is you'll be taking away our weapons." I asked pointedly, "You think I'm going to take away your hunting rifle?" Nobody responded.

I vetoed the bill on September 9, and we kept up the pressure. President Bill Clinton hailed our assault weapons ban as a national model and called on Congress to adopt the Brady Bill to outlaw assault weapons nationwide. (It took another two years, but Congress did pass that bill and Clinton signed it into law for a period of ten years.) The namesake of that federal law, James Brady, came to my office in a wheelchair to show his support. Gregory Peck made a television commercial urging residents to oppose efforts in the legislature to override my veto. Even my predecessor as governor, Tom Kean, said of his fellow Republicans' effort to repeal the law, "It's dead wrong. I don't know what the lawful purpose could be in owning an assault weapon."

An Eagleton Poll taken shortly before the assembly scheduled a vote to override the veto found that 90 percent of New Jerseyans favored the assault weapons ban. In my veto message on September 9, I had recommended that instead of calling for an override vote, the legislature should let the public decide in referendum whether the ban should be retained or repealed. A few lawmakers got cold feet, including four Republicans who bucked their party's leadership in the assembly by voting to sustain the veto, but the lower house voted to override by the barest possible two-thirds majority, 54–23, on February 25, 1993—despite the public's overwhelming support for the ban.

Now it was up to the senate, which lived up to the role our Founding Fathers envisioned: it performed as the more deliberative legislative body. Senate President Donald DiFrancesco (affectionately referred to by his colleagues on both sides of the aisle as "Donnie D.") was being pressured behind the scenes by several Republican senators who had voted for repeal, and even by some assembly members who had voted for the veto override, not to post the override bill. He also let it be known in the GOP caucus that he personally felt that overriding the veto was not in his party's interest. In addition, the only Republican senator who had voted for the assault weapons ban and against repeal, Bill Gormley of Atlantic County, made it clear he wasn't about to change his mind.

These two Republican senators earned my deepest gratitude for standing up to the extraordinary pressure brought to bear on them by the NRA. Even more, they deserve the gratitude of all New Jersey citizens for their courageous decision to do what was right, to put the public interest ahead of a powerful special interest.

By the time the override bill reached the senate floor on March 15, 1993, the momentum that had driven it through the assembly had ground to a halt, and support for it in the upper house had evaporated. In the end, twenty-six senators—Senate President DiFrancesco, Senator Gormley, fourteen of their fellow Republicans, and ten Democrats—voted to sustain the veto; the other fourteen senators abstained. Not a single member of the senate of either party cast a vote to override the veto.

The assault weapons ban stood—and it still stands today.

⋘

Two months later, on May 24, 1993, I had the honor of accepting the fourth annual Profile in Courage Award from the trustees of the John F. Kennedy Presidential Library and Museum. It was one of the proudest moments of my life.

The award citation read, in part:

> On May 30, 1990, under Governor Florio's leadership, New Jersey passed the strictest gun control law in the nation, banning the sale and severely restricting the possession of assault weapons in the state. The action was a significant legislative victory for Florio, who was then engaged in a public and political battle over his reforms to the state tax and education systems. The 1990 gun control victory launched a

Profile in Courage
May 24, 1993
Governor James J. Florio of New Jersey

Taking a strong stand against the rising tide of weapons and violence in his state, James Florio became one of the first and few governors in America to defy the national gun lobby and all its political forces and resources. He courageously vetoed a new and hostile legislature's repeal of a statewide ban on assault weapons, and mobilized the people of his state to sustain his veto. He waged this battle at a time when his prospects for reelection were in continuing grave jeopardy from his decision, upon taking office in 1990, to deal boldly with the state's unprecedented fiscal crisis, its unconstitutional school finance system, and its unjust property tax assessments. His far-reaching plan of educational, budget, and tax reforms has enhanced educational quality and fiscal stability in his state, and has provided a model for the nation of wise political vision and courageous political leadership in facing up to the economic and social challenges of our times.

President,
John F. Kennedy
Library Foundation

Chairman,
Profile in Courage
Award Committee

Governor Florio's "Profile in Courage" award citation

three-year-long battle with the National Rifle Association, gun rights activists, sports organizations, and the state legislature.

In 1991, after an intense lobbying effort by the NRA and gun rights activists, the same Democratic-controlled legislature that passed the assault weapon ban voted to weaken it—even though 80 percent of New Jersey voters supported it. Although Governor Florio vetoed the amendments, the NRA refused to concede defeat and strengthened their efforts. In 1992, the new Republican-controlled legislature voted to overturn the ban and legalize the sale and possession of assault weapons. Determined to maintain a firm stand against the special interests of the gun lobbyists, Governor Florio again vetoed the bill.

Despite legislative attempts to override his vetoes and tireless efforts by gun lobbyists, who spent nearly one million dollars to defeat the assault weapon ban, Governor Florio succeeded in mobilizing the people of New Jersey into an unprecedented counterforce against the NRA and in support of the ban, demonstrating, as Florio said, that "the State of New Jersey will not be held hostage by the lobbying efforts of the National Rifle Association." In March 1993, the state senate voted . . . to uphold the Governor's veto.

In my acceptance speech, I focused on what was, and has always been, my abiding philosophy about government, politics, and public life:

As special as this day is for Lucinda and me, I must tell you, I look forward to another day—when public servants who follow the dictates of their conscience are regarded not as heroes worthy of awards, but simply as men and women worthy of the offices to which they are entrusted.

We don't get to choose the times in which we live, but we do get the chance to determine how we respond to those times. We can consign our children to inadequate schools, or we can choose to make our schools better. We can stand by and watch our economy slowly crumble, or we can choose to invest again in our people and their potential. We can cower at the threats of powerful special interest groups who would put the deadliest weapons into the hands of criminals, or we can dare to break their grip and take back our democracy.

It's up to us.

In New Jersey, we're trying to live up to our responsibility by standing up to the gun lobby on behalf of safety and sanity, and standing up for the right of every child to get the education that will allow them to live up to their boldest dreams.

You know, the first thing I learned as governor is that you can't please everybody. The second thing I learned is, some days, you can't please anybody. So be it. Conflict is inevitable. It's the price we pay for change in a democracy.

If I've taken stands that have sometimes upset some people—and I have—it's not because I hold their opinion in contempt. It is because, as President Kennedy wrote in *Profiles*, I have "faith in people's ultimate sense of justice, faith in their ability to honor courage and respect judgment, and faith that in the long run they will act unselfishly for the good of the nation."

As governor, I've seen that faith in action. And I've had my own faith strengthened by it.

⋘

Winning the battle over assault weapons wasn't a victory for me. In fact, it may very well have been one of the key reasons I lost my bid for re-election in 1993. It was, however, a decisive victory for the people of New Jersey over a powerful, vocal, and well-organized special interest.

Such battles are not easily won. Whether they are fought in Washington, in state capitals, or in city or town halls across the country, efforts to enact change always run up against opposition from those who benefit from keeping things the way they are. Every local zoning amendment has the potential to adversely affect a business, a homeowner, a landlord, or a tenant who will rise in protest. Every adjustment to the formula for allocating state aid to school districts will provoke outrage from teachers, students, and/or those who pay property tax. Every serious attempt over the last thirty years to reform the federal tax code (as opposed to simply cutting taxes for the wealthy) has been doomed to failure because there are so many people—and so many organized, powerful, and vocal groups—who have a vested interest in preserving the status quo.

But our experience in New Jersey shows that it is possible, when citizens are engaged and informed, for the public interest to prevail over even the most organized, powerful, and vocal special interest. It takes hard work. It takes an appeal to reason over emotion. It takes implicit faith in people's understanding that the strength of our democracy comes not from satisfying everyone's self-interest but from assuring the achievement of our collective interest, our shared well-being, our common good.

That is why I don't consider the ban on assault weapons a personal triumph. I think of it, instead, as one of New Jersey's finest achievements.

Today, just 12.3 percent of New Jersey's residents own guns. Only Hawaii and the District of Columbia have lower rates of gun ownership. In 2015, New Jersey residents registered a total of 54,612 weapons, compared to 225,377 in neighboring Pennsylvania. In 1990, the year before our assault weapons ban took effect, New Jersey ranked twenty-fourth in the nation in the incidence of violent and property crimes. In 2015, it ranked forty-ninth.

Regrettably, what we have achieved in New Jersey has been the exception, rather than the rule. The federal assault weapons ban that was adopted by Congress and signed into law by President Clinton in 1994 expired in 2004, and the number of firearms manufactured in the United States has skyrocketed since then, from a little more than three million in 1994 to nearly eleven million in 2013.

The United States has by far the highest rate of gun ownership in the world—88.8 per 1,000 residents, far ahead of second-place Yemen's 54.8 per 1,000 residents. At the same time, even without gun control at the national level, the percentage of American households with guns has dropped from 46 percent in 1989 to 31 percent in 2016. A recent study by

Harvard and Northeastern universities found that the 242 million adults living in the United States possess 265 million guns; remarkably, half of these guns belong to only 3 percent of the adult population.

Virtually every mass shooting that has taken place in the United States in recent years has been carried out with assault weapons: Aurora (2012), Newtown (2012), San Bernardino (2015), Orlando (2016), and Las Vegas (2017). The NRA response to these massacres has been to make a sales pitch for weapons manufacturers. If moviegoers in Aurora, teachers in Newtown, office workers in San Bernardino, nightclubbers in Orlando, and country music concertgoers in Las Vegas had been armed with their own cache of weapons, the NRA contends, the carnage would have been avoided.

This isn't just nonsense. It's a clarion call to turn twenty-first-century America into a vigilante state, a modern version of the Wild West. The Bureau of Alcohol, Tobacco, and Firearms announced recently that there are now more guns than people in the United States. And the NRA thinks that's not enough?

The NRA hides behind the Second Amendment to the Constitution, which holds that a "well regulated Militia, being necessary to the security of a free State, the right of the people to keep and bear Arms, shall not be infringed." There is nothing in this language that says it is unreasonable to impose restrictions on gun ownership and the types of guns available. The courts have consistently held that reasonable regulations on the sale and use of firearms are clearly constitutional.

Isn't it reasonable to believe that hunters don't need thirty-, fifty-, or one hundred-round clips for their firearms?

Isn't it reasonable to be concerned that the purchasers of weapons at gun shows, who represent an estimated 40 percent of gun owners, aren't subject to background checks?

Isn't it reasonable to ask why someone on the terrorist watch list can't board a plane, but can buy a gun?

Isn't it reasonable to question why we buy protective vests for police officers and then allow the sale of cop-killer bullets?

An overwhelming majority of Americans consistently tell pollsters that steps to limit the sales of such guns and ammunition are eminently reasonable, that state and federal lawmakers are defying public sentiment when they refuse to take a common-sense approach to gun control. The reason so many of them don't can be summed up in a single word: fear.

We have learned throughout history that a dedicated minority—a cadre of people who are true believers in a cause and have the resources to back up their beliefs—can prevail over the general public by striking fear into the hearts of politicians who are more concerned with getting re-elected than with doing what's right or even what's popular. The NRA has used this tactic most effectively. They are not at all subtle about threatening any incumbent who would dare oppose them, and they can use me as Exhibit A. You want to know what we do to politicians who cross the NRA? Ask Jim Florio.

To take my experience as a lesson in why I should *not* have pushed the assault weapons ban, however, is to miss the fundamental principle that should guide political action and public service. I stood up to the NRA, and they were instrumental in denying me re-election. But they did not prevent the assault weapons ban from becoming law, nor were they successful in their persistent efforts to repeal the law. This was a conflict between the NRA and the people of New Jersey. And the people won.

CHAPTER 2

From Red Hook to Camden

Values Start with the Family

Looking back on my childhood, thinking about the neighborhood where I grew up, and the personality characteristics I inherited from my parents, no one would have believed that my chosen profession would be politics. Only in retrospect did I come to understand that, as with most people, my values and many of my subsequent actions were largely shaped in my formative years.

I was born in a public housing project in the Red Hook section of Brooklyn, a rough-and-tumble neighborhood with a historic past. Robert Fulton's steamboat was launched from the Brooklyn Navy Yard in Red Hook; so were the *Monitor*, the nation's first ironclad ship, and the *Maine*, whose sinking triggered the Spanish-American War. The USS *Arizona*, destroyed in the Japanese attack on Pearl Harbor that sparked the United States' entry into World War II, and the USS *Missouri*, on whose deck the Japanese signed the surrender that ended that same war, were both built at the Brooklyn Navy Yard.

Red Hook was more than the shipyard, however, and its surrounding streets took on a notorious character, perhaps best described by author Tim Sultan in his 2016 memoir, *Sunny's Nights: Lost and Found at a Bar on*

James Joseph Florio receives Birth Certificate No. 28118 following his
August 29, 1937, arrival at Cumberland Hospital in Brooklyn, New York.

the Edge of the World. The neighborhood around Sunny's Bar on Conover
Street, he wrote, was a place where "bootleggers distilled, arsonists lit,
nuns crossed, longshoremen hauled, unions agitated, kids pelted, gangs
brawled."

By the time I was born in 1937, there weren't many bootleggers left, and
I don't recall knowing any arsonists—but there were plenty of nuns, longshoremen, unions, kids, and gangs. You could certainly call it a "color-
ful" neighborhood, and that is where my family lived for the first four or
five years of my life.

We moved out of Red Hook in the early 1940s to a rented row house on
East Seventh Street in Flatbush, a block east of Ocean Parkway. The neighborhood was peppered with Italian, Irish, Polish, and other identifiable
ethnic enclaves, but this part of Flatbush was predominantly Jewish. From
the time we moved there until I joined the navy a dozen years later, I actually thought that most of the rest of the world was Jewish.

Our house had a front porch and a little bit of lawn. We lived on the first floor; there were neighbors on the second floor, and people lived in the attic as well. I had my own bedroom. After my younger brothers, Bill and Dick, were born, they shared another bedroom. It was a coal-fired house, and my first (unpaid) job was to take out the ashes every night.

My first paid job, at the age of twelve, was delivering the *Brooklyn Daily Eagle*. Later I was a delivery boy for Harold Goodman's grocery store. Then the store next door, Louis Balitsky's Kosher Meat Market, lured me away, and I began delivering Jewish delicacies to families, most of them Reform Jews, in the area along Ocean Parkway. Still later, I was employed by the city's park system. I pushed a little cart in Prospect Park offering ice cream and frozen Milky Ways for sale, and at the end of the summer I got promoted to be the balloon guy. I had a helium tank in the shape of a big clown and would blow up balloons and sell them.

Even from a young age, I was always a worker. I didn't mind hard work; in fact, I enjoyed it. And there was the added incentive from my mother, who told me I could keep all the money I earned and use it to buy clothes. The proceeds from selling ice cream, frozen Milky Ways, and balloons had me decked out in style—peg pants with pistol pockets and a snazzy pair of blue suede shoes.

⋘

The saying that every child combines the characteristics of his or her parents certainly applied to me: I was truly a blend of my father and mother. From my Italian Catholic father I inherited my drive, my competitiveness, and my desire to achieve goals that were sometimes beyond my reach. I inherited my love of books, my seriousness, and my sometimes overly guarded manner from my Irish Protestant mother.

My father's name was Vincenzo, but everybody called him Jimmy. (In fact, he told us he never knew his name wasn't Jimmy until he registered for the draft.) He didn't go to high school. He started working when he

Lillian and Vincenzo Florio, Jim's parents

was about twelve. He was a painter—and a good one—who was employed for most of his working life at the Brooklyn Navy Yard.

In addition to being a hard worker, my father was a big gambler. He never read newspapers, but he studied the racing sheet that came out every day and he knew what to look for. He would take his vacation days and travel to tracks up and down the East Coast. (Years later, when

Father and son share a toast. When Congressman Florio was able to obtain tickets for his father to attend the Kentucky Derby, it was Vincenzo's lifelong dream come true.

I was in Congress, I asked a colleague from Kentucky for tickets to the Kentucky Derby and gave them to my father. It was his lifelong dream come true.) My father was also a crafty gambler who knew how to play the odds. After World War II, when the shipyards closed down for a while and he was out of work, we lived off his poker winnings for eighteen months.

My mother Lillian, known by her friends as Lilo, was much more sedate, very quiet, almost reclusive. Like my father, she had no formal education of any sort. But she was a consummate reader, and she made sure I was too. We had a set of Mark Twain's books and a set of John Steinbeck's books, and I read them all. Every month, she would spend enough at the local A&P to earn a volume of the *Wonder Book of Knowledge*; over a period of a year or two, I read the whole set, from A to Z.

My father was a first-generation American; both his parents came from Italy. My mother's father came from Ireland, but her mother was born in the United States. My father's side was Catholic, my mother's side Protestant. When my father and mother, against their parents' wishes, ran off and got married, both their families disowned them. Then I came along, the first grandson, and the families managed to get past their differences and treat my parents (if not each other) with relative civility. This was the first time I functioned—though not consciously—as the peacemaker, the mediator, the consensus builder.

My father was rough around the edges. He teased my mother a lot, sometimes more harshly than he intended, but she understood that he wasn't trying to be mean. All these years later, I sometimes find myself teasing Lucinda, and she knows I do it with love—but I have to wonder if I may inadvertently be channeling one of my father's less endearing qualities.

My mother doted on me, especially before my two brothers were born. She took me to see Frank Sinatra in a live concert at the Paramount Theater, and she took me to the movies. We would go walking on Flatbush Avenue. When I was good, we would go to Horn & Hardart, put a coin in the slot, and out would come a sandwich. It was a big deal.

She also filled me with advice, much of which has guided me throughout my life. To this day, I finish every meal that is put in front of me. "Eat all the food off your plate," my mother would tell me. "There are hungry people in Europe." Another of her favorite sayings was, "Never be late. To be late is to be rude." People who know me well, people who have worked with and for me over the years, will attest to the fact that I have always been nauseatingly punctual—a characteristic, I have found, that differentiates me from many politicians.

There was another, darker side to my mother's admonitions. "Never get too close to anybody," she would caution me. "People turn on you." Although I have lived most of my adult life in the public sector, I nevertheless tend to be a very private person, to be introverted, not at all what you would call a "natural politician." I had to work very hard to develop the accepted

Vincenzo Florio poses with his three sons; from left, James, Richard, and William.

practices—the hand shaking, the backslapping, the baby kissing—of retail politics. I don't know what event in my mother's life caused her to be so guarded and defensive. But because she was so wary of getting too close to people outside the family, it took me a long time to recognize that meaningful professional and personal relationships had to be built on trust.

Above all, my mother was frugal—another adjective I would unhesitatingly apply to myself. (Lucinda puts it more bluntly: she says I'm cheap.) When it became clear to my mother that my father, my two brothers, and I would go through a jar of strawberry jelly in no time because we liked it so much, she started buying apple-mint jelly, which nobody liked. It lasted much longer, of course, which pleased her greatly.

"Be clean," she constantly told us. "Clean is everything. We're poor, but we're clean." Her obsession with cleanliness, however, didn't necessarily rise to the level of godliness, because it would sometimes come into conflict with her frugality. On Saturday nights, for example, because she didn't want to run up the gas bill by using the water heater too much, she would draw only one tub of bathwater. I'd get the first bath because I was the oldest. My brother Bill got the second bath, and Dick got the third.

My father was not a churchgoing Catholic, and my mother was more of a social than a spiritual Methodist-Episcopalian. In those days, however, families in Flatbush would never even consider the idea of mixing their children's religious upbringing—or, worse, providing them with no religious upbringing at all. My father was Catholic; therefore, I was going to be brought up Catholic. End of discussion.

Among my earliest and happiest memories, however, was attending a big Protestant event with my mother every year in Prospect Park. I have no idea what was being celebrated, but there was always a big parade, and they served cookies and ice cream at the back of the church. I looked forward to it every year, mostly because of the cookies and ice cream.

Among young Jim Florio's earliest and happiest memories is attending a "big Protestant event" with his mother every year in Brooklyn's Prospect Park.

Maybe it was because they knew my mother wasn't Catholic that representatives of the church decided to show up at our house one day and let us know, in no uncertain terms, that I was expected to attend church every Sunday and go to religious instruction on Sunday and Wednesday afternoons. "You have to make sure he goes to church," they implored my mother. "He's Catholic."

So I did. I went to St. Rose of Lima Church every Sunday—by myself. The church was on Parkville Avenue, about six or seven blocks away, so I walked there. My mother would give me two quarters each week to leave in the collection plate. One minister, Father O'Malley, was an especially enthusiastic supporter of Senator Joseph McCarthy, and I would listen to his sermons intently. I distinctly remember him preaching from the pulpit how "our good Senator McCarthy" was protecting us from communists, both foreign and domestic.

It would be some years before my own political views started to take shape in quite a different direction from those of Father O'Malley. It would take about the same amount of time for my adherence to Catholicism to fade into agnosticism.

In school, I was also an intent listener. And because I did so much reading at home, I was a good student. The first of the many teachers I would credit with having a very strong influence on me was my sixth-grade teacher at P.S. 179, Mrs. Braverman. She got me hooked on *My Weekly Reader*. The last page of each issue was a current events quiz, and I started reading newspapers—the *Brooklyn Daily Eagle*, the New York *Daily News*, and the New York *Daily Mirror*—so I would score 100 on the quiz. This got me interested in newspapers, in current events, in public affairs—not just in reading but also in absorbing and learning.

I was also becoming a more discriminating reader. The *Brooklyn Daily Eagle* featured only local news, and I was more interested in national and international events. So I started paying more attention to the *Daily News* and the *Daily Mirror,* until it dawned on me that a murder in the Bronx or a rape in Central Park might be less deserving of the front page than a more significant national or international event. I began to realize that reading two or three newspapers wasn't enough to make someone aware of what was really going on in the world—and that my own sense of what was important didn't necessarily coincide with what the editors of tabloid newspapers thought.

Mrs. Braverman also paid me one of the nicest left-handed compliments I have ever received. Our class was observing "Friendship Day," celebrating diversity, and Mrs. Braverman was explaining that we shouldn't apply stereotypes to people. "I mean look at little Jimmy Florio," she said. "He's Italian—and he's smart."

At Erasmus Hall High School, I got good grades. I became particularly interested in subjects related to earth science, geology, and weather—which, perhaps not surprisingly, became my area of specialty in the navy. There was a point in my life where I knew the names of all the dinosaurs; later I enjoyed reading stories about dinosaurs to my children and still enjoy talking about them with my grandchildren. As a kid, I was also able to identify all kinds of birds; today, Lucinda and I enjoy keeping tabs on the many varieties of winged visitors who flock to the bird feeder in our yard. I wasn't exactly a whiz kid, but I enjoyed learning about subjects that interested me.

The Boy Scouts were also a very important part of my life. Our troop went on trips from Brooklyn to the wilds of Staten Island, and even deeper into the backwoods of Bear Mountain State Park on the west bank of the Hudson River in Rockland County. In the summers, I would take a week off from whatever job I had at the time to go to Boy Scout camp.

But my real passion, like every kid in Brooklyn, was the Dodgers. I was a devoted fan. Pee Wee Reese lived in our neighborhood; Gil Hodges was a milkman in the off-season. Ebbets Field was on the other side of Flatbush Avenue, so I'd take a bus to get there, and I think it cost $1.50 to get in. I learned mathematics by calculating batting averages. Years later, I can still cite all sorts of arcane Dodgers statistics, like the fact that Carl Furillo, a rifle-armed outfielder who hit .344 in his best year and finished

A family portrait from January 1955 shows seventeen-year-old Jim Florio flanked by his parents and brothers.

with a career batting average of .299, earned a salary of $28,500 his last year in Brooklyn. How times have changed!

My interest in baseball was purely as a spectator, not a participant. We played some stickball around the neighborhood, but it didn't take long for me to realize that baseball was not my game.

Still, I was reasonably well-coordinated, and I had a lot of energy. As a growing boy, I definitely needed some kind of athletic activity to put all that energy to some recreational use.

I hung around at a couple of places in my early teenage years: the Police Athletic League, because they gave out free tickets to movies and other events, and the Flatbush Boys Club on Bedford Avenue, because they had a lot of organized activities—everything from gymnastics, swimming, and arts and crafts to ping pong, billiards, and outings to Ebbets Field.

And they had boxing.

I was just roaming around the Flatbush Boys Club one day when a guy named John Doucette came up to me and asked, "How would you like to box?" I thought to myself, "Sure, why not?" He told me, "In amateur boxing, if you have a good left jab, that's really all you need to survive." So he put me in front of the heavy bag and had me practice left jabs, which I did hour after hour, for about two weeks. That was my training.

Once I graduated from the heavy bag into the ring, I understood almost immediately that boxing is as much about brain as brawn. I used my brain—and my left jab—first to reach the point where I wasn't embarrassing myself and then to develop enough ring sense to become marginally successful. The next thing I knew, I was signed up to compete in the Golden Gloves.

In the 1950s, in Brooklyn, the Golden Gloves were a very big deal. Professional boxing was in its heyday; the Friday night fights aired by the Mutual Broadcasting System on WINS radio drew a huge New York audience, later eclipsed by the televised Gillette Friday Night Fights on NBC and the Pabst Blue Ribbon Wednesday night bouts on CBS. The Golden Gloves were like the upper-level minor leagues in baseball, where talented youngsters showed the skills that would turn them (well, a few of them at least) into the future stars of the sport. One of them, Floyd Patterson, rose from the streets of Brooklyn to become heavyweight champion of the world and an idol to every youngster who ever put on a pair of gloves at the Flatbush Boys Club.

I was a competent but unexceptional welterweight, and I had no illusions about boxing becoming my professional career. But I was competitive, and although I lost my Golden Gloves match, I won my father's admiration. He came to the match with my Uncle Tony, a rather obnoxious guy who used to harass me all the time about how I wasn't a real man because I didn't want to go fishing with him. Uncle Tony stopped harassing me after he saw me in the ring. And my father, who couldn't relate very much to my academic interests or my penchant for reading and studying, could definitely relate to my being a boxer: he was very proud of me.

Maybe it was my father's newfound pride, or my mother's resolve never to discourage me from doing anything I wanted to do, or just the fact that I had always played the role of bringing the family together that caused both my parents to defer to me when I told them I wanted to quit high school at the end of my junior year. I was bored with school. I wasn't getting guidance or counseling from any adult, either at Erasmus Hall or at home. I didn't know what to do, and I didn't know what I was going to do with my life. I felt I needed some structure, some direction, some self-discipline. "Well, I guess you know best" was my parents' response.

In retrospect, that is how my parents always treated me, even from a young age. It wasn't that I was spoiled; they certainly didn't give me everything I wanted. It was more that they sought my approval for things we did as a family. My father was hardly shy and retiring, but I think he was aware of his own limitations, and as it became clear that I was not only a pretty good student but also a pretty clear thinker, he began respecting and deferring to my judgment. Whenever a family decision had to be made, he and my mother would ask me what I thought, and more often than not, they would do as I suggested. It was almost as if I was the parent and my parents were the children.

My father did draw the line, however, when I told him I wanted to join the U.S. Marines. I was only seventeen and needed his permission to enlist. I had been impressed by some of the war movies I had seen about the Marine Corps, how structured and disciplined they were. But my father, who had served in the National Guard at Fort Drum in upstate New York, refused to sign the enlistment papers. "The army and the

Though he would soon join the navy, Jim Florio dons a borrowed Merchant Marine uniform in an effort to impress a young lady he was hoping to date.

marines live in dirt," he said. "I don't want you living in dirt. If you want to join, join the air force or the navy."

I chose the navy.

※

One thing the navy does very well is match the skills and interests of its enlistees with the specialties the service requires. The keen interest I developed in school in subjects related to earth science was reflected in the scores on the aptitude tests I took on entry into the navy, and it was no surprise then that I wound up being a weatherman.

I enjoyed the navy. I enjoyed the camaraderie. I enjoyed learning about the country. I served in Maryland, Oklahoma, Florida, New Jersey, and Alaska where I met people from all walks of life. The navy really broadened my horizons. It also ended my boxing career.

After boot camp in Bainbridge, Maryland, I was sent to Norman, Oklahoma, where I was enrolled in a forty-day course in naval aviation. For most of the next two years I was stationed in Key West, Florida, where I trained to be a weatherman or, as it is known in navy parlance, an aerographer's mate in naval aviation. That's where I also resumed boxing.

The Key West Naval Air Station regularly hosted evenings of boxing events called smokers. A notice was posted asking for volunteers, I applied, and thanks to my earlier training at the Flatbush Boys Club and my participation in the Golden Gloves, I did pretty well. I became sort of a navy hero because in one of my first bouts, I knocked out my opponent, who happened to be a marine. The navy guys really thought I was hot stuff. I ended up with a fairly respectable 12–3 record in those smokers.

After Key West, I had six months of additional weather training in Lakehurst, New Jersey, before being sent to my final posting in Alaska. There, in Kodiak, my boxing days ended—with a bang *and* a whimper.

I had a reputation by then. Several times, guys I was scheduled to fight backed out, and I felt pretty cocky. One night, when yet another scheduled opponent withdrew suddenly, saying he was sick, there was a second bout scheduled, but only one of the boxers, a fellow from Louisiana named Sherman White, showed up. I foolishly volunteered to fight him.

I was a 156-pound light middleweight. Sherman was a 172-pound light heavyweight. He hit me about three or four times and broke something every time—my jaw, my nose, my lip. I somehow managed to make it through the final round, but my jaw was wired up for the next two months. I survived on milkshakes, while nursing a badly bruised ego.

The Florio brothers join the navy; from left, Bill, Jim, and Dick.

Seaman Florio, second row, third from left, poses with his Aerographers Mate School classmates at Lakehurst Naval Air Station, New Jersey.

My boxing days behind me, I focused on my job as a weatherman. Kodiak was the fleet's weather central, where we did monitoring and forecasting using a very complicated process involving precision instruments, weather balloons, and detailed maps. Before there were computers, this was all done by personal observation and analysis. At exactly five minutes to the hour we had to go out and take a balloon reading to determine the wind direction and speed; then exactly on the hour we had to read the temperature; and then we had to teletype it to central headquarters, where all the readings from all over the country would be gathered and analyzed.

Meanwhile, we had to draw maps. We had to take all these little dots representing coded information and draw lines between them indicating wind pressure, air pressure, the dew point, and all manner of detailed weather data. It was very detailed, precise, analytical work.

Years later, I would impress my children by telling them what the weather was going to be. "Today it's going to rain slightly," I would say, "and then it's going to rain hard with thunder and lightning." They would ask, "How do you know that?" Well, by the time I left the active navy as a first-class petty officer, I was pretty accomplished at forecasting the weather.

That wasn't all I learned in the navy. I had lived so provincially in Brooklyn that I never knew anybody from Kentucky, or Texas, or Minnesota. I had never met a black man from Chicago or a Puerto Rican from Miami. When I was on leave in New York City from boot camp, a guy from Oklahoma had to show me around Manhattan because I didn't know where to go or what to do.

A whole bunch of people in boot camp were from West Virginia. I made friends with men from Harlan County, Kentucky, and Enid, Oklahoma, great guys who had a totally different perspective on life from my own. In my time in the navy, I never served on a ship, never went overseas. But it was an eye-opening experience for me. For the first time in my life, I experienced real diversity.

When I left active duty, I immediately affiliated with the Active Naval Reserve out of Lakehurst, New Jersey. I drilled regularly one weekend a month and two weeks in the summer for eighteen years, giving me a total of twenty-two years of service. Starting out as a high school dropout seaman recruit, I retired from the navy in 1974 as a lieutenant commander.

꧁

Nobody in my family ever talked about college. In our family, you had made it if you got a city job. The most successful members of our family, including all the distant relatives, worked for the sanitation department, the fire department or, if they were really lucky, the police department. This was the post-Depression generation. If you got yourself a half-decent salary and a pension, you had made it.

I had earned my GED, a high school equivalency diploma, through a correspondence course while I was in the navy, which qualified me to apply for a job as a New York City cop. The starting salary was $5,000, big money for me. If I had followed in my family's footsteps, I would almost certainly have traded in my navy whites for NYPD blue.

But as I was about to leave the navy I got the idea that maybe I should go to college instead. My parents had earlier moved to New Jersey because the Brooklyn Navy Yard had closed, and my father was working out of the shipyards in Bayonne and Hoboken. They had rented a summer cabin in Lake Hopatcong, which they bought and converted into a year-round house. So I no longer had a home in Brooklyn; I was now a New Jerseyan.

While still stationed in Alaska, I had started looking through some college catalogues, and my interest was drawn to the pictures and descriptions of one particular teacher's college in my newly adopted state. After four years in the navy, including the last two on an Alaskan island that had a population of about 7,000 people and 3,500 Kodiak bears, what I found especially appealing was the school's undergraduate gender ratio: seven women to every man.

I vividly remember standing at a mailbox in Kodiak, with two envelopes in my hand. One was an application for the New York City Police Department, the other an application to Trenton State College. I sent the one to Trenton State.

When I got there, in September 1958, I was older and more mature than most of the students. But they were coming straight out of high school, and I hadn't been in a classroom, other than on a navy base, in four years. I started out not really knowing a whole lot about what was going on or what to expect, but I caught on fairly quickly.

One of my English professors, Hugh Ford, awakened in me an understanding of what education, especially higher education, was all about. He taught me how to look into books, how to read more deeply into what they really meant, how good authors went beyond a superficial presentation to convey deeper thoughts and meanings. It was thanks to Professor Ford that I realized *Moby Dick* wasn't just a story about a whale.

Aerographers Mate First Class Florio prepares to leave active duty in the navy and enroll at Trenton State College. He would spend the next eighteen years in the Active Naval Reserve, retiring as a lieutenant commander.

One of my textbooks, S. I. Hayakawa's *Language in Thought and Action*, was very influential in my thinking. Dr. Hayakawa, who later became a senator from California, was a great semanticist. He described how different kinds of words—purr words, snarl words—could be used symbolically, how they could convey inferences and judgments, how language could be used for good or for evil. These were eye-opening concepts for me.

I spent a lot of time in the library. I worked there part-time, for $1.50 an hour, and the librarian, Felix Hirsch, was another influential educator in my life. Like Professor Ford, he urged me to read in depth, to get more out of books than a superficial understanding or a simple message. To this day, I tend to read books that challenge me to think, to analyze, to look for deeper meaning. My mother encouraged me to read books; my professors taught me how to understand them.

In my freshman year, I read the little-known book by John Steinbeck, *In Dubious Battle*, and it really shaped my thinking about the difference between right and wrong, between what's fair and unfair. Like many of Steinbeck's books, it's about farm workers in California, and it paints a picture of desperation, of good people who just can't catch a break. Everybody was against them: the railroad people, the farmers, the media, the police, the officials, and yet they fought back. It's a classic story pitting fairness against unfairness, and it left an indelible impression on me. It is part of the reason I became inclined later in life to fight against things I considered to be unfair, and to sympathize with and often take on the cause of the underdog.

After living in an off-campus apartment as a freshman because the college didn't have enough dormitory space, I moved into a dorm my sophomore year. My roommates, Joe Britta and Val Raugas, were fraternity guys. They were into wearing beanies and playing games and partying. I was into studying and working at the library. They teased me a lot for working too hard and getting straight A's; I teased them a lot for wearing beanies and partying.

We got along well, however. The teasing was all very innocent and play-ful. When I decided to run for student body president in my junior year, I had to go before the student council leaders to answer their ques-tions. Asked how I was doing academically, I replied that I was doing all right. "He does all right?" my former roommates blurted out from the back of the room. "He got straight A's."

I got involved in student politics because I enjoyed going to many of the forums the school sponsored, but I didn't much like the speakers they were inviting. I thought the student body would be better served by hearing from more prominent and distinguished speakers, and I fig-ured I would be able to invite them if I were in a position of student leader-ship. I decided to run for student body president, which was the first time I ran for anything. Almost by accident, I discovered what elections are all about.

First of all, you have to have a message. Mine was bringing better speakers to the campus. Second, you have to have a campaign strategy. Mine was to take my message to those in the student body who weren't part of the "in crowd," the BMOCs and beauty queens who hung around the student center. Instead I campaigned in the sorority houses, the dor-mitories, the library—the places that were filled with students who, like me, spent more time studying than socializing.

Third, you have to be lucky. My opponent in the race for student body president was Vince Segal, who later became a judge and a personal friend. He was a football player who hung out in the student union and was popu-lar with all the pretty girls. He was confident his campus celebrity would be enough to win him election. It didn't. One of the main reasons I won—by a vote of 910–187—is that I was lucky enough to run against an opponent who didn't think he needed to mount a vigorous campaign.

I was a social studies major, with a concentration in Russia and East-ern Europe, and a minor in geography. I was very interested in Russian history and government, and I was fascinated by the life and times of Alexander Kerensky, the former Russian prime minister who fled to Paris after the Bolsheviks took power and eventually settled in the United States. I invited him to speak and he accepted.

Among the other speakers I brought in were Arnold Toynbee, the acclaimed British historian; John Hope Franklin, a prominent civil rights activist, academic, and historian; and Norman Thomas, the six-time presidential nominee of the American Socialist Party. I worked very hard to get these prominent people, the school extended invitations to them, and the forums were very well-attended. I made good on my campaign promise.

I also learned a very valuable lesson—about human interaction and, by extension, about politics—from an incident involving a position I took that put me in conflict with the college administration. I don't even remember what my position was, but it led to my being called into the office of Dean of Students Charles McCracken. After I explained that I had very strong views about the particular issue under discussion, he offered me an analogy: "I would like to go to work here every day without a tie," he told me, "but that's not acceptable around here, so I wear a tie every day. It's not worth picking a fight over whether I have to wear a tie. It's a matter of perspective. You can't have fights all the time. Pick your fights well and make sure you fight for things that are worth fighting for."

This was more or less the verbal equivalent of the physical lesson I should already have learned from my last boxing match. From that point forward, I decided I would try (though I was not always successful) to pick my battles wisely.

⋘⋙

Bringing speakers to the college wasn't my only extracurricular activity at Trenton State. At a mixer on one of my first nights on campus I met a young woman, Maryanne Spaeth. She was very smart, very organized, and a very devout Catholic. Here I was, fresh out of the navy, looking for some stability and organization in my life. I found that in Maryanne.

We were married at the end of our sophomore year. Nine months later, our first son Christopher was born. He was followed eighteen months later by our second son whom, in my fixation on all things Russian, I wanted to name Gregor, after the central character in Mikhail Sholokhov's *Quiet Flows the Don*—but Maryanne put her foot down and he became Gregory. Our daughter Catherine was born two years later. (Yes, she was named after Catherine the Great.)

Tuition at Trenton State in those days was $150 a year. I was able to afford it because I was getting $70 a month from the Korean War GI Bill. After we got married, I got $80 a month. I would tease Maryanne that she was worth $10.

We lived a block off campus, in two rooms that were part of a larger house. We didn't cook there; we ate all our meals at the college. Later we moved to a three-room apartment over a barbershop on East State Street in Trenton, out by the New Jersey State Fairgrounds. We were able to cook for ourselves there, but I remember there was one month when the GI Bill check came late, and we were down to about three or four potatoes. But we always made do. I never really thought about money. I hadn't grown up with much, and I didn't anticipate that I would ever really make a lot.

We both graduated magna cum laude, and I was awarded a Woodrow Wilson Fellowship to study for a year at Columbia University, which was a big deal for someone from Trenton State College. We moved from our three rooms in Trenton to a little bungalow in New Shrewsbury, part of a housing project built for workers at Fort Monmouth during World War II. Maryanne and the kids settled in there, while I roomed during the week at the International House near the Columbia campus in New York City and came home on weekends.

Living in the International House was a fascinating experience. I was surrounded by foreign students, most of whom were very rich. I didn't get to know them well, since I was spending most of my weekdays in classes or studying and my weekends in New Shrewsbury. I was struck, however, by the social difficulties experienced by a lot of the young men, especially those from Middle Eastern countries. They didn't interact well with American women, and they were very frustrated by that. This made me think that much of the hostility we have in the world comes from people who have spent time in the United States, never felt comfortable, and went home with unpleasant memories.

Like Mrs. Braverman at P.S. 179, and Professors Ford and Hirsch at Trenton State, a teacher at Columbia opened my eyes to a bigger world and my mind to new ideas. I had arrived at Columbia thinking I might want to get a degree in Russian studies or American government and go on to teach, maybe even at the college level.

Then I took Richard Neustadt's class.

At Trenton State, I had read *Presidential Power*, Professor Neustadt's acclaimed book that examined the strengths and weaknesses of the American presidency. And here he was, in the flesh, a political science icon who had served in the Truman White House and was now one of the most influential advisors to the Kennedy administration.

I found his lectures spellbinding, his message inspirational. He was the living, breathing embodiment of JFK's credo, "Ask not what your country can do for you; ask what you can do for your country." His example made me stop thinking about studying and teaching about government and concentrate instead on becoming involved in government.

I had the pleasure of meeting Professor Neustadt again about fifteen years later, when I was serving in Congress. I told him, "I just want to let you know, for the good or for the bad, that you inspired me." He was pleased.

Most of the people I knew, or had read about, who were involved in government were lawyers. I didn't really have a deep interest in the law. I wasn't even sure I ever wanted to practice law. But as my year at Columbia was drawing to a close, I had firmly decided that I wanted to be involved in government, and since I thought that meant I probably should become a lawyer, I applied to Rutgers Law School in Camden and was accepted.

There was only one problem: we didn't have any money. One look at our bank account, and a quick calculation of our living costs, made it clear there was no way I could afford to spend the next three years in law school. Instead, I went out and got a job, as the assistant to the executive director of the Glassboro Housing Authority. My arrival there turned what had been a one-person office into a two-person office. It was my first and only job on the administrative side of government until I became governor.

⟋⟋⟋⟋⟋

The following year, I reapplied and was reaccepted at Rutgers, and I spent the next three years studying law. We had saved money from my job in Glassboro, and then in the summer I worked as a construction laborer, which gave us enough money to be able to get through the first year. Then I got a job as a night watchman at Woodrow Wilson High School in Camden, which helped get us through the second year. During my third and final year in law school, I worked as a clerk in the office of the Camden city attorney, Joe Nardi, who later became mayor.

I found law school pretty interesting, and I did well academically. Even though I wasn't there to become a practicing lawyer, but rather to gain the credential I thought I needed to go into government, the actual study of law—learning about process and procedure—really shapes your mind into thinking in a certain way. It forces you to have the mindset that prepares you to defend somebody one day and prosecute them the next. I think everything really clicked for me when I was studying for the bar exam. I only really became a lawyer, in my own mind, just before the bar exam, which I took at the Robert Treat Hotel in Newark in the middle of the 1967 race riots. Inside were all the would-be lawyers sweating over the exam; outside were gunshots.

The day I learned I had passed the bar exam, October 12, 1967, I was working in the father-and-son law office of Frank Lario Sr. and Jr. in Camden. They were social friends as well, and from the moment I was notified of the good news in the morning, no more work was done in that office for the rest of the day. The Larios, Joe Nardi, and a few other friends and associates decided we had to celebrate. We drove to a restaurant in Hamilton Township, next to Trenton, called Chick & Nello's Homestead Inn, where we spent the whole day—and a good part of the evening—in celebration.

This group of friends and colleagues was very active politically. Joe Nardi became the mayor of Camden; Frank Lario Jr. became a judge. These friends weren't white-shoe lawyers; they were lawyers of the people. Frank Lario Sr. represented a lot of Italian farmers, who would sometimes pay him with produce, like a bag of tomatoes, which he gratefully accepted.

These were my early mentors and lifelong friends. The Larios had a spare office, which they rented to me. There was no secretary, just an answering machine and me. Every afternoon, I would sit at my desk and dictate into a tape recorder. Then, after work, I would drive to Elsie's house (I have no idea what her last name was) and drop off the tapes. She would transcribe them, and I would pick them up the next morning. My first year as a lawyer, I made $12,000. My second year, I made $60,000. Much to my surprise, I was actually practicing law—and making money at it.

I was also making connections. Most of my practice was in municipal court, but I started picking up appointments to represent local public bodies. I was named solicitor for a few government agencies. I was retained as the lawyer for the Board of Education in Lindenwold. There was a large Polish American community in Camden, and I started doing volunteer work with the Polish-American Citizens Club, drawing up free wills for its members.

Camden was now our home. We lived in East Camden, which was in many ways reminiscent of my old neighborhood in Flatbush—it was a solid, ethnically diverse, working-class community. The city still had a thriving manufacturing base; the shipyard was still open, RCA had a big work- force, Campbell Soup had production lines of people.

In the next few years, that would all change. So would my life.

CHAPTER 3

Bitten by the Political Bug

When you take on the jobs nobody else wants, you advance with little opposition and you gather knowledge. When you gather enough knowledge, you find that knowledge is power and you advance more rapidly.

I entered public life in an era when the political structure, especially in urban areas, was a well-oiled hierarchical machine run by entrenched bosses. By the time I won a seat in Congress a decade later, the machine was breaking down; political power was shifting from the bosses to the people.

I was a young man in a hurry in the early 1960s. On arriving in Camden, even before I started law school, I wrote a letter to the Democratic mayor, Alfred Pierce. I told him I was a college graduate, a veteran, and a hard worker who wanted to become active in the Democratic Party. I was having some difficulty finding a way to get involved, and I asked if he might give me some direction.

In response Mayor Pierce sent Armand Paglione to my home. Armand was the ward leader of Camden's 12th Ward, where I lived. He was a rough, tough guy who immediately took a liking to me. During the year that I worked at the Glassboro Housing Authority, as often as not I would come home after work and meet up with Armand. We would drive around the city and meet for coffee with guys who were known by names like "Chester the Squirrel" and "Charlie Debauch," characters straight out of a Damon Runyon story.

Armand was my first political mentor, and he appointed me to the post of "district leader" of the 7th District of the 12th Ward. It turned out that this was more than an honorary title. There were 600 voters in my district, and I was designated as the person they should call with their complaints, requests, concerns, and problems. If somebody's garbage wasn't picked up, I got the call and notified the Sanitation Department. If somebody's street wasn't plowed after a snowstorm, I got the call and notified the Public Works Department. If somebody wanted to set up a meeting with the mayor, I got the call and notified City Hall.

The motive for this hands-on involvement for the Democratic Party was securing votes; every problem solved was a likely Democratic vote in the next election. My personal motive was to show my loyalty to the party; every problem solved was a feather in my cap, my ticket of entry into the world of Democratic powerbrokers—a world in which an Irish American, Jim Joyce, was the powerful county chairman, and an Italian American, Angelo Errichetti, was the powerful city chairman.

What I discovered, almost to my surprise, was that my real satisfaction and enjoyment didn't come from climbing the political ladder: it came from helping people. This was my first grassroots experience in good old-fashioned constituent service, and I took seriously my responsibility to meet the daily, nitty-gritty needs of the residents of the 7th District of the 12th Ward of the City of Camden. In later years, I tried to continue to pay the same close attention to people's needs, and I derived the same satisfaction and enjoyment from addressing them, in the assembly, in Congress, and in the governor's office.

Angelo Errichetti was my second political mentor. Like me, he had gotten involved in local Democratic politics through Mayor Pierce, whom he had served as an administrative assistant. When he took me under his wing, he was the city's purchasing agent. Later he would climb up the political ladder to be public works director, mayor, state senator, and one of the most powerful men in South Jersey before the FBI brought him tumbling down in the Abscam investigation. Before that fate befell him, he and I had parted ways—but I learned a lot, both about what to do and what *not* to do in politics, during our tempestuous relationship.

Errichetti was very impressive in a hard-edged way. He enjoyed near-heroic stature in Camden, having carved out a reputation as an exceptional athlete and all-state high school football player before he entered politics. He was very smart and very capable administratively. He had great political instincts, knowing how to motivate people and which buttons to push to get things done.

I spent a lot of time with Errichetti in his office, and I saw how he operated, how he used his position to gather information, and then how he used that information, for better or worse, as an instrument of power. I would be sitting there when somebody would come in and tell him something. Then the next person would come in, and he would share the information he had just learned with that person, but he would do it in a way that intimated he was the source, rather than the recent recipient, of the information. I marveled at how effectively he used this technique of gathering and dispensing information to achieve and hold political power, to be the central figure of authority, the hub that connected and held together all the spokes of the wheel.

At the same time, I was developing the disquieting feeling that Errichetti saw the accumulation of power as an end in itself, rather than as the means to an end of pursuing policies for the benefit of the people. To be sure, he cast himself as a champion of the people, and he sincerely tried to do things for his city, which was literally dying from white flight and shuttered manufacturing plants. However, he also started to believe he was above the law, that he could do anything and get away with it. Unfortunately, he was surrounded by sycophants, who followed him with blind adoration—which, like too many politicians, he found intoxicating.

I got my first glimpse of the way Errichetti operated when I saw him place a phone call to Camden's chief of police, Harold Melleby, ordering him to set up a police stakeout of his political opponents. None of the targets of the stakeout was suspected of doing anything criminal; rather, it was clear that Errichetti simply wanted to intimidate them or get something on them. I thought about suggesting that this might not be an appropriate deployment of the city's Police Department's resources, but I bit my tongue. I was still the new kid on the block and maybe more than a little intimidated by Errichetti myself.

From that point on, however, our relationship, which might have been described early on as almost as close as father to son, deteriorated into a rivalry and, ultimately, complete estrangement. As I began to build my own political base, I could see my bond with Errichetti turning from an asset into a liability.

In the spring of 1964, I left my job with the Glassboro Housing Authority and went to work as a laborer. I was working on a bridge at the intersection of Cuthbert Boulevard and Route 70, known locally as Marlton Pike, in Cherry Hill. (My kids always referred to it as "daddy's bridge.") I enjoyed the hard, hands-on work, and I made good money. I also learned a lot about the working world and about my own work habits, after a couple of union members chastised me for loading my buggy with too much concrete. What I was supposed to do instead, they told me, was to load it with less concrete to make the job last longer.

By this time I had parlayed my role as district leader of the 7th District of Camden's 12th Ward into the chairmanship of the Camden County Young Democrats. It was in this capacity that I enjoyed my first involvement in national politics, playing a cameo role in a drama of historic political significance.

The 1964 Democratic National Convention in Atlantic City was, for the most part, not a very suspenseful affair. Once President Lyndon Johnson announced that his vice presidential running mate would be Minnesota senator Hubert Humphrey, the only remaining drama centered around the question of who would represent Mississippi on the convention floor. Would it be the all-white delegation chosen by the Mississippi Democratic Party or the mixed-race, mostly black delegation representing the Mississippi Freedom Democratic Party?

The dispute was to be decided by the convention's Credentials Committee, headed by New Jersey governor Richard J. Hughes. As the competing delegations sought to convince the committee why they should be seated, and protesters jammed the Boardwalk outside Convention Hall (and filled the television screens on the nightly newscasts), Governor Hughes urged state Democratic chairman Thorn Lord to round up some warm bodies to sit in the seats reserved for the Mississippi delegation during the convention's preliminary sessions while the Credentials Committee worked to resolve the dispute.

Thorn Lord called Jim Joyce, the county chairman; Joyce called Angelo Errichetti; and Errichetti called me. All I was told was that there might be a problem at the convention, and they needed volunteers to play some kind of role in helping to resolve it. My job was to round up the Camden County Young Democrats and go with them to Atlantic City. So I got a bunch of people from our club and we headed for Convention Hall, having no idea what we were going to be told to do once we got there.

On arrival, we received our orders: occupy the seats of the Mississippi delegation until further notice. The reason President Johnson, Governor Hughes, and the rest of the Democratic leadership insisted that the seats be occupied, it turned out, was that they didn't want the television audience to see any empty seats on the convention floor.

The all-white delegation ultimately took the seats. Senator Humphrey tried to broker a compromise, which would have granted two nonvoting seats to the Mississippi Freedom Democratic Party, but the insurgent group rejected the offer. To the best of my knowledge, none of the television commentators ever raised questions about the identity of those "ringers" who had been sitting in the seats of the Mississippi delegation during the preliminary sessions.

Three years later, after I graduated from law school and passed the bar, I got a phone call from Joe Cowgill, a state senator who represented part of Camden County. He had gotten to know me through my involvement with the Young Democrats, as well as in my new role as assistant to Assemblyman John Horn during my last year in law school.

"Congratulations on passing the bar," Senator Cowgill said. "I'm going to give you your first patronage position." This political plum was an appointment as rate counsel for the state in contesting an application by Public Service Electric & Gas Co. (PSE&G) for a rate increase. I thanked him profusely, before pausing to consider that I knew absolutely nothing about what a rate counsel was supposed to do, what an application for a rate increase looked like, and how the process for contesting it was carried out. But I was sent a ten-pound bag of documents in preparation for the case, and I religiously read through everything. At the hearing before the Public Utilities Commission (later renamed the Board of Public Utilities), it was me against a veritable army of PSE&G lawyers, accountants, economists, and other experts.

I don't remember all the details of the case, but in essence PSE&G wanted a 12 percent increase, I advocated on behalf of the state for a 10 percent increase, and the Public Utilities Commission, in Solomon-like wisdom, approved an 11 percent increase. To me this was a very satisfactory result. And for my service to the State of New Jersey, I was paid the princely sum of $300.

Although I spent four years at Trenton State College, I really didn't know Trenton very well. The college is actually located not in the city, but in suburban Ewing Township, and my off-campus housing was far away from downtown Trenton. If I had ever visited the State House (the formal name of New Jersey's capitol building) during my college years, it certainly hadn't left a lasting impression.

During my final year in law school, however, I started spending quite a bit of time at the State House as the assistant to Assemblyman John Horn. In those days, neither the legislature itself nor individual legislators had much of a staff. There was a modest stipend for individual legislators to hire staff, but not enough to attract more than a part-time glorified "gofer," which is essentially what I was.

The Office of Legislative Services, which today provides a full range of services to members of the assembly and senate, had not yet been created. What existed at the time was a small, loosely knit, nonpartisan professional staff that performed various legal, research, and fiscal functions at the direction of two extraordinarily capable men: Arthur Applebaum (whose son David later became one of my longest-serving assistants) and Samuel Alito (whose son Samuel Jr. later became an associate justice of the U.S. Supreme Court).

But my experience as the assistant to John Horn, to borrow from the tag line of the MasterCard ad, was priceless.

John was a labor guy. His base was the United Transport Union, and the bus drivers loved him. His approach to his responsibilities as a lawmaker was to push whatever cause the unions were pushing; in return, the unions were always there for him.

My primary job as assistant was not to research legislation or write position papers or attend committee sessions. It was to follow him around, to watch how he interacted with his labor supporters, to learn from him. John taught me a lot of things, some of them good, some of them not so good. He lived by two political commandments. Number 1: Keep your base; never walk away from your base. Number 2: Don't make decisions prematurely. I had no difficulty accepting the first commandment as an indisputable fact of political survival. But I found that my own take on the second commandment differed considerably from John's.

Here's how I interpreted how politicians should make decisions. Issues that come before the legislature, or any public body for that matter, tend to be complicated and multifaceted. There are almost always strong, compelling arguments to be made on both sides of the issue. The responsible way to approach decision making is to gather as much information as you can from both sides, study it, analyze it, and then, when you have considered all the pros and cons, make your decision.

John's approach was a bit different. It wasn't so much that he wanted to study an issue before he made a decision. It was more that he didn't want to make a decision at all, until or unless it was unavoidable.

I remember asking John why he told one person that he agreed with him in support of a particular bill and then turned around and agreed with someone else who was opposed to the same bill. "Well, you know, you say these things," he told me. "Most of these things don't even come to completion, so why alienate somebody early on by telling them? Tell them what they want to hear, and then when you have to make a decision, you make a decision—but try to avoid making decisions as long as possible."

I was actually getting similar advice from Armand Paglione. When I told him I wanted to run for a seat on the Camden Board of Education, he said, "No, you don't want to do that." Later, when I said I wanted to run for the Camden City Council, he counseled, "No, you don't want to do that either." I pressed him for an explanation. "Skip over those jobs," he said. "Those are the kinds of jobs that will get you locked into a place where you don't want to be, because you have to make all these hard decisions."

But I was determined to run for office. In 1969, I told Armand I wanted to run for a seat in the General Assembly. Surprisingly, he didn't try to talk me out of it, though he didn't think I stood much of a chance. It was a gubernatorial election year, and the Republican candidate at the top of the ticket was popular South Jersey congressman William T. Cahill. "It's going to be hard," Armand said of my candidacy, "because Bill Cahill is going to kill everybody down here in the campaign."

Errichetti was also supportive, but similarly unimpressed with my likelihood of success. "Why not?" he said when I asked him if I should jump into the assembly race. "I mean you're a fairly attractive candidate. We have nobody else, so you can do it."

He was right: there was nobody else. The Camden County Democrats would not normally run a thirty-two-year-old whippersnapper with no experience in elective office for a seat in the assembly when there were hardened, grizzled political veterans around who were more experienced, were better known, and had paid their dues to the party over a long period of time. But with Cahill considered a shoo-in for governor and Republicans anticipating a South Jersey sweep, nobody else wanted to run.

So I did.

Assembly District 3D, one of three legislative districts covering parts of Camden County, was one of the most competitive districts in New Jersey in the late 1960s. In 1967, it was one of only two districts in the state that split its ticket, electing one Democrat and one Republican to the lower house. In 1969, I had the benefit of running with the Democratic incumbent, a man I knew well: John Horn. The Republican incumbent, Lee Laskin, chose not to seek re-election. He decided instead to run for a seat on the county freeholder board—a place from which patronage flows, in the form of jobs and contracts—making it a much more fertile field for county party leaders than the state legislature or even Congress.

So there was an open seat. Democratic Party leaders were not at all optimistic about capturing it, but the rank and file held out hope that perhaps Assemblyman Horn, as an incumbent with a strong labor base, could withstand the Cahill landslide. Their attitude about me was more like, "OK, kid, go ahead, throw yourself into this. If you lose, it's no big deal."

I did throw myself into the race. I enjoyed enthusiastic support and assistance from the members of the Camden County Young Democrats, many of whom lived in Cherry Hill and other suburbs outside the district, but who went door to door campaigning for me in Camden. I was also encouraged by the turnout at a bunch of coffee klatches we scheduled for me to meet and mingle with voters. I invited John Horn to join me, but I think he had already decided I was a little too aggressive for my own good (and certainly for his), so he ran his own, more laid-back campaign.

In the end, Cahill did win in a landslide, largely because his opponent, former governor Robert Meyner, had antagonized the Democratic organization in Hudson County. Without Hudson, then as now, no Democratic candidate has a prayer in a New Jersey election, and Cahill breezed to a 500,000-vote victory statewide. He carried Camden County by a 2-to-1 margin. But Assembly District 3D bucked the trend. John Horn got 19,687 votes, and I followed with 18,303, which was 381 votes more than the closest Republican competitor, John Mohrfeld.

Bill Cahill and I did not exactly get off on the right foot. As a young Democratic assemblyman, I wrote a letter to the editor of one of the papers, I think it was the *Philadelphia Inquirer,* criticizing Cahill's tax proposal as unfair to the City of Camden. (The irony of this position on taxes, one of my earliest as a fledgling legislator, was not lost on me, nor was it ignored by my political opponents, a couple of decades later.) I got a call the next day from the governor's office, asking me to meet with Cahill the following Monday, when the assembly would be in session.

No sooner had I walked in Cahill's office than he was waving the newspaper clipping at me and demanding, "Why did you write that letter? What, do you want to start fights?" I said, "No, no, these are just my thoughts." He started to get all red in the face and yelled, "Are you an agitator or are you just somebody that wants to pick political fights all the time?" I replied, "No, no, no." I was really taken aback, but he kept going on and on. "Governor, don't be paranoid," I finally said. He went ballistic.

Years later, when I was a congressman and he was a former governor, we actually became very friendly. When I ran for governor, Cahill, along with many of the people who had been involved in his administration,

In January 1970, newly elected Assemblyman Florio ascends the steps at the State House in Trenton to attend his first session as a member of the New Jersey legislature.

most of them Republicans, supported me. After I was elected governor, I appointed his son Bill Jr. to a seat on the State Commission of Investigation, and our relationship grew stronger. Like the so-called Presidents Club about which so much has been written, current and former governors of New Jersey usually share a bond, regardless of party, that is forged by our common experience.

I took my seat in the assembly in January 1970 with no staff and no prior experience in elective office. But since I had been a staff person to Assemblyman Horn for two years, I had a pretty good understanding of how the legislative process worked. Although the committee system was not especially sophisticated, I felt that familiarizing myself with legislation in its formative stages and then getting involved as it worked its way through committee and onto the floor were the way to gain real influence over the direction of public policy.

I spent a lot of time during my first assembly term in the State Library, where I researched subject areas that interested me or came to my attention through constituents. One of the first areas that captured my interest—and led to my sponsorship of a significant piece of legislation, which subsequently passed—was franchise protection.

At that time a number of gas station operators in South Jersey were complaining that they felt oppressed by the oil companies. I remember one gas station franchise holder who told me he was forced to work on Christmas Day because the oil company that held the lease to the station insisted on it. Owners of automobile franchises also felt oppressed by the auto companies. One man who had a Ford dealership came to me and said that Ford was harassing him to do things that he felt were inappropriate and burdensome. These franchise holders had virtually no bargaining power, which tapped right into my aversion to unfairness.

So I worked on researching and then writing a bill that protected franchise holders. I shepherded the bill through committee, sponsored it in the assembly, pushed for its passage by the senate, and had the satisfaction of seeing it signed into law. New Jersey still has one of the nation's

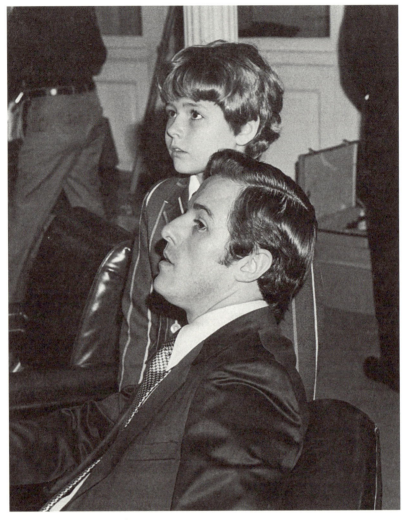

Assemblyman Florio and his son Gregory watch the proceedings from the floor of the assembly chamber.

most stringent laws protecting franchise holders, rather than franchise granters.

I also got involved in tenants' rights. Dennis Riley, a fellow South Jerseyan who headed the New Jersey Tenants Organization, came to me with reports of abuses that were being committed against renters; he told me about cases of people being locked out or even thrown out of their homes. So I got involved in researching and writing legislation to address this problem, and we passed some very strong laws protecting tenants' rights, not landlords' power.

Both of these issues, franchise protection and tenants' rights, represented battles between competing interests in which one side clearly won and the other lost. A less confrontational, more moderate approach might have been to seek a compromise that both sides could live with. Instead, we ended up with a situation in New Jersey where franchise granters felt they had no protection and landlords felt they were the ones being oppressed.

So I definitely violated John Horn's second commandment. I made decisions—and in the process I made some enemies. But I was faithful to his first commandment. I kept my base. In fact, because I was not afraid to make certain decisions, I actually expanded it.

I was very much a hands-on, retail politician. I held coffee klatches on a regular basis, and constituents would regularly bring issues to my attention. Some of them were strictly personal—a problem with the Division of Motor Vehicles or a missed unemployment check. Others were of a broader nature, like the problems faced by franchise holders and tenants. When people bring problems like these to your attention, it is your job as an elected official to try to solve them. And when you commit yourself to solving people's problems, there's a pretty good chance they'll become part of your base.

Tenants' rights groups became part of my base. So did franchise holders. So did veterans and environmental groups and scores of individual constituents who had come to me for help. I also enjoyed strong support in the Polish American community, dating back to my days writing wills pro bono for members of the Polish-American Citizens Club. I still went to all of their social events, and they backed me with their contributions and their votes.

This was an age when political machines, run by party bosses, were powerful in New Jersey. The almost dictatorial power once enjoyed by county chairmen had been lessened by the U.S. Supreme Court's "one-man, one-vote" ruling, which divorced legislative districts from the boundaries of county lines, but party bosses were still very much in evidence in Democratic bastions like Hudson and Essex Counties and in Republican strongholds like Atlantic County.

I had an intuitive understanding that to be totally reliant on a single political organization was a mistake. You never want to make your political life or death dependent on anyone other than yourself. You need to have your own organization, separate and distinct from the party machine, if you want to have any independent leverage. I've always worked from the premise that having an outside game—people who support you because of who you are, not what organization you represent—is every bit as important as the inside game, a universe where your star may rise or fall on the whim of a power broker.

So I proceeded to form my own political organization—a "citizens' machine," if you will—independent of the city and county organizations. It was made up of people who supported me because I was responsive to their concerns. For as long as the party machine's interests and my own interests were compatible, the machine and my organization hummed along in uninterrupted harmony. In 1971, with the backing of the party organizations and my own growing group of supporters, I won re-election by nearly 8,000 votes, a tremendous increase from the 381-vote margin in my first election.

Emboldened by my electoral success, I decided to take on a more quixotic challenge. New Jersey's 1st Congressional District had been represented by Republicans for 116 of the previous 118 years, but its boundaries were redrawn following the 1970 Census to reflect a significant shift in population from rural Salem County to suburban and urban Gloucester and Camden Counties. I felt certain this demographic change would make this district more competitive politically.

Assemblyman Florio and his three children; from left, Gregory, Catherine, and Christopher.

I also felt I had nothing to lose and everything to gain by running for Congress. For one thing, legislative elections in New Jersey are held in odd-numbered years, so I could run for a seat in the House of Representatives in 1972 without having to give up the seat I won in the assembly in 1971. For another, launching a bid for Congress was a way of gaining name recognition and enhancing my reputation as a tireless campaigner, a champion of the working people, and a staunch supporter of progressive causes.

My first run for Congress had a striking similarity to my first run for the General Assembly. There was little doubt that 1972 was going to be a big Republican year, with incumbent president Richard Nixon considered an overwhelming favorite for re-election over Democrat George McGovern. If I was going to win this race, I would again have to overcome a landslide at the top of the ticket, as I had in 1969 when Bill Cahill was cruising to victory.

꧁

My opponent in the 1972 race for Congress was the incumbent, John Hunt, a stereotypically conservative Republican who was seeking his fourth term after succeeding the more moderate Cahill in the House of Representatives. Hunt was a World War II veteran, a former state policeman, and Gloucester County sheriff and state senator before being elected to Congress. His base had primarily been in reliably Republican Salem County, which was no longer part of the district. Now he had to count on support from the rural but increasingly suburban communities of Gloucester County and eastern Camden County. My base was in the city of Camden.

It was a crazy campaign. The Camden County Democratic organization pretty much wrote off the congressional race, concentrating instead on trying to win freeholder seats. My campaign had practically no money— I think we raised a total of about $25,000—and my only real strategy was to work my tail off. I had assumed Hunt's strategy would be to ignore me, but I was heartened when I found out he was actually starting to take me seriously. I knew he was when he began attacking me.

The Hunt campaign dubbed me the candidate for "the three A's: amnesty, acid, and abortion." This was a common Republican line of attack against Democrats running on the same ticket as the liberal McGovern, even if it bore no resemblance to the candidate against whom it was lodged. In my case, amnesty for draft-age men who left the country to avoid service in the Vietnam War was not part of my platform; I'm not sure I even knew at the time what "acid" was; and I studiously avoided raising or commenting on the contentious issue of abortion (though I was later to become, and still am, strongly pro-choice).

My campaign got its share of coverage in the local media. We pulled one stunt that was very effective, if slightly gimmicky, when Hunt didn't show up for a scheduled debate. We knew he wasn't coming, so we carried in a straw dummy with a sheriff's badge on its back, and I proceeded to engage it in debate. Another stunt was done without my approval and was not at all helpful. The rambunctious Gloucester County Democratic chairman, Kenny Gewertz, decided to buzz a big Republican picnic with a helicopter that spread dust all over the participants, drawing outrage over the "dirty tricks" employed by Democrats.

We hosted coffee klatches all over the district. I walked door to door from one end of Delsea Drive in Westville to the other end in Franklinville, knocking on doors and introducing myself to voters in Gloucester County who didn't know much about me. I was helped enormously in the campaign by a small cadre of volunteers who worked every bit as hard as I did. Three people in particular—Joe Salema, Steve Weinstein, and Chuck Manella—would go on to form the core of many of my subsequent campaigns and become very close personal friends, for years to come.

I lost by a little more than 10,000 votes out of 186,000 cast. I carried Camden County by about 1,600 votes and lost Gloucester by more than 11,000. But I was heartened by the results: Nixon won Camden County by 36,000 votes and Gloucester by 19,000. I was already looking ahead to the 1974 midterm election, when the prospects for a Democratic candidate would be improved—though I hardly knew at the time just how much better they would turn out to be.

My wife and kids were with me at campaign headquarters the night I lost my first congressional race. They were sad; at least one of the kids,

The Florio family is all smiles awaiting the results of the 1972 congressional election. Hours later, the defeated Democratic candidate would tell his tearful children and their mother Maryanne, "Really, this is something we learn from. We don't cry. We don't do that sort of stuff. We take what I did wrong this time and we do it better next time."

maybe two, maybe even all three were crying, and I remember as we were driving home, I told them, "Really, this is something we learn from. We don't cry. We don't do that sort of stuff. We take what I did wrong this time and we do it better next time." My children vividly remember that incident to this day.

A really important lesson to learn about democracy is that there are no permanent winners or losers—or, at least, there shouldn't be. If you lose an election, it doesn't mean you're dead forever. It means you have to do something different the next time. You have to put together more forces. You have to persuade more people. And advocacy is really the essence of democracy, with everybody advocating for what he or she thinks is in the public interest. The uniqueness of the democratic process is that we have these vehicles—elections—that enable us to change things.

So I went back to the assembly, winning re-election handily in 1973 in the Democratic wave that swept Brendan Byrne into the governor's office. Many of my newly elected colleagues were older than I was, but because I was entering my third term, I enjoyed an unusually lofty status of seniority. I became chairman of the State Government Committee, with jurisdiction over congressional redistricting. This was a very hot (and very complicated) issue.

An earlier redistricting plan, based on the 1970 Census, had been put in place for the 1972 congressional election by a three-judge federal court. The legislature wanted to redraw the districts, but Governor Byrne said he would sign a new redistricting plan only if its implementation date was delayed until 1976. With the ever-growing Watergate scandal looming large over the upcoming 1974 congressional election, a lot of incumbent members of Congress—and a lot of would-be congressional candidates— were jockeying for position. As a result, some of the governor's emissaries paid a bit more attention to me, and to my votes, than they might have otherwise.

State Treasurer Dick Leone was particularly attentive. Credited as the mastermind behind Byrne's successful campaign, Leone was known around the State House as one of the governor's "whiz kids." He was brilliant—and he was brutal. Ultimately, it was the friction that developed between Leone and me that would terminate my relationship with Angelo Errichetti.

Over time, I came to have enormous respect for Dick Leone's intellect, his grasp of public policy, and his commitment to progressive government. What he did not possess, however, at least in his dealings as state treasurer with legislators in the first year of the Byrne administration, was any hint of charm. He pressured me all the time, badgering me with questions about why I couldn't support the governor on this or how I should back the governor on that. And his behavior was over the top. His demeanor was in-your-face harassment.

Like virtually every governor before and since, Byrne was grappling at the time with the issue of taxes. The administration was working on a proposal that would include adoption of the state's first income tax, and Leone was the point person, feeling out how individual legislators would vote on various components that might be included in the tax package. In keeping with my own interpretation of John Horn's second commandment, I felt that I should wait and see what the final package looked like, study it, analyze it, and then, having considered all the pros and cons, make my decision.

This did not sit well with Dick Leone. He wanted me to support whatever tax package the administration put together, and I wasn't about to make any such commitment. (As it turned out, I would unquestionably have voted for the income tax package the legislature finally did adopt in 1976, but by that time I was no longer in the assembly: I was in Congress.) Even if I had been inclined to offer my unequivocal support for Governor Byrne, my testy relationship with State Treasurer Leone had stripped away whatever loyalty I might otherwise have felt.

Four years later, I was in my second term in Congress when I got a call from Angelo Errichetti regarding the 1978 Democratic primary for U.S. Senate. By this time, Errichetti was the undisputed head of the Camden Democratic organization. The Senate seat was held by Republican Clifford Case, and the two leading candidates for the Democratic nomination were Leone, who had the backing of Byrne and many of the state party leaders, and former New York Knicks star Bill Bradley.

I didn't know very much about Bradley. I wasn't a basketball fan, and I had never met him. But because he wasn't Leone, I was strongly inclined to support him. Errichetti was not. "We're all supporting Dick Leone," he told me. "Well," I replied, "I'm not." I explained that my interactions with Leone during my time in Trenton had been less than cordial.

Errichetti implored me to meet with Leone. "He's going to make nice with you," he said. So I drove up from Camden on a cold, snowy day and met Leone at the Forsgate Country Club in Jamesburg. We had a civil but curt conversation, in which he told me, flat out, that I had no choice but to support him because Errichetti was supporting him. I promptly drove back to Camden and told Errichetti I was supporting Bradley.

"Fine," Errichetti said. "Then you're off the ticket." I would be running in the Democratic primary for my third term in the House of Representatives, and Errichetti's threat meant my name would not appear in the column with candidates endorsed by the party for U.S. Senate, the county freeholder board, and all local offices.

In those days, in order to have your own separate line on the primary ballot, you had to have a slate of freeholder candidates—and county bosses cared much more about freeholders, whom they could control, than about congressmen and senators. So I went out and lined up a slate of people to run for freeholder on the same ticket with Bradley and me.

Errichetti's people contacted me immediately. "No, no, don't do that," they said. "We'll get you a line." They went to court and somehow got a judge to issue an order allowing a column to be placed on the ballot with my name and Bradley's, but without freeholder candidates.

In the primary, Bradley clobbered Leone in Camden County by nearly 12,000 votes and carried Gloucester by a 7-to-1 margin. I won without opposition; the Errichetti machine apparently couldn't find anyone to put on the organization-backed ticket against me, and Bradley was elected to the U.S. Senate, where he would serve for eighteen years.

The following year, I put together a full ticket of legislative and freeholder candidates against the Errichetti machine. They all won. And that was the end of my relationship with Angelo Errichetti.

⟨⟨⟨⟩

In my third and final run for the General Assembly in 1973, the Republican campaign against me was centered on my ambition. "Florio isn't interested in going to the assembly," the GOP campaign charged. "He just wants to go to Congress again." They were right. I did want to go to Congress. And on my second try, in 1974, I succeeded.

Looking back, I am reasonably confident, based on my showing in 1972, that I could have won the congressional race two years later even under normal circumstances. The fall of 1974, however, was anything but a normal time in U.S. politics.

The "two-bit burglary" that took place at Washington's Watergate Hotel on June 17, 1972, had turned into a constitutional crisis by the spring of 1974. The nation was gripped by the televised hearings of the Senate Select Committee on Presidential Campaign Activities, headed by North Carolina senator Sam Ervin, and of the House Judiciary Committee, chaired by New Jersey's own Peter Rodino.

At the end of July, the House Judiciary Committee approved three articles of impeachment against President Nixon. On August 8, rather than face a trial in the Senate, the president resigned. Vice President Gerald Ford was sworn in as president and declared that "our long national nightmare" was over.

It was not over, however, for Congressman John Hunt. Along with fellow New Jersey Republicans Charles Sandman and Joseph Maraziti, Hunt was an outspoken defender of President Nixon. Sandman and Maraziti both served on the House Judiciary Committee, and they were among a distinct minority who voted against all three articles of impeachment. In November, their constituents responded by voting them out of office. Hunt suffered the same fate.

The results in the 1st Congressional District weren't even close. My margin in Camden County soared from 1,600 votes in 1972 to 26,000 votes in 1974. In Gloucester County, my 11,000-vote loss in 1972 turned into a 500-vote victory in 1974. On election night I told my kids, "Remember when I talked to you two years ago about losing and running? Well, we did. We lost. We knew how we lost and we corrected it." In retrospect, my explanation may have been a bit brash. Richard Nixon may have had a lot more to do with correcting it than I did.

My larger point, though, had to do with setting goals for yourself and pushing yourself to meet those goals. You're always testing yourself. Even if you fail at whatever you're trying to do, you'll learn something about yourself, about what you can do and what you can't do. Losing means pushing yourself to the very edge, seeing if you can do something, and then doing it well. If you can't, then you know what your limit is, and you know how to improve your effort to make sure that, next time, you don't lose.

Maybe that's the old boxer in me, the light middleweight who took on the light heavyweight and got his clock cleaned. Nowadays I walk. I walk fast with weights, and I do different exercises while I'm walking. I set a target, say ninety paces, but when I get to that place, particularly when I do hard exercises, I tell myself, "OK, ten more feet"—and then maybe another ten feet. If you try to push yourself a little bit more than you anticipated, you will go as far as you can go—and then farther.

I never made a secret of my political ambitions. In the seven congressional races I ran after 1974, the Republicans always rolled out the same campaign theme they had used against me when I ran for the assembly. "He's not interested in being your congressman," they said. "He just wants to be governor." They were right that I wanted to be governor, but they were wrong that I wasn't interested in being their congressman.

CHAPTER 4

The Congressional Years

Democracy is a mechanism for achieving stability by harmonizing diverse and divergent views. Through harmony, you find consensus— and consensus delivers results.

I entered the U.S. House of Representatives with one of the largest and least politically experienced congressional classes in American history. We were the "Watergate babies"—seventy-five Democrats elected just three months after President Nixon's resignation. We were young, relatively new to public office, and absolutely convinced that we would be the agents of change in an ossified, out-of-touch Congress.

As one of my newly elected colleagues, Tim Wirth of Colorado, put it, "We were the children of Vietnam, not World War II. We were products of television, not of print. We were products of computer politics, not courthouse politics. And we were reflections of JFK as president, not FDR."

Many in our class, both Democrats and Republicans, went on to have long and distinguished careers—some in the House, others in the Senate, still others in governor's mansions. They included Norm Mineta and Henry Waxman of California; Chris Dodd and Toby Moffett of Connecticut; Abner Mikva and Paul Simon of Illinois; Chuck Grassley and Tom Harkin of Iowa; Paul Tsongas of Massachusetts; Jim Blanchard of Michigan; Max Baucus of Montana; Bill Hughes, Millicent Fenwick, Andy Maguire, and Helen Meyner of New Jersey; Tom Downey and Dick Ottinger of New York; Larry Pressler of South Dakota; Harold Ford of Tennessee; Jim Jeffords of Vermont; and Bob Kasten of Wisconsin.

Before I took the oath of office, I was one of a dozen incoming representatives selected to attend the Bipartisan Program for Newly Elected Members of Congress at the Kennedy School at Harvard. It was a series of lectures and discussions about the lawmaking process, the committee system, relations with the executive and judicial branches, and a wide range of domestic and foreign policy issues. I did have some relevant experience from my three terms in the New Jersey General Assembly, but there are many more differences than similarities between being a state legislator and being a congressman. Learning about those differences, and gaining an intellectual appreciation of how the legislative branch of the federal government works (or is supposed to work), was excellent preparation for serving in Congress.

Perhaps the biggest difference between the New Jersey legislature and the U.S. Congress is the importance of the committee system. In New Jersey, most legislation was initiated by the governor's office, the leaders of the majority party, or both. It was then given a perfunctory review by the relevant committee and sent to the floor of both houses for an up-or-down vote. All bills in Trenton were required to relate to one issue and one issue only; no unrelated riders could be added to them.

In Congress, legislation typically goes through a time-consuming process of rigorous review by professional staff, followed by markup, economic and budgetary analysis, hearings, amendments, rehearings, and other procedural milestones, all of which are spelled out in meticulously detailed House and Senate rules, before reaching the floor. Once there, one or more riders may be attached, turning an otherwise deliberative process focused on addressing one particular policy issue into a free-for-all of competing interests fighting for pieces of an omnibus package, many of which are aimed at satisfying a whole host of single-issue constituencies.

This process, while Byzantine, was not necessarily unproductive. Getting an omnibus bill passed often relied on the now-unfashionable use of "earmarks," the practice of gaining members' votes for a bill by adding projects that benefited their districts. This was frequently the key to achieving the consensus necessary to advance important legislation.

Although this kind of horse trading could easily be abused—and certainly was on more than a few occasions—its abolition in recent years may be one of the main causes of current congressional dysfunction, with Democrats and Republicans, liberals and conservatives, and Northerners and Southerners in Congress unable to find consensus on just about anything. Occasional earmarks were easy to villainize, but overall they were a very effective lubricant for keeping the wheels of government moving.

I quickly realized that if I wanted to accomplish anything of substance as a member of Congress, I had to get a seat on the right committees. So I went to see Phil Burton.

⪡⪡⪡

A big, outgoing, self-described "fighting liberal," Phil Burton of California was entering his sixth term in Congress in 1975. He had made his name in Washington by leading the successful movement to dismantle the controversial House Un-American Activities Committee. By the time I arrived, he was chairman of the House Democratic Caucus. More important, as far as I was concerned, was his chairmanship of the Democratic Steering and Policy Committee, the body that hands out committee assignments.

Each member of Congress was assigned to one major committee and one minor committee—and not always the ones of his or her choice. Had I not forged a relationship with Phil Burton, I might very well have ended up on the Post Office Committee, or the Banking Committee, or any of a number of other committees in which I would have had little interest and even less expertise.

I told Phil I was particularly interested in environmental issues. I had read and been deeply moved by Rachel Carson's *Silent Spring* a few years earlier, and threats to the environment were becoming a source of considerable anxiety back home in New Jersey. My district was home to a number of major manufacturing plants (RCA, DuPont, and Monsanto, among others), as well as oil refineries and other heavy industries, and my constituents were voicing serious concerns about air pollution, water quality, exposure to toxic substances, and other environmental threats. The district was bordered on the west by the Delaware River, with Camden on one side and Philadelphia on the other. Visions of smoke and flames that arose from another river, the Cuyahoga, that flowed past another gritty city, Cleveland, were still fresh in people's minds.

I also had a strong interest in protecting the New Jersey Pine Barrens, the heavily forested and lightly populated area that covers parts of seven South Jersey counties and sits atop an aquifer that covers 3,000 square miles, nourishing the forest and providing drinking water for more than one million residents. There had been a lot of talk a few years earlier about building a 32,500-acre jetport, along with a new city of 250,000 people, in the middle of the Pinelands.

More recently, there was a move to authorize offshore oil drilling along the New Jersey coast. Contracts were being drawn up, and companies coming in from Louisiana were renting property around Atlantic City. From there, they were planning to transport oil from offshore to refineries along the Delaware River—via a pipeline that would run directly through the Pinelands and into my district.

Phil Burton directed me to the two committees appropriate to my interests. The major committee, which had jurisdiction over environmental issues, was the Interstate and Foreign Commerce Committee, chaired by Harley O. Staggers of West Virginia. (It was later renamed the Energy and Commerce Committee.) The minor committee, which would have jurisdiction over protection of the Pinelands, was the Interior and Insular Affairs Committee, chaired by James Haley of Florida. (It has since been renamed the Natural Resources Committee.)

The Commerce Committee has a long and storied history. Under one name or another, it is the oldest standing legislative committee in the House of Representatives, created in 1795 as the Committee on Commerce and Manufactures. Its heyday was between 1933 and 1936, during the presidency of Franklin D. Roosevelt, when much of the legislation crafted to carry out the New Deal was guided through the committee by its very capable and politically savvy chairman, Sam Rayburn of Texas. He would go on to serve as Speaker of the House for a record seventeen years.

For reasons that still baffle me, there was no subcommittee on the environment at the time, so bills related to the environment went through the Subcommittee on Commerce and Transportation, which I promptly joined. I also joined the Subcommittee on Health, a field in which I also had considerable interest.

The Subcommittee on Commerce and Transportation was an especially good fit for me. In addition to the environment, transportation issues—everything from auto safety, highways and bridges, railroads, and public transit systems to regulation and oversight of pipelines, airports, and seaports—were of great significance to my district and to all of New Jersey. There were also a number of energy-related bills that came before the subcommittee, and energy had become a very hot topic in New Jersey. Everyone had vivid memories of the 1973 Arab oil embargo and the resulting long lines that greeted motorists at gas stations through the first several months of 1974.

The chair of the subcommittee was Fred Rooney of Pennsylvania, a nice, easy-going guy who was not averse to letting junior members play a significant role in the development of legislation. He gave me both the encouragement and the latitude to throw myself into the lawmaking process, allowing me in my first term to take a leadership role in passage of the Resource Conservation and Recovery Act (RCRA) of 1976, a landmark law that gave the U.S. Environmental Protection Agency (EPA) cradle-to-grave authority over the generation, transportation, treatment, storage, and disposal of waste that posed a threat to human health and the environment. With Fred Rooney's blessing, I wrote the section of the law that dealt in considerable detail with the regulation of hazardous waste.

I was also instrumental in passage of the Toxic Substances Control Act (TSCA) of 1976, another major piece of legislation that provided the EPA with authority to regulate the manufacture and sale of chemical substances in commercial products—a very significant issue in New Jersey, with its heavy concentration of petrochemical plants. My involvement in both the RCRA and TSCA laws earned me a measure of prominence that was unusual for a freshman member of Congress.

Meanwhile, the Interior Committee turned out to be a perfect place for me to focus attention on the Pinelands and to gain support from some unusual sources. Most of the members of the committee came from states like Wyoming and Utah, places where the biggest and most popular national parks are located. So they might have wondered whether this freshman from New Jersey was someone with whom they were going to find common cause. They probably felt the same way about Paul Tsongas, who also joined the Interior Committee.

It turned out that Paul was there because he wanted to create a national park in Lowell, Massachusetts. I was there because I wanted to protect the Pinelands in South Jersey. We both believed we would get a sympathetic response from our Western brethren, especially if we also supported their pet projects. We were right.

❧

In my second term, Morris "Mo" Udall of Arizona replaced James Haley as chairman of the Interior and Insular Affairs Committee. Mo's brother, Stewart, had served as secretary of the interior in the Kennedy and Johnson administrations. The Udall family name was already synonymous with environmental activism, and that reputation was cemented during Mo's thirty years of service in the House of Representatives. In 1992, Congress established the Udall Foundation as an independent executive branch agency "to honor Morris K. Udall's lasting impact on this nation's environment, public lands, and natural resources."

The National Parks and Recreation Act of 1978 was an important piece of the Udall legacy. I wrote Section 502 of this law, creating the Pinelands National Preserve. It gave the secretary of the interior thirty days to request that the governor of New Jersey establish a planning entity to develop a comprehensive management plan for the preserve and spelled out in detail the membership of the entity that would develop this plan. It was this level of specificity that allowed the Byrne administration and the New Jersey legislature to pass the landmark Pinelands Protection Act in 1979, establishing the state Pinelands Commission and setting the stage for adoption of the Comprehensive Management Plan that today guides land use, development, and natural resource protection in the Pinelands.

Protecting the Pinelands wasn't just an important environmental goal; it was a public health and economic imperative. The soil in the Pine Barrens is very porous, and any foreign substance—a pesticide applied to crops on farmland, oil from a spill, natural gas from a ruptured pipeline—can easily seep into the aquifer below, causing widespread contamination. The Pinelands and its aquifer may be thought of primarily as a South Jersey issue, but the fact is that the health of all New Jersey residents and the economy of the entire state are dependent on a pristine supply of water. We used to think we could just dump stuff in the ground and it would go away. Now we know better. It doesn't go away: it goes into our drinking water.

Writing Section 502 was an arduous task. It required extensive research into the ecology of the Pinelands and its rich diversity of plant and animal species; its critical importance as a source of drinking water; and its significant natural, cultural, recreational, agricultural, economic, and public health benefits. It also required working hand in glove with key people in the Byrne administration to ensure that what we were doing in Washington was compatible with what they were doing in Trenton.

The effort to preserve and protect the Pinelands was not universally popular back home in New Jersey. There were landowners who feared that designating the Pinelands as a national preserve would diminish the value of their property. There were farmers who were concerned that their ability to plant and grow crops, and to draw the large amounts of water necessary to sustain them, would be adversely affected. There were county and municipal elected officials who were annoyed that decisions made at higher levels of government would supersede theirs. And there were plenty of developers, real estate people, and bankers whose visions of replacing sections of the pine forest with profitable shopping malls and housing developments would be dashed.

There was even a secession movement that found a receptive audience among conspiracy theorists in South Jersey. Convinced that my plan to protect the Pinelands aquifer was actually part of a plot by North Jersey to steal South Jersey's water, this movement circulated petitions to put a public question on the ballot asking if voters in the seven counties affected by the Pinelands initiative favored seceding from New Jersey and establishing their own state. Fortunately, there weren't enough conspiracy theorists in any of the seven counties to bring this question to referendum.

Aside from the secessionists, I had to explain to a lot of people that I recognized and appreciated their short-term interests, but that I believed their own longer-term interests—as well as the public interest—would be better served by taking action now to protect the Pinelands against rampant development, environmental degradation, and unhealthy water. Not all of them agreed, but the process of engaging and informing the public about the critical importance of the Pinelands as an environmental and economic asset to New Jersey succeeded in building a groundswell of popular support for the initiative, easily overcoming the self-interested opposition.

The public wasn't the only audience that needed to be engaged and informed. It was also necessary to educate my fellow members of the Interior and Insular Affairs Committee, who knew practically nothing about the 1.1 million acres of land (22 percent of New Jersey's total landmass) that would become the largest area of protected open space on the Mid-Atlantic seaboard between Richmond and Boston.

We invited Secretary of the Interior Cecil Andrus, a former governor of Idaho, to do a helicopter tour of the Pine Barrens region. He was stunned; nothing could have been further removed from his perception of New Jersey than getting a bird's-eye view of this vast scenic and environmentally sensitive area in the middle of the Northeast megalopolis. Secretary Andrus became a strong advocate for the Pinelands Preserve.

Paul Tsongas and I worked together, as the Eastern contingent, to acquaint our committee colleagues with the environmental interests and concerns of our constituents. At the same time we looked for ways we could help satisfy their concerns about issues like grazing rights, getting a new restaurant approved in a national park, or obtaining an increased appropriation for a project in their district or state. Some of these efforts were significant, others almost trivial.

The California delegation on the committee, which included Democrats Phil Burton and George Miller and Republicans Donald Clausen and Robert Lagomarsino, were pushing a proposal, similar to my Pinelands initiative, to create the Santa Monica Mountains National Recreation Area and establish a comprehensive management plan "to preserve and enhance its scenic, natural, and historical setting." Another committee member, Democrat Teno Roncalio of Wyoming (the last Democrat to represent Wyoming in Congress), was interested in changing the name of the Fort Laramie National Monument to the Fort Laramie National Historic Site and revising its boundaries. The ranking Republican on the committee, Samuel Devine of Ohio, wanted increased appropriations of $1.5 million for the William Howard Taft National Historic Site and $4.2 million for Perry's Victory and International Peace Memorial in his home state.

In virtually every case, I said I would be happy to support these worthy causes, and I would appreciate it if, in turn, the Pinelands National Preserve would receive their support. Paul Tsongas made the same overtures to gain approval of the Lowell National Historic Park. In the end, the bill that came out of committee might be described by critics of the traditional legislative process as a "Christmas Tree" package—a pile of presents wrapped up by members of the Interior and Insular Affairs Committee to give to themselves and each other.

To the contrary, I believe that it was an example of the kind of collaboration that used to make Congress an effective lawmaking body. Admittedly, there may have been more than a few items in the eighty-four-page National Parks and Recreation Act of 1978 that amounted to little more than fulfillment of bringing-home-the-bacon boasts for their sponsors. But without the inclusion of these items, there might not have been enough votes to create the Pinelands National Preserve, and New Jersey might have been deprived of what we consider today to be one of our state's most precious natural resources.

<center>~~~~</center>

Thomas P. "Tip" O'Neill was the House majority leader when I arrived in 1975, and he became Speaker of the House two years later. He is perhaps best remembered for his oft-stated maxim, "All politics is local."

I was very much a disciple of this credo. My background in politics was local, starting in the streets of the 7th District of the 12th Ward of the City of Camden, and I continued my attention to local interests, issues, and concerns as a member of Congress. I placed great emphasis on constituent service. My standing order to the people I hired for both my Washington office and my district office was to be attentive and responsive to every constituent's needs, regardless of who they were, how they voted, or what they needed.

There are two overarching reasons a member of Congress needs to be attentive and responsive to constituents. The first is purely political. If you do something for your constituents—find their lost Social Security check, contact the Veterans Administration about a benefit, help get their relative into a nursing home—you have their vote forever. If you don't do these things, you aren't likely to be a member of Congress for very long.

The second reason is more fundamental: it's your job.

When I was in the state assembly, if I got a call from a woman saying, "Help, my husband beats me," I'd get in touch with the local police chief and ask him to check it out. If I got a request from someone who wanted a liquor license or help with a car registration problem or an answer to a letter sent to an administrative agency, I'd look into it and see what I could do. Even if I couldn't do anything, the fact that I tried was clearly appreciated.

That's retail politics. People count on their elected representatives to help solve their problems. It doesn't matter if you're a member of the town council or the county freeholder board or the state assembly or the U.S. Congress. And it's very satisfying as an elected official to be able to see tangible demonstrations of your positive impact on people's lives.

There is one very important distinction, however, between the level of constituent service provided by a member of Congress and that provided by a state or local officeholder. In the assembly, I made practically all those phone calls and answered nearly all those requests myself. In Congress, I had a staff of about a dozen people doing it.

I greatly appreciated not only the luxury of staff but also the access to information that was available in Washington. If a constituent had a problem with the Social Security Administration, we had an established contact in the agency who could get quick action. If we had a question about the navy, we'd call a high-ranking officer in the Pentagon, who would make arrangements to bring anyone we needed to our office and give us a briefing. Things like that never happened in Trenton.

My first congressional office was on the seventh floor of the Longworth Building. I used to walk up from the basement every day, partly to stay in shape and partly because the elevators took so long. I chose that office because it had a lot of storage space, which we converted into staff facilities. Unfortunately, this office also had a fairly high population of mice, which made it a less-than-desirable work environment for the staff. So I moved into the Rayburn Building, which is both a classier structure and, at least in my experience, mouse-free.

I lived a block from the Capitol in a rent-controlled, one-room efficiency apartment above a liquor store, which featured a flashing light that kept me up half the night. I paid rent of $200 a month for the entire fifteen years I served in Congress. One of the happiest people when I left Washington was the landlord, who promptly raised the rent to $1,400 a month. Like many members of Congress, especially those from the East Coast, I spent my weekdays in Washington and every weekend back home in the district.

One casualty of this arrangement was my marriage. Maryanne and I both realized that we had married too young and too quickly, without giving either of us the chance to mature into the adults we would become or the time to ensure that our interests, our lifestyles, and our aspirations would be compatible. She was an admirable and wonderful mother to our children, but we had grown apart; we were separated, geographically if not formally, by my work in Washington and her home with the kids in the Camden County suburb of Runnemede.

⊰⊱

I was blessed, from the very start, with a great staff. In Washington, my first chief of staff was Wally Johnson, who had served as an administrative assistant to Senator Harrison Williams. Wally had been on Capitol Hill for a long time, and his style was the complete opposite of mine. I liked to spend the bulk of my time reading and researching legislation; he liked to spend his time schmoozing. And he was an expert schmoozer. I remember him going to somebody and saying, "You know, my congressman needs this, and if I don't get it for him, I'm going to get fired. I have a wife. I have a daughter." Wally could be outrageously theatrical—but he was very effective.

Wally was with me for my first two terms. Peter Newbould served as my chief of staff for most of the following years until I left the House to assume the governorship of New Jersey in 1990.

My district office, ably staffed by the quartet of Joe Salema, Viola Foster, Chuck Manella, and Cass Honer, was located during my first year in Congress behind a diner in Somerdale; a year later, we moved it to a strip mall on Colby Avenue in Stratford, and that's where it stayed for the next fourteen years.

Joe Salema had just graduated from college when he volunteered in my unsuccessful 1972 congressional campaign. His aunt was the municipal chairman in Monroe Township in Gloucester County, and she introduced us. I really didn't know my way around Gloucester County, which made up a significant portion of the district, so I relied on Joe to drive me around and help me get to know the lay of the land. He moved up from volunteer to hired staff for the 1974 campaign, and then onto the congressional payroll to work in the district office. Viola Foster was from Burlington County, part of which was moved into my district after the 1980 Census. Chuck Manella and Cass Honer were from Camden County.

They were the point people for constituent service, and they did a wonderful job. Any problem, no matter how trivial, got a response. Sometimes the response wasn't what the constituent wanted to hear. Sometimes it took longer than we had hoped to get a response from Social Security, the Veterans Administration, the Internal Revenue Service, or some other federal agency. I was almost pathologically concerned about making sure that everybody got some kind of response within a couple of days; if we didn't have the answer yet, we would let the constituent know we were working on it and would provide regular updates.

Joe, Viola, Chuck, and Cass kept records of every call and letter we received, what kind of problem or issue was presented to us, and what we had done to address it. We hoped our constituents would remember our efforts and support me in the next election. Many of them did, and I am convinced that strong constituent service was one of the main reasons I won re-election handily in every race from 1976 to 1988.

We also attracted skillful volunteers to help out in the district office. Two retirees, Jack Williams and Dave Halsey, offered their services after hearing me talk at a town meeting. Jack had worked for the Veterans Administration; Dave had worked for the Immigration and Naturalization Service. Whenever a veteran had an issue, Jack was on it. Whenever an immigration issue arose, Dave took care of it. Their contribution to our constituent service was invaluable.

While still in Congress, I taught a course in politics and public policy for about a year and a half at Rutgers University's Eagleton Institute of Politics. Every Monday morning, I would teach a 9:00 a.m. class in New Brunswick, then get a ride to Newark, board the train, and head down to Washington. (Later, I taught a Monday morning class in administrative law at Rutgers Law School in Camden, got a ride to Philadelphia, hopped on the train, and headed down to Washington.) Two of my best students at Eagleton—David Applebaum and Bob Sommer—subsequently came to work in my Washington office, and David continued to work for me through my term as governor. Another longtime loyal employee, Amy Mansue, started as an intern from the University of Alabama to work with me on the Subcommittee on Health, stayed on my staff when the internship ended, and then served as an extremely valuable policy advisor on health during my administration in Trenton.

My campaigns and my Washington and district offices were also places where romance bloomed. Working there brought together Steve Weinstein, who managed my successful assembly campaign in 1969 and my unsuccessful first run for Congress in 1972, and his wife Karin Elkis; Dan Dalton, an early campaign volunteer who came to work in my Washington office, and his wife Suzanne; and Chuck Manella, part of the quartet in my district office, and his wife Maria. All of them worked very hard for me and became good friends.

I won't point the finger at any of them for an embarrassing episode that took place early in my congressional career. I had two cars: a beaten-up Ford Escort, which I used very occasionally in Washington, and a Mercury, which I used when I was in the district. The Mercury's license plate, provided by the state, featured two gold shields, the words "U.S. Congress," and the number 1 (for the First Congressional District). I told my district office staff to use the car during the week if they had to—until it was brought to my attention that the car was spotted one night at a motel. I don't know to this day who took the car, but I wasted no time getting rid of those courtesy license plates.

It may be hard to believe, given the raucous reception many members of Congress have experienced in recent years when they've met with constituents, but one of the things I loved about serving in Congress was holding town hall meetings. I held them on average about twice a month, all over the district. I would spend about fifteen minutes or so on whatever was the issue of the day and then let the audience go at me for the next hour and a half. I sometimes think it was this experience that inspired me, in my life after politics, to become a teacher.

People would come to these meetings, tell me what they thought about this or that issue, and then ask me to comment. What did I think about Medicaid coverage of abortion, affirmative action in college admissions, mandatory recycling, nuclear weapons for NATO, or foreign aid to Israel? Some of the questioners were openly hostile, but I tried very hard to treat everyone with respect. I would explain that I appreciated the fact that different people took different positions on issues and then would go on to describe what I felt were the most persuasive arguments in favor of a particular position. I didn't shy away from taking a stand, but always tried to base it on facts, logic, and a sense of fairness. Even if my arguments weren't always persuasive to some, I think people generally came away from these meetings with the feeling that I was a rational and reasonable representative.

In addition to the town meetings, I made a point of accepting invitations to speak before groups that I knew were not on my side. I enjoyed going to meetings of organizations like local Chambers of Commerce, fully aware that my well-known and enthusiastic support for issues like environmental regulation marked me as the opposition. Speaking before a hostile group could sometimes be uncomfortable, but more often than not it had a salutary effect. For one thing, people tend to be a little more courteous when they know they have you outnumbered. If nothing else, they give you grudging respect just for showing up. More important, there may be a handful of people in that audience who are at least open to the idea that certain environmental regulations are actually in their best interest. If you go into a hostile setting and come out with even one convert, it's a victory.

Every meeting I attended, whether the audience was made up of individual constituents or members of an interest group, made me keenly aware of the extent to which people are often motivated, appropriately or inappropriately, by self-interest. A lot of the comments I heard at meetings reflected people's hopes and fears about how a particular government program or action would affect them. In cases where such concerns were justified, and where a particular program or piece of legislation could be tweaked to avoid unpleasant consequences without causing harm to anyone else, I tried to do something about it. In other cases, where the broader public interest came into conflict with the constituent's or group's self-interest, I tried to find ways to reduce the level of conflict as much as possible by presenting alternative views of what I regarded as their real interest.

There are, of course, some personal interests that simply cannot be reconciled with the public interest. If somebody from the Chamber of Commerce wanted the RCRA law to be gutted because it adversely affected his business, or a constituent at a town meeting wanted citizens to have unfettered access to guns, there was no way I would be supportive—and, conversely, there probably was no way the people raising these issues were going to vote for me. In most cases where somebody's self-interest couldn't be reconciled with the public interest, all I could do was express my sympathy and explain that I had a constitutional responsibility to serve all the people to the best of my ability. Only on the rarest occasions, like when somebody wanted to put more guns on the street, did I express no sympathy at all.

Before the "Watergate babies" arrived in Washington, there was a time-honored tradition that members moved up the chain of command in their committees and subcommittees on the basis of seniority. The longest-serving member of the majority party became chairman; the longest-serving representative of the minority party became the ranking member. There was rarely a contest for a committee or subcommittee chairmanship.

Our class of 1974 changed the rules. We insisted that the chairs of the standing committees be elected by the full Democratic caucus, rather than enthroned by their longevity. And we wasted no time putting the new rules into effect.

The longtime chairman of the House Armed Services Committee, F. Edward Hébert of Louisiana, was the first victim. He was already in the crosshairs of many of his younger, antiwar colleagues because of his chummy relationship with the Pentagon. Then, he pretty much alienated everyone who was elected in 1974 by dismissively referring to us as "boys and girls." When he was asked in the caucus how he felt about women serving in the military, he replied that he thought women were nice, but they had no place in the armed forces. He also made some extremely insensitive remarks about African Americans. He was abruptly replaced as chairman by Charles Price of Illinois.

The same thing happened to a pair of Texans, Wright Patman and William Poage. Patman lost the chairmanship of the Banking, Currency, and Housing Committee to Henry Reuss of Wisconsin, and Poage was replaced as chair of the Agriculture Committee by Tom Foley of Washington.

The contrast between the older members of Congress and the "Watergate babies" was like night and day. I was surprised by how passive many of the entrenched members were. They didn't get involved early on in the committee or subcommittee process, but waited instead for bills to come to the floor before they expressed any interest in them. There seemed to be an entire older generation of members of Congress who faithfully followed the second commandment laid down by my former assembly colleague John Horn: don't make a decision until or unless you have to.

Those of us who felt it was our job to make decisions were emboldened by the changeover of committee and subcommittee chairmanships from the old guard to the new and by the sense that a new wave of activism was sweeping through the House of Representatives. During my second term in Congress, which coincided with the first two years of Jimmy Carter's presidency, we created the U.S. Department of Energy, enacted the National Energy Conservation Policy Act, made major changes to the Clean Water Act and the Federal Water Pollution Control Act, and passed the first law promoting solar photovoltaic energy research and development.

The 1978 congressional election was a turning point for me. The Democrats lost fifteen seats, a fairly modest number for a party holding the White House in a midterm election. One of the Democrats who lost his seat, however, was Fred Rooney, chairman of the Subcommittee on Commerce and Transportation.

Under the old rules, the subcommittee chairmanship would automatically have gone to the next senior member, David Satterfield III, a conservative from Virginia who was entering his seventh term. I felt that my diligence on the subcommittee, my leadership on the RCRA and TSCA bills, and my involvement in many other pieces of legislation during my two terms entitled me to some consideration for the chairmanship.

During the subcommittee's deliberations, Congressman Satterfield emphasized his many years of experience; I talked about substantive environmental and transportation issues and enumerated all the things I had accomplished in the previous four years. The subcommittee members opted for substance over experience and elected me chairman.

I made several changes right away. First, I changed the name of the subcommittee to Commerce, Transportation, and Tourism. Next, I made it clear that subcommittee meetings would start on time. My very first meeting as chairman was scheduled to begin at 10 a.m. When I arrived, the only other person in the room was the court reporter. I gaveled the meeting to order and started calling the names of people who were supposed to be there as witnesses. None had shown up yet.

This unheard-of punctuality by a subcommittee chairman found its way into an edition of *The Hill*, prompting some attention and a whole lot of questions. What's going on here? Who is this guy? Who ever heard of committee or subcommittee meetings starting on time? After a while, both the subcommittee members and the people we called to testify were embarrassed enough to start showing up on time.

This may have been an early indication to anyone who might have been watching of the discipline I would later attempt—with limited success— to impose as governor. In any event, I know I made my mother proud.

One of the great benefits of chairing a congressional committee or sub-committee is the staff that comes with the position. Now, in addition to my staffs in the Washington and district offices, I had the opportunity to put together a subcommittee staff. I had heard good things about Greg Lawler, who had established a solid reputation while working for another member of Congress. Shortly after assuming the chairmanship, I interviewed Greg and hired him on the spot.

Greg, who was later to serve as legislative counsel during my governorship, helped me assemble an outstanding subcommittee staff, made up of people who were not only good on substance but also understood the legislative process. Chief among them was Rena Steinzor, who served as staff counsel to the subcommittee; her contribution to our success in writing and passing landmark legislation protecting the environment was indispensable. She went on to become a professor at the University of Maryland Law School.

Another attorney on the subcommittee staff, Richard Huberman, had tremendous expertise in railroad and consumer protection issues. And another outstanding subcommittee staffer, Stavroula Lambrakopoulos, was so professional and competent I later hired her as director of federal relations when I became governor. A few years later, she earned her law degree, with honors, from George Washington University Law School and went on to become a partner in one of the top law firms in Washington.

Knowing how the legislative process worked was critical. My own tutorial in congressional process came from two sources of almost completely opposite comportment and temperament: John Dingell of Michigan, who succeeded Harley O. Staggers as chairman of the Energy and Commerce Committee in 1981 and served in that capacity for the next fourteen years; and Paul Rogers of Florida, who chaired the Subcommittee on Health.

John Dingell was the consummate deal maker. He could be bombastic one day, courtly the next. He could be a ruthless partisan or a charming consensus builder. He was a tireless advocate for the automobile industry, which conflicted with my support for tightening fuel economy and air quality standards, and an outspoken defender of unfettered gun rights, a position with which I also strongly disagreed. But he knew how to work the system, how to find common ground among Democratic and Republican members of subcommittees and committees, and how to round up the votes on the House floor from both sides of the aisle to get important legislation through Congress.

I acquired a lot of his knowledge by viewing him in action. His abiding principle was perhaps best expressed when he announced in 2014 that he was stepping down after a record sixty years in the House of Representatives: "Congress means coming together, the great coming together of the American people," he told the *New York Times*. "Compromise is an honorable word."

Paul Rogers couldn't have been more different. The embodiment of the courtly Southern gentleman, Rogers approached lawmaking by publicly acknowledging some merit in whatever anyone said while, at the same time, deftly steering his subcommittee toward the result he wanted. He accomplished this by subjecting the Subcommittee on Health to interminable hearings, patiently gathering testimony and politely encouraging members in a direction that ultimately led to his desired outcome. You could almost call it legislation by attrition and courtesy; after a while, even the most stubborn subcommittee member just gave up and said OK.

I did not adopt the full Rogers technique in running my own subcommittee, partly because I didn't always have a preconceived idea of exactly where I wanted our deliberations to take us. Nor did I think my desired outcome, if I had one, was necessarily the best one or the only one I could support. But I did learn from Paul Rogers how courtesy, politeness, and patience can go a long way toward developing the kind of bipartisan camaraderie any legislative body—whether it's a subcommittee, a full committee, or the entire 435-member House of Representatives—needs to be productive.

Thanks to John Dingell and Paul Rogers, I was keenly aware that a bill coming out of a unified subcommittee had a much greater chance of becoming law than one that was supported by members of one party and opposed by the other. Partisan bills voted out by a subcommittee had to go through a time-consuming, and often futile, effort to achieve consensus at the full committee level. Bills that come out with concurrence of both the majority and minority have a much smoother route to passage.

There were seven Democrats and five Republicans on the Subcommittee on Commerce, Transportation, and Tourism, and I was determined that, as often as possible, the bills we reported out to the full committee would have at least some Republican support. Thankfully, there were two Republicans— one on the subcommittee, the other on the full committee—who were collegial, smart, and a pleasure to work with. Ed Madigan of Illinois was the ranking member of the subcommittee. Norman Lent of New York, who served on the full committee, represented a Long Island district that was affected by many of the same environmental and transportation issues facing my New Jersey district. The three of us worked very closely together, always looking for ways we could find common ground. We talked about our differences on bills, which were sometimes considerable. I would ask them, "Have you thought about this?" And they would respond, "Well, have you thought about that?" I often found that I hadn't, and I needed to rethink my position. So this was a very useful and productive process.

An important lesson I learned from my interaction with Madigan—and in some respects reflecting the Paul Rogers approach—was to keep discussion and negotiation open for as long as possible in an effort to achieve consensus. Forcing a decision prematurely hardens people's positions. Getting politicians to accept the same thing they rejected last week is hard, if not impossible. But if you take the time to find out what their concerns are, you can modify a bill, even if only cosmetically, and allow them to change their mind without sacrificing their principles.

I came to recognize that every subcommittee member had to have a piece of what we were dealing with, that everybody had to be engaged—intellectually, emotionally, or some other way—in doing the public's business. Sometimes, the outside game was just as important as the inside game. Maybe a key decision maker on the subcommittee, regardless of party, would be responsive to a labor leader, or a businessman, or an environmental activist, or a transportation expert. Get to know your colleagues, figure out what makes them tick, get the outside forces engaged, and you'll have a greater chance of success. Harmonize your interests with their interests. Find out if there's a piece of legislation, an amendment, or even a slight change in language that can satisfy everyone's interests.

As indulgent as I tried to be in attending to the interests of my subcommittee members, I was almost prosecutorial in my treatment of witnesses. I strongly discouraged them from giving canned testimony. I routinely gave a witness five minutes to talk before opening the proceedings to questions. And I asked tough questions, even of witnesses with whom I agreed. To me there was nothing more boring, not to mention unproductive, than calling witnesses who shared the same views held by the Democratic or Republican members of the subcommittee so they could all ask softball questions and then nod their heads in agreement.

I remember one subcommittee meeting on insurance that featured Ralph Nader as a witness. He gave us all the reasons he thought every action in the bill we were contemplating would be a terrible thing to do. So I asked him, "Well, Mr. Nader, would you please give us your thoughts as to what you would tell us if you were the president of Metropolitan Life Insurance?" He couldn't bring himself to play that role. "All those things," he said of the measures we were considering, "are just no good."

In the course of researching and writing the section of the RCRA law dealing with the regulation of hazardous waste, I uncovered countless examples of toxic substances that had been disposed of improperly before the law took effect. All over the country dumpsites were contaminated with toxic materials, such as benzene, toluene, and PCBs, that were known human carcinogens.

If RCRA worked as it should, we would put a stop to the practice of dumping toxic waste in a manner that posed a threat to human health and the environment. But stopping the dumping of hazardous substances wouldn't do anything about dumpsites that already existed. We needed an inventory of places where hazardous substances had been dumped before RCRA took effect, and we needed legislation that addressed this issue retrospectively, authorizing and financing the cleanup of these dangerous dumpsites.

As chair of the subcommittee with jurisdiction over environmental matters, I felt it was my obligation to meet this issue head-on. I studied it intensely. I researched the available scientific information on the human health effects of thousands of chemical substances. I met with representatives of petrochemical companies, waste haulers, and landfill operators who feared regulation of their industries' practices; environmental groups who were supportive of such regulation; bankers who would be involved in financing the cleanup of hazardous sites; and legal firms that specialized in cases regarding the assessment of environmental liability.

What emerged from this process was a 162-page piece of legislation called the Comprehensive Environmental Response Compensation and Liability Act (CERCLA)—or, as it is more familiarly known, the Superfund law. I was the principal sponsor, and getting it passed was by far the most difficult battle I faced as a legislator at both the state and federal levels.

The underlying principle of the Superfund law was a simple one: the cost of cleaning up pollution should be paid by the polluter. This concept was vigorously disputed not only by companies that produced or used the substances that ended up in hazardous waste sites but also by those that transported or dumped them there. They contended that society as a whole benefited from the manufacture of these products and that society should therefore bear the burden of cleanup. Environmentalists countered that the companies had benefited economically from the irresponsible disposal of these wastes and should therefore bear the cleanup costs.

There was another, even stickier, point of contention in the legislation— the application of both strict liability and joint several liability, two crucial concepts in tort liability law. The legislation empowered the EPA to levy cleanup costs on a polluter on the basis of strict liability, meaning the agency did not have to prove that the polluter had been negligent or acted in bad faith. Even more contentious was the application of joint several liability, which meant that if a number of different property owners were involved in the disposal of toxic waste that required remediation, all of them would be held jointly liable for the cleanup costs—unless a party could prove that it was responsible for only a specified percentage of the pollution present at the site, in which case its share of the cleanup cost would be allocated proportionally.

It took months of hearings and intense negotiations to get the bill through the subcommittee, the full committee, and onto the House floor. If it is true that timing is everything when it comes to getting a controversial piece of legislation enacted, we were fortunate that dramatic environmental disasters in two places—one in Bullitt County, Kentucky, and the other in Niagara Falls, New York—captured widespread public attention just as the bill was making its way through the legislative process, and they embodied the critical need for the Superfund law. I use the term "fortunate" advisedly. Supporters of the bill were fortunate; the people who lived near these two places were not.

A. L. Taylor owned a dump truck, a crane, and a seventeen-acre field about twenty miles south of Louisville in Bullitt County. He made a living hauling away liquid waste from many of Kentucky's largest industries and dumping them in his field. When state officials responded to a complaint that a nearby creek had caught fire, they visited the site, where they found 100,000 steel drums filled with sulfuric acid, solvents, paints, auto transmission fluids, chemical degreasers, and a variety of exotic industrial chemicals with names like cyclohexanone, n-prophyl acetate, isocyanate, Triton-X, and arapol 892X60.

The A. L. Taylor field became widely known as the Valley of the Drums.

The second site was a three-block tract of land on the eastern edge of Niagara Falls where, in the early days of the twentieth century, William T. Love had envisioned the development of a dream community. He would build homes and industries in the neighborhood and would generate hydroelectric power for them by digging a short canal between the upper and lower Niagara Rivers. His dream was shattered in 1910, a casualty of both an economic downturn and the discovery of cheaper ways to transmit electricity.

Construction of the Love Canal, however, had already begun.

At some time during the 1920s, the Love Canal was turned into a municipal and industrial chemical dumpsite. In 1953, the Hooker Chemical Company, which had taken ownership of the site, covered the canal with earth and sold it to the City of Niagara Falls for $1. By the end of that decade, about one hundred homes and a school had been built on the three-block tract.

In 1978, as we were writing the Superfund law, corroding waste-disposal drums were showing up in residents' backyards, along with puddles of toxic substances. Trees were turning black and dying. The air in the

Congressman Florio, chairman of the House Subcommittee on Commerce, Transportation, and Tourism, joins fellow sponsors and cosponsors of the bill deregulating the nation's railroads as President Jimmy Carter signs it into law.

neighborhood was described as having a faint, choking smell. Children were returning from the school playground with burns on their hands and faces. The neighborhood was experiencing an alarming cluster of miscarriages and birth defects.

Spurred into action by the Valley of the Drums and Love Canal, Congress approved the Superfund bill, and President Carter signed it into law as one of his last official acts on December 11, 1980. A little more than a month later, Ronald Reagan was sworn in as president. I would spend most of the next eight years trying to get his administration, which was openly hostile to the law, to implement and enforce it.

Teaching a course at the Rutgers Law School for two semesters in 1982 allowed me to blend my academic interest in the subject of administrative law with my practical experience in Congress. I had a pretty thorough understanding of how the laws passed by the Congress, which inevitably contain language that is open to interpretation, are interpreted, refined, and implemented by the regulatory agencies in the executive branch that are responsible for carrying them out.

The Superfund law, for example, was not without its ambiguities. Its provisions call for cleaning up toxic waste dumpsites. But how do you define toxic? How do you define cleanup? How clean is clean? An administrative agency, in this case the EPA, has to answer these questions. If you have an administration that supports the law, the agency will adopt regulations that define what constitutes an acceptable level of cleanup with some degree of specificity and establish a scientific standard for measuring compliance. On the other hand, if you have an adverse or hostile administration, the EPA could direct responsible parties to brush the site up with a whisk broom.

Worse, what a hostile administration can do is withhold funding for any program it doesn't want to implement. It was clear, almost from the outset, that this is exactly what the Reagan administration intended to do with the Superfund. Democrats, who still held the majority in both houses of Congress, went on the defensive: we had to stop bad things from happening, as opposed to making good things happen.

Reagan's EPA administrator, Anne Gorsuch Burford, was an avowed opponent of many of the laws her agency was charged with enforcing. She shared the president's view that environmental laws, rules, and regulations were killing the oil companies, the chemical companies, and other polluting industries. In her first year in office, she slashed the EPA budget, relaxed Clean Air Act regulations, and dropped cases against polluters. Then she took aim against the Superfund. That was her big mistake.

By 1982, the second year of the Superfund's existence, it was clear that funds that were supposed to be used to clean up toxic waste sites were not being used for their intended purpose. In fact, it appeared that

$1.6 billion in Superfund money was being mishandled by the EPA. At that point, Congress ordered Administrator Burford to turn over the records of the Superfund program. She refused, claiming the records were covered by executive privilege. She subsequently became the first agency director in history to be cited for contempt of Congress.

Several months later, the Reagan administration dropped the claim of executive privilege, the EPA turned the documents over to Congress, and in March 1983, Administrator Burford resigned. Less than a year later, her assistant, Rita Lavelle, who had direct responsibility for administering the Superfund program, was sentenced to six months in prison and fined $10,000 for lying to Congress. Altogether, twenty-two EPA officials resigned or were fired in connection with mismanagement of the Superfund program.

Thanks to their overzealous efforts to undermine the Superfund, these EPA officials inadvertently saved it, though we did have to continue to battle during the rest of the Reagan administration against repeated attempts to circumvent or shortchange it.

The administration was very clever. For example, it couldn't get rid of the Clean Air Act, so it mounted an attack through the appropriations process. Here's your appropriation, the administration would say, but a footnote would state that none of the money could be used to implement this rule or that rule, and so on. We still had a Democratic majority in Congress, but we weren't able to fight off a lot of these measures. We lacked the votes to override a veto.

Another example of the administration's maneuvering was President Reagan's food stamps initiative. The law states that children must be provided a nutritional lunch that contains proteins, carbohydrates, and other specified nutrients. What constitutes these nutrients, however, is left to interpretation by the agency responsible for adopting regulations pursuant to the law. The Reagan administration interpreted ketchup and relish as vegetables for the purposes of meeting the definition of a nutritional lunch.

The frustration I and other Democrats in Washington felt most acutely during the Reagan years was with the administrative agencies. They were openly flaunting the clear intent of laws we had worked on or sponsored. The agencies exploited these laws' ambiguities, interpreting them in a way the administration wanted to interpret them, often in direct contradiction to the intent of Congress.

⋘⋙

Conflict between a Democratic Congress and a Republican administration was hardly unique to the Reagan years. Nor was the source of the conflict unusual. It pitted a familiar Republican argument—that over-regulation of industry costs too much money and too many jobs—against a traditional Democratic position, that regulation is necessary to protect public health, promote worker safety, and deliver a host of other social and economic benefits.

I have always made the argument that environmental laws in particular, designed to clean up our air and water, are extremely important for jobs. If you let toxic dumpsites spread, what happens to the food processing industry, which is very water-intensive? If you don't ensure that water is of the highest quality, what happens to the chemical and pharmaceutical industries? If you dump sewage in the ocean, what happens to the tourism industry?

At the same time, if you strengthen regulation of what comes out of the smokestacks of power plants and effectively shift the nation's energy appetite away from fossil fuels toward more sustainable sources, you create jobs in a growing sector of the economy researching and developing solar, geothermal, wind, and other clean, sustainable sources of energy. Likewise, programs like the Superfund don't just create jobs; they create an entire industry dedicated to cleaning up hazardous waste sites and further spur economic growth by making cleaned-up property suitable for redevelopment.

I wish I could brag that I introduced the Superfund legislation because I knew my constituents back in New Jersey would be its primary beneficiaries. I didn't. I had no idea that New Jersey would lead the nation in the number of hazardous waste sites identified for remediation under the Superfund, and I'm not at all sure that New Jersey took pride in this distinction. Nevertheless, we were able, despite the Reagan administration's lack of enthusiasm for the program, to identify and authorize the remediation of seventy-five Superfund sites in New Jersey between 1983 and 1989, including the notorious GEMS and Lipari landfills in Gloucester County, the Kin-Buc Landfill in Edison, and the dioxin-contaminated Passaic River in Newark, a byproduct of Agent Orange manufactured by the Diamond Alkali Company during the Vietnam War.

New Jersey still has more than one hundred active Superfund sites that are in need of cleanup, an average of about five per county. In our densely populated state, nobody lives far from a site that poses, in the words of the Superfund law, "imminent and substantial endangerment to human health or the environment." There is still a lot of work to be done.

Although my clear emphasis throughout my time in Congress was on environmental issues, there are three other legislative accomplishments of which I am especially proud—the Railroad Retirement Solvency Act, enacted early in the Reagan administration; the Korean War Veterans Memorial bill, adopted midway through Reagan's two terms; and the Exon-Florio Amendment related to foreign investment, which was passed as Reagan was leaving office.

In 1981, I was the principal House sponsor of the Northeast Rail Service Act, which essentially saved the Consolidated Rail Corporation (Conrail) by relieving it of its obligation to operate passenger service and turning that obligation over to Amtrak. Over the next couple of years, the Reagan administration talked openly about the possibility of breaking up Conrail's freight service and selling or privatizing Amtrak. We were successful in fighting off both these efforts.

The administration also proposed shifting railroad retirees out of the financially troubled Railroad Retirement Program into the less-generous Social Security program. I sponsored the Railroad Retirement Solvency Act of 1983, which saved the Railroad Retirement Program by modifying the tax rules, adjusting the eligibility requirements for disability benefits, recalculating annuities, amending the program's borrowing authority, and enacting a host of other provisions that allowed retirees to continue drawing benefits from the program. More than three decades later, a railroad man in Washington told me, "I still think about you because you saved the railroad pension system."

In 1984, I left the Interior and Insular Affairs Committee and joined the Veterans Affairs Committee. Shortly thereafter, at one of my town meetings in Gloucester County, a Korean War veteran named Otto Gollon stood up and asked me why there was no memorial in Washington honoring those who had served in Korea. He felt that he and other Korean War veterans had been slighted and denied their rightful share of the nation's appreciation.

Although I joined the navy several years after hostilities in Korea ended, I nevertheless benefited from the Korean War GI Bill, for which I was deeply grateful. I also agreed with Otto. Congress had already authorized a memorial to Vietnam veterans, who served their country two to three decades after those who served in Korea. So I sponsored the Korean War Memorial Act, authorizing construction of a monument to honor members of the armed forces who served in the Korean War.

I was proud to attend the dedication of the Korean War Veterans Memorial on July 27, 1995, the forty-second anniversary of the armistice that ended the war. It occupies a prominent site near the Lincoln Memorial, just south of the Reflecting Pool on the National Mall.

In 1988, I cosponsored, with Senator James Exon of Nebraska, the National Security Test for Foreign Investment Bill, which came to be known as the Exon-Florio Amendment. This provision granted the president the authority to investigate and block any mergers, takeovers, and/

or acquisitions that could result in foreign control of domestic companies if, in the president's judgment, the transaction would threaten national security. The bill was a response to concerns about a recent rash of foreign takeovers of American firms that produced high-tech goods and services and to the fear that the United States was becoming too dependent on foreign sources for defense-related production.

What was interesting about this bipartisan measure was the almost contradictory motivation behind conservative Republican and liberal Democratic support for it. Those on the Right saw the amendment as a way to protect American businesses from foreign competition, while those on the Left believed that giving the president the power to investigate and block transactions would ensure that decisions regarding national security would be made at the highest levels of government, not by the private sector.

This example illustrates how legislating is often the art of finding common ground among uncommon allies. It's a matter of aligning personal interests with political interests, of convincing people on polar ends of the political spectrum that somewhere in the middle lies a position that they can support without sacrificing their principles.

Serving in Congress is an eye-opening experience in many ways. Learning about issues you never even thought about before, meeting people from states you've never visited, listening to a well-reasoned argument from someone whose opinion couldn't be more diametrically opposed to your own—these are all the kinds of experiences that leave a deep and lasting impression on a kid from Brooklyn.

As a child, I never traveled anywhere outside New York and New Jersey. In the navy, I spent time in Maryland, Florida, Oklahoma, and Alaska. As a congressman, I discovered the world.

One of my most interesting trips out of the country was to the Soviet Union in 1986. I went there at the behest of some Jewish "refuseniks," who wanted me to see firsthand the oppressive nature of life under the Communist Party. When corporate leaders at Campbell's Soup, one of Camden's biggest employers, learned I was going to Moscow, they asked if I could also make some inquiries on their behalf.

Campbell's Soup was interested in the possibility of establishing some kind of relationship with the Soviet government. The company's leaders explained to me that because the Soviets didn't have a modern, sophisticated system for food processing and distribution, many of their food crops, particularly tomatoes, were rotting before they got to market. Campbell's Soup was hoping someone in Moscow might be interested in pursuing some sort of a venture partnership with the world's most famous producer of tomato soup.

Once in Russia, I had an opportunity to raise this idea at a cocktail party attended by the Soviet minister of agriculture, who told me his government would be interested in such a venture only if Campbell's Soup put up the money and then turned management over to the Soviets. That put a quick end to any discussion of détente between Campbell's Soup and the Soviet Union.

After the minister had a little more to drink (well, actually a lot more), I summoned up the nerve to point out that it was pretty clear to me, even in my brief visit, that the housing stock was falling apart, Muscovites were standing in long lines outside the stores, and the whole Soviet economy looked like it was in shambles. How, I asked him, despite these obvious difficulties, had his country nevertheless managed to make such great advancements in space exploration?

"The truth of the matter," he confided, "is the space program really doesn't work very well. What we do is, if we need one part for a space operation, we order 100 parts—and maybe one out of 100 will be effective." I was surprised at his answer, both for its bluntness and its admission that what we in the West thought were the most productive features of Soviet society were, in fact, spectacularly unproductive. We found out a few years later that this nearly defined the whole Soviet economy, and that's why it all fell apart.

Another fascinating trip I took was to the Philippines. It was a fact-finding tour with a contingent that included my House colleague (and later Senator) Bob Torricelli. The most memorable part of that trip was our meeting with the archbishop of Manila, Jaime Sin (widely known as "Cardinal Sin"), with whom Congressman Torricelli promptly got into a debate. Why, he asked, if the population of the Philippines was rising faster than the government's ability to feed and house it, did the archbishop not support abortion as a birth control measure? Needless to say, he didn't get the answer he was hoping for.

On the same trip we stopped in South Korea, where other members of the delegation went on a shopping spree. After Manila, Seoul seemed like one giant supermarket. I was impressed by the modern skyscrapers and the hustle and bustle of the streets, but I am definitely not a shopper—never have been, never will be. The rest of the delegation was buying up $100 suits that would have cost three times as much at home. Our flight back to Washington carried a lot more luggage than our flight to Manila, but mine was still a single beaten-up old suitcase.

My most interesting trip, which I did largely because many constituents pushed me to go, was to Israel. I knew that Israel was a little bit smaller than New Jersey, but I had never considered what life would be like if Pennsylvania were Egypt, New York were Syria, and both were openly hostile to New Jersey. That's what living in Israel is like, and when you can drive from the Syrian border to the Gaza Strip in just a few hours, you get a real appreciation for the very tenuous situation there.

This gave me an insight into Israel that I didn't have before and helped me understand why it is so difficult to find a peaceful solution to the problems that plague the Middle East. It all comes down to a matter of trust. Israel and Egypt were able to reach a milestone peace agreement at Camp David, built on trust developed between Israeli prime minister Menachem

Begin and Egyptian president Anwar el-Sadat. No such trust has been
forged, however, between Israel and the Assad regime in Syria or with Pal-
estinian leadership in the West Bank and Gaza. Without trust, the only
sentiment that deepens is suspicion.

≪≪≪

Trust is not just the key to resolving some of the world's most difficult and
dangerous conflicts. It is also the foundation of the relationship that needs
to exist between the American people and their elected officials.

There is an all-too-common belief, frequently expressed on talk radio
and elsewhere, that "all politicians are crooks." This is an especially widely
held view when the politicians in question are from New Jersey. For better or worse, the Garden State has a reputation of being a fertile field for
political corruption.

When I first got elected to the assembly, I had an office on Cooper
Street in Camden. People would park their car on the street and come to
my office. Then, when they got back to their car, they would find a parking ticket. Some of them would come back in and ask if there was anything I could do about it. "Sure," I said. "I'll take care of it." And I did: I
paid the ticket.

At some point between my election to the assembly in 1969 and my
election to Congress in 1974, I realized that I would never do anything like
that again. Maybe it was the impact of Watergate. Maybe we had entered
a new era in which public figures were being held to a higher standard of
honesty and integrity. Whatever the reason, I felt it was always necessary
to be overly cautious about separating any actions I took as a public official from any hint of personal gain.

It isn't always easy in public office to differentiate a campaign contribution from a bribe. Did you get that donation from a constituent, an
organization, or an interest group because they appreciate your service or
as payback because they benefited financially from a vote you cast? Did
you sponsor a particular bill because it was the right thing to do or because

a wealthy donor asked you to? Did you appoint a contributor to a board or commission based on merit, or was the appointment a quid pro quo for the contribution? In this day and age when campaigns have become multimillion-dollar enterprises, it is especially difficult to escape the dangerous grip that money holds on elective office.

Sometimes, allegations of corruption come from places you least expect. When I was in Congress, my subcommittee held many hearings dealing with the waste industry, a field that has known more than its share of dishonest behavior. I learned about a Rhode Island television station that ran a news story about the solid waste industry, which featured a clip from the testimony given at one of our hearings by an informant who was shielded to protect his identity.

"Everybody in New Jersey that was involved with the garbage industry is mobbed up," the clip showed the informant saying. This was immediately followed by another clip: "Florio is very involved in the congressional effort to deal with solid waste." The clear implication of these two statements, pieced together, was that I was "mobbed up."

I was outraged. There was no question in my mind that this was a clear case of defamation. I immediately called my former law partner, Carl Poplar. When he picked up the phone, I introduced the case by asking him, "Carl, how would you like to own a television station?"

I knew that suing a television station or any media outlet for defamation is usually a headline-grabbing but legally futile gesture for a public figure like a member of Congress. To win such a case, the public figure must prove malice—and that is a burden of proof few plaintiffs are able to meet.

Nevertheless, we went ahead and sued the station. Through discovery, we reviewed all the tapes the station had gathered, both from our subcommittee hearing and from follow-up interviews with the informant who had testified. What the station had not included in its broadcast was the part of the interview in which the informant was asked, "Well, what about Florio?" He replied, "Florio is straight. He's out of the whole thing." This

was sufficiently suggestive of malice to prompt the station to pay a substantial sum to settle the case.

Then there was Abscam.

I was one of several members of Congress approached by a guy named
Joseph Silvestri, who told me he represented a group of Arabian sheiks
who were requesting my assistance. He suggested that I meet with the
sheiks and some of their representatives in Georgetown. If I agreed to help
them, he said, they would return the favor by helping me obtain funding
for projects in Camden.

What really turned me off about this guy was how he bragged that he
"owned" Congressman Rodino and Senator Williams. I knew that Harrison Williams had a drinking problem, and I worried that Silvestri might
actually have something on the senator. But I also knew that Peter Rodino
was above reproach, and I didn't believe for a minute that this guy, or anybody he represented, "owned" the chairman of the House Judiciary
Committee. I wanted nothing at all to do with him or his sheiks, so I
didn't go to meet with them in Georgetown.

My colleague from the neighboring Second Congressional District, Bill
Hughes, had the same experience. We talked about it later, about how
this guy had approached us, and how neither of us wanted anything to do
with him. But I thought later how easy it would have been to get ensnared
in Abscam—which, it turned out, was an FBI sting. I might have taken the
meeting if I hadn't been so turned off by Silvestri's brash and boastful
attitude.

Yet I certainly wouldn't have taken a brown bag with $50,000 in cash
from the undercover FBI agents, as Congressman Michael "Ozzie" Myers
of Pennsylvania did—for which he was expelled from Congress, convicted
of bribery and conspiracy, and sentenced to three years in prison. But Senator Williams and New Jersey congressman Frank Thompson of Trenton
got "stung" in a different way.

Neither of them took a bundle of cash in a brown paper bag. Instead,
they were convicted of using their office to further a business venture in

which they had a hidden interest or otherwise aiding the Arabs (or, as it turned out, the FBI agents posing as Arabs) with certain immigration problems in return for money for projects in New Jersey. To this day, I am certain that alcohol played an outsized role in both Senator Williams's and Congressman Thompson's downfall. I do not believe that either of them, had they been sober, would have betrayed the public trust as they did.

Back in New Jersey, Angelo Errichetti's downfall wasn't caused by alcohol: it was the product of sheer hubris. Serving as both mayor and a state senator at the time, he bragged to the undercover FBI agents that he could use the sheiks' money to get a gaming license for a group of partners in Atlantic City. He said he would use the money to grease the palms of politicians and state officials to ensure the success of the casino application—a boast that led to his conviction on bribery and conspiracy charges, removal from both his city and state offices, and a six-year prison term, of which he served thirty-two months.

"I can only blame myself for the tremendous ego I developed, the kind of ego that gets a politician into trouble," Errichetti was quoted as saying on his release from prison. Earlier, having learned that I had spurned the overture to meet with the sheiks, he was recorded on tape dismissively referring to me as a "Boy Scout." That is a badge I have always worn with honor.

≪≪≪≫

Let me share one final thought about my fifteen years in Congress.

Washington has always been a partisan place, but it was not nearly as combative and divisive in the 1970s and 1980s as it is today. My primary interest was in accomplishing things for New Jersey, and that meant working with my Republican as well as my Democratic colleagues in the state delegation.

There were many issues, of course, on which we did not all see eye to eye. I sometimes found myself in profound disagreement with Republican congressman Ed Forsythe, whose district abutted mine and included

large portions of Burlington and Ocean Counties that fell within the
Pinelands National Preserve. But we worked together to find as much
common ground as often as we could. In 1989, I ran for governor against
another fellow congressman, Jim Courter, and while that race was hotly
contested, there were any number of issues on which we had earlier cast
identical votes for the benefit of the citizens of New Jersey.

Our delegation came together to preserve the Pinelands; to clean up
hazardous waste sites; to protect the Jersey Shore; and to provide federal
aid to our cities, our schools, our police departments, and other institutions important to our state. I believe everyone in the New Jersey delegation can point with pride to the actions we took in those years, collectively, to
benefit our citizens.

I had very cordial and mutually respectful relationships with Republicans in the New Jersey delegation, on my committees and subcommittees,
and across the aisle of the House of Representatives as we worked together
on environmental, transportation, health care, and other policy issues.
That, in large measure, is how and why we got things done in Congress
during the years I spent there. In my judgment, the loss of cordiality and
mutual respect is, regrettably, a major reason things do not get done today.

CHAPTER 5

If at First You Don't Succeed . . .

One of the best ways to learn how to run a successful campaign is to run an unsuccessful one.

The New Jersey governorship is a very desirable position. It is (or was, until a 2006 amendment to the state constitution created the office of lieutenant governor) the only statewide elective office in New Jersey. The governor of New Jersey enjoys one of the most powerful executive offices in the country. He or she appoints every judge; nearly every cabinet officer serves at the governor's pleasure; and every individual line of the state budget is subject to the governor's veto.

I made up my mind fairly early in my political career that if I wanted to accomplish as much as I possibly could for the citizens of New Jersey, being governor would be a whole lot more effective than being a congressman.

Not that serving in Congress isn't attractive. The legislative branch of government has the closest connection to people. It's the place where you can solve constituents' individual problems directly and where you can serve their collective interests by formulating and advancing important public policy initiatives. It's also a place where you can delve deeply into subject areas that are of particular interest to you, specializing in issues such as the environment, transportation, and health care.

The greater reward that comes from serving in the executive branch is implicit in its name. While the legislative branch is responsible for *making* the laws, the executive branch is responsible for *executing* them. The governor gets to carry out the laws that provide services to the people—the environmental laws that preserve land and protect public health, the education laws that benefit our schoolchildren, the labor laws that help our workers, the consumer protection laws that guard our pocketbooks, the criminal laws that keep our streets safe.

After winning my congressional race in 1974 by about 26,000 votes, I was re-elected in 1976 by 80,000 votes, and I felt my seat in Congress was secure. So I made my first run for governor in 1977. Because New Jersey holds its state elections in odd-numbered years, that meant I could run for governor without having to give up my seat in Congress if I lost— just as I had made my first, unsuccessful run for Congress in 1972 without having to give up my seat in the state assembly. And, just as my congressional campaign represented an opportunity to gain name recognition beyond my assembly district, so was the run for governor a chance to gain name recognition beyond my congressional district.

I probably would not have given a moment's thought to throwing my hat into the gubernatorial ring at such a young age (I was only forty) and so early in my political career were it not for the fact that the incumbent Democratic governor, Brendan Byrne, was so unpopular. Having pushed through the state's first income tax, he was widely dismissed as OTB ("One-Term Byrne") and given little chance of re-election. An April 1977 poll by the Eagleton Institute of Politics showed Byrne's approval rating at 17 percent.

In fact, there were strong hints coming out of the governor's office that Byrne would not even run for re-election. A large number of Democrats were talking openly about running in the primary if Byrne decided not to, including at least three members of his cabinet: Human Services Commissioner Anne Klein, who had finished second to Byrne in the 1973 primary; Labor Commissioner Joe Hoffman, who had a following in

Middlesex County; and Secretary of State Don Lan, whose base of support was Union County.

In addition, one of my congressional colleagues, Bob Roe, who hailed from Passaic County, was definitely interested. So was state senator Ralph DeRose, who was mobilizing his Essex County base (he also had strong support in Hudson County) and gearing up for another run after finishing third behind Byrne and Klein in 1973.

I contacted Governor Byrne early in 1977 and I told him, point-blank, "I'm thinking about running for governor if you don't." But, I added, "I won't run if you do. Please let me know as soon as you decide."

He did not tell me his plans. With the deadline for filing fast approaching, I still hadn't heard from the governor or any of his operatives, so I went ahead and collected all the signatures I needed (actually many more than I needed) and got my name on the primary ballot. Then, at the very last minute, Governor Byrne filed his paperwork to run. Anne Klein did not; neither did Don Lan. Joe Hoffman was the only one of Byrne's cabinet officers who did, but six other challengers, including Jersey City mayor Paul Jordan, jumped into the race.

I found out years later from Dick Leone, who had resigned as state treasurer to run Byrne's re-election campaign, that the plan all along was to make the primary field as large as possible, thereby splitting the anti-Byrne vote and allowing the governor to squeak by. Roe would win Passaic County, Hoffman would carry Middlesex, and the two of them would split the labor vote in the rest of North Jersey. DeRose would pile up votes in Essex and Hudson Counties. They needed me in the race to prevent the rest of the field from picking up enough votes in South Jersey to knock off Byrne.

It was incredibly clever—and hugely successful. Byrne won the primary with about 31 percent of the vote. Roe followed with 24 percent, DeRose with 18 percent, and I finished fourth with a little less than 16 percent. Hoffman trailed with 10 percent. I carried Burlington, Camden, Cumberland, Gloucester, and Salem Counties, which is exactly what

Byrne and Leone were counting on. I got absolutely crushed in the northern counties, especially Hudson, where 89,649 votes were cast—and I got only 1,327 of them.

⋘⋘⋙

I learned a lot from that experience, particularly that the days of the party bosses, the smoke-filled rooms, and the unrivaled power of county chairmen had not yet come to an end in certain parts of New Jersey. Later, with the suburbanization of New Jersey's population, political power would become much more diffuse. But in 1977, organizations led by powerful county chairmen could still deliver endorsements and votes, by fiat.

As I was contemplating running, I had my first encounter with the legendary Essex County Democratic chairman, Harry Lerner. We met at the venerable Essex Club on Park Place in Newark, the kind of private club with thick red carpets and oak-paneled rooms where political strategy used to be plotted and deals used to get made. He sat me down, immediately ordered a double bourbon, and asked me what I would have to drink. "Just a Coke," I said. He looked aghast. "No, no, no," he said. "What will you have to *drink*?" I got the hint and said, "OK, I'll have a double bourbon."

I have no memory of the conversation that followed. I was wiped out for the rest of the afternoon.

Middlesex County meanwhile was firmly in the grip of the Wilentz organization, which dated back to the 1930s, when state attorney general David Wilentz gained international fame for his successful prosecution of Bruno Richard Hauptmann in the Lindbergh kidnapping case. David's son Warren had run unsuccessfully for the U.S. Senate against Clifford Case in 1966. His other son Robert served two terms in the assembly before Byrne appointed him chief justice of the state Supreme Court, a position he held for seventeen years.

If you wanted to gather any support from Democrats in Essex County, you needed the nod from Harry Lerner. If you had any hope of picking up Democratic votes in Middlesex County, you needed the thumbs up from the Wilentz organization. Two other North Jersey counties, Hudson and Passaic, had similar, machine-like Democratic Party organizations. And Camden County in South Jersey was still firmly in the grip of Angelo Errichetti.

Another important lesson I learned in the 1977 race was that a campaign for statewide office was entirely different from a state legislative or congressional campaign and it required a totally different mindset. In the 1977 gubernatorial primary, I did what I had done earlier in my congressional races: I gathered my friends and supporters from Camden County, and we took off by bus on Saturday mornings to different neighborhoods, where we would do door-to-door canvassing. The difference in the statewide campaign was we were canvassing in neighborhoods that were unfamiliar to us; we were going to parts of the state that we knew virtually nothing about— and where the people we were meeting knew nothing about me.

Our canvassing had virtually no impact. You just can't run a statewide race that way. When you're running for a local office or even on a state legislative ticket, you can do retail politics. It's a little more difficult when you're running for Congress, because the district is so much larger. You have to put more emphasis on mass communication, though you can still do a fair amount of door-to-door campaigning.

Running for governor is a whole different ballgame. If you want to go door to door, you make sure you do it with a camera crew, filming you so that thousands of people can later see a television commercial of you going door to door. That's more or less the wholesale way of doing retail politics.

We ran that 1977 primary race on a shoestring. Bob Roe raised and spent more than $1.1 million to secure his second-place finish. Governor Byrne's winning campaign cost about $700,000. Ralph DeRose spent $440,000, and Joe Hoffman spent $337,000. My campaign spending totaled a paltry $290,000.

One footnote to the financing of that campaign would take an ironic twist more than a decade later. The largest single campaign contribution

I received—$2,500—was from the National Rifle Association Political
Victory Fund.

⟨⟨⟨⟩

In 1977, I was the provincial South Jersey candidate in a losing primary.
In 1981, I became a statewide candidate in a winning primary.

Several noteworthy things happened between 1977 and 1981. The first
was my break with Angelo Errichetti. By the time he was indicted (and
subsequently convicted) of bribery in the Abscam sting, I was fortunately
no longer in a position to suffer guilt by association.

Another was my ever-increasing vote margins in congressional elections. After my 1977 gubernatorial primary run, I was re-elected to
Congress in 1978 by 80,000 votes. In 1980, while Reagan was carrying
Camden and Gloucester Counties by 18,000 votes, I won re-election by
102,000.

In addition, the bill creating the Pinelands Preserve was signed into
law in 1978, and the Superfund law was enacted in 1980. I now could
point to two major pieces of legislation as evidence of my commitment
to environmental protection and of my ability to get things done for New
Jersey.

Finally, I had the good fortune to find myself in a field of primary candidates in 1981 that was even more crowded than it was in 1977. Bob Roe was
making another run from his Passaic County base. Ken Gibson, the mayor
of Newark, was one of two Essex County candidates; the other was Pat
Dodd, former state senate president. Joe Merlino, the sitting state senate
president, was the Mercer County candidate. Jersey City mayor Tommy
Smith was the Hudson County candidate. Bill Hamilton, the former General Assembly Speaker, was the Middlesex County candidate. Assembly-
woman Barbara McConnell was the Hunterdon County candidate. Former
state attorney general John Degnan, a close Byrne confidante, had the
support of the outgoing governor. Anne Klein, who had run in 1973 and
passed up the chance to run in 1977, was back on the ballot in 1981.

I won the 1981 primary by doing what I didn't do in 1977: I ran a state-wide campaign. I went out and actively recruited supporters from areas beyond my South Jersey base. Instead of heading home to Camden from Washington on the weekends, I headed to Newark, Jersey City, Paterson, and other North Jersey cities and towns.

We still brought up busloads of enthusiastic supporters from my congressional district to campaign in the northern part of the state, but we also reached out to people at the local level to join them. Mike Perrucci, who would later become my law partner, was the Democratic chair and an early and active supporter in Warren County. George Zoffinger, who would later serve in my administration as commissioner of the Department of Commerce and Economic Development, was the Democratic chair in Sussex County and a strong supporter.

Primary elections are won on turnout. We concentrated on gathering support around the state and then motivating those supporters to go to the polls on primary day. And that's how we won.

The primary votes split pretty much as expected along county lines. Roe carried the northern tier of Passaic, Bergen, Morris, and Sussex Counties, ending up with 15.6 percent of the statewide vote. Gibson carried Essex and Union Counties, gaining 15 percent of the statewide vote. Merlino carried Mercer for 11.2 percent, Smith carried Hudson for 9 percent, Hamilton carried Middlesex and Somerset Counties for 2.7 percent, and McConnell carried Hunterdon for 2.5 percent.

I carried Atlantic, Burlington, Camden, Cape May, Cumberland, Gloucester, Monmouth, Ocean, Salem, and, thanks to Mike Perrucci, Warren Counties. Just as important, I finished second in Essex, Mercer, Middlesex, Somerset, and, thanks to George Zoffinger, Sussex Counties. And I ran a respectable third in Hudson and Union Counties. I won the statewide balloting handily with 26 percent of the vote.

My opponent in the general election was Tom Kean. We knew each other, though not well, because we had served together in the New Jersey legislature. He was the General Assembly Speaker during my second two-year term in Trenton because of a deal the Republicans made after the 1971 election with the Democratic delegation from Hudson County. With the assembly then made up of forty Democrats, thirty-nine Republicans, and the independent Anthony Imperiale, four Hudson County Democrats, headed by Assemblyman David Friedland, cast their votes for Kean for Speaker; in return the Democrats were given chairmanships of key assembly committees.

David Friedland deserves special mention. In the mid-1960s, he made history when he successfully argued that the makeup of New Jersey's legislative districts violated the U.S. Supreme Court's "one-man, one-vote" principle. In the early 1980s, his fame would turn to notoriety. After his conviction on racketeering charges for taking kickbacks for arranging loans from the Teamsters' Pension Fund, he turned state's evidence and then, in a bizarre twist, faked his own drowning death off Grand Bahama Island before his scheduled sentencing. He was ultimately captured on the Indian Ocean island nation of Maldives, where he was running a scuba diving business.

Honestly, when it comes to some corruption cases involving New Jersey politicians, you can't make this stuff up.

Let me begin my description of the 1981 general election campaign with the punch line: I lost—by 1,797 votes out of 2,290,201 votes cast. Or, to put it another way, the final tally was Kean 50.04 percent, Florio 49.96 percent. It was (and still is) the closest statewide vote in New Jersey history.

A lot of people who worked on that campaign still sit around and wonder what we might have done differently, how we might have swung less than one vote per precinct to turn a loss into a win. I do not spend my time second-guessing a whole lot about that campaign. I worked my tail off, losing something like fifteen pounds. I got up before dawn every morning to go to RCA, Campbell's Soup, or another factory to meet people going to work, and then I would head off to other places around the state.

Following his own advice—to take what he did wrong and do it better next time—Congressman Florio loses the Democratic primary for governor in 1977, turns around and wins it in 1981, only to lose the general election by 1,797 votes, the closest margin in New Jersey history.

I campaigned from early morning until late at night. I had a strategy and a schedule, and I stuck to it.

Tom Kean rarely did that sort of electioneering: he ran a more laid-back campaign. While I was running all over the state—shaking hands at factories at dawn, speaking at small gatherings at lunchtime, going door to door at night—he let the media convey his message. I thought mine was a good strategy for the kind of frenetic person I am; his was a smart strategy for the more placid person he is.

A statewide general election campaign is entirely different from a primary campaign. In the primary, your goal is to convince your own party's registered voters that you would be the best candidate to represent it and to make sure enough of them get to the polls to put you over the top. In the general election, the goal is to convince voters who aren't affiliated with either party that you will do a better job than your opponent in representing their interests. If the key to success in a primary is turnout, the key in a general election is image.

What I learned about strategy from the 1981 general election campaign reinforced what I had already discovered in the 1977 primary: you cannot run a retail campaign statewide. There are more than eight million people in New Jersey, and no matter how many plant openings you attend, no matter how many hands you shake, you will never have direct contact with more than a fraction of the electorate. I met with farmers, state workers, VFW members, the American Legion, and dozens of other organized groups, but even as I gained their individual or collective support, they did not come close to constituting a majority of voters. They represented a good cross-section, but not a majority.

What I gleaned from Tom Kean's success is that a statewide election is thematic. You've got to develop a theme and an image that people associate with you, as opposed to trying to touch people one by one. You have to develop a persona to which people can relate. This is done primarily through the media, both paid (advertising) and free (appearances on news and talk shows). In that arena, Tom Kean was simply more effective than

I was. Our public images were a pretty accurate reflection of who we were: the genial, soft-spoken, serene Tom Kean versus the hard-driving, pugnacious, street-smart Jim Florio.

Despite the stark differences in our personalities, the 1981 general election campaign was, by and large, an extremely civil contest. Tom Kean and I both ran positive campaigns. We treated each other with respect. We talked about issues, not personalities. Even in the days after the election, when the results were still in question, our lawyers and political operatives who oversaw the recount were cordial and courteous to each other.

There were two minor exceptions to this cordiality. Both were my fault, and I regret them to this day. At a debate in South Jersey, Tom began by saying he was "happy to be here on Delby Drive in Glassboro." I should have just let it go, but when my turn came, I said, "I want everyone to know that I'm here on Delsea Drive" (the correct name of the street)—and all the South Jersey people whooped it up. It was a cheap shot.

At another event (I think it was a joint NAACP appearance), I took another cheap shot. Tom was talking about how he had ridden through Camden a few days earlier when he saw some "19-year-old boys" standing on the corner. When my chance came, I said, "When I see 19-year-old people, they're 19-year-old men, not boys." I still hadn't learned the lesson that some thoughts are better left unspoken.

When I formally conceded defeat twenty-seven days after Election Day, I talked to the new governor-elect on the phone for fifteen minutes, offering not only my congratulations but also my pledge to work with him and his administration when I returned to Washington. "We share the goal to make New Jersey a better place," I said.

One place in New Jersey I would have certainly liked to make better was our statewide headquarters for the 1981 campaign—a dive in East Orange that pompously called itself the Evergreen Hotel. It was anything but a hotel. You might generously call it a motel; a more accurate description would be a collection of unkempt rooms, many of which were occupied for no more than an hour at a time. The clientele, other than our campaign workers, fell into two categories: hookers, who rented rooms by the hour, and enormous cockroaches, who took up more permanent residence.

In any close election, the number of factors that could have turned the result around might equal or exceed the number of votes that separated the candidates. I won't try to recount the 1,797 reasons I lost, but let me point out several factors I believe were decisive.

First, while New Jersey may be thought of today as a reliably Democratic state, the governorship has tended to swing back and forth between the two parties. Since New Jersey adopted its state constitution in 1947, changing the term of governorship from three years to four and allowing the governor to serve two consecutive four-year terms, only once have the voters elected a governor of the same party for more than two consecutive terms. I was seeking to follow two-term Democrat Brendan Byrne.

Second, protection of the Pinelands was very popular across the state, but there was a deep pocket of resistance and opposition to it in Atlantic County. That is where the South Jersey secession movement was still going strong and where the myth that creation of the Pinelands Preserve was a plot by North Jersey to steal South Jersey's water had the most resonance. I swept the rest of the South Jersey counties, but lost Atlantic County by 2,750 votes. If I had carried Atlantic, I would have won the election.

Third, I had a lot of support in the Polish community, dating back to my pro bono legal work for members of the Polish-American Citizens Club in Camden. In Middlesex County, there was a very influential newspaper called the *Polish Eagle*, whose editor, Chester Grabowski, was running for governor as an independent. A couple of weeks before the election, he announced he was dropping out and was endorsing me. But his formal editorial endorsement in the *Polish Eagle* wasn't published until the day after the election. Meanwhile, his name was still on the ballot, and he got 4,496 votes.

Fourth, my candidacy drew less than enthusiastic support from the Democratic organizations in both Middlesex and Union Counties. In 1977, Brendan Byrne carried Middlesex by 32,000 votes; in 1981, I won it by only 6,000. In 1977, Byrne won Union County by about 4,500 votes; in 1981, I lost it by nearly 14,000.

In Middlesex County, the Wilentz organization simply did not generate the kind of support a gubernatorial candidate should expect coming out of a Democratic county. Maybe it was because Robert Wilentz had served with Tom Kean in the state legislature (and was subsequently reappointed chief justice of the New Jersey Supreme Court by Governor Kean, over the vehement opposition of many of Kean's fellow Republicans).

In Union County, Tom Dunn, the mayor of Elizabeth, a former state senator, and a fellow Democrat, told me he would enthusiastically endorse me in the general election. "I'm very impressed with you," he said. "I heard all these good things. You have my support." The very next day, he held a press conference and endorsed Tom Kean. Mayor Dunn's political opponents never hesitated to brand him a pathological liar; I would say simply that he had a passing acquaintance with the concept of integrity.

Fifth, and by far the most significant factor leading to my defeat, was the underhanded Republican effort to interfere with voters on Election Day. In Newark and other cities, the Republicans hung up posters in neighborhoods with large black and Hispanic populations that read, "WARNING: This area is being patrolled by the National Ballot Security Task Force. It is a crime to falsify a ballot or to violate election laws."

The National Ballot Security Task Force, a front for the Republican National Committee, spent $75,000 in the 1981 election to dispatch teams of off-duty police and sheriff's officers—some in uniform, others wearing armbands, many carrying weapons and two-way radios—in a clear attempt to intimidate voters in precincts where Democratic candidates traditionally performed well. There's no doubt in my mind that many more than 1,797 people were intimidated into not showing up at the polls.

The Democratic National Committee filed a $10 million federal lawsuit against the Republican National Committee, charging that the tactics employed by the National Ballot Security Task Force violated the Voting Rights Act. Both the Republican National Committee and the New Jersey Republican Committee signed a consent decree in November 1982 affirming that they would not conduct "ballot security activities" in areas with large concentrations of minority voters "where a purpose or significant effect of such activities is to deter qualified voters from voting."

The Republicans have made repeated efforts over the years to amend or terminate the consent decree, contending it is antiquated and unnecessary. In response, the courts have extended the consent decree and expanded its reach; it now covers not only New Jersey but all fifty states, and it requires Republican organizations to obtain judicial preclearance to ensure that any effort to assist or engage in ballot security activities complies with the consent decree.

In my view, all of these factors played a role in the outcome of the 1981 election. I don't think there is anything I could have done to change the minds of voters who opposed Pinelands protection in Atlantic County, or to keep Chester Grabowski's name off the ballot, or to overcome the lack of enthusiasm for my candidacy by the Democratic organizations in Middlesex and Union Counties, or to stop the National Ballot Security Task Force from carrying out its intimidating tactics.

The actions of the National Ballot Security Task Force left an especially bitter aftertaste for many of my supporters and led a number of Democrats to cast a suspicious eye, if not an outright accusatory stare, at Tom Kean. After the recount was concluded, a lot of them wanted me to challenge the governor-elect, to publicly accuse the Kean campaign and its dirty trickster accomplices of "stealing" the election.

I refused to do so for two reasons. The first is that I took Tom Kean at his word; I believed him when he said had no personal knowledge of "the people posting notices and wearing armbands." The second is that I felt questioning the legitimacy of the election would undermine public trust and confidence in the integrity of the political process. I saw nothing that could be gained by casting a shadow on the Kean administration as it was starting to take on the challenges of governing New Jersey.

As I told Tom Kean on the phone the day I conceded, "We share the goal to make New Jersey a better place."

Two criticisms dogged me in the wake of the 1981 campaign. A number of Democratic strategists around the state said I spent too much time attacking Ronald Reagan and the Republicans in Washington, and too little time attacking Tom Kean and the Republicans in Trenton. And people close to Governor Byrne were annoyed that I didn't publicly defend the decision by the Sports and Exposition Authority to name its new basketball and hockey venue the "Brendan Byrne Arena."

As much as I admired Governor Byrne's wit and wisdom (he was known to quip that he picked up a lot of support among Italian voters who thought his name was Brendan Byrne Arena), the decision to place his name on the arena was enormously unpopular. A poll in October 1981, taken just before the election, found that 7 percent of respondents favored naming the arena for Byrne, compared to 48 percent who said the name should be changed and 42 percent who said it didn't matter.

I actually thought I was doing Governor Byrne a favor by *not* joining the chorus of vocal critics—including a large number of loyal Democrats—who were offended by what the *New York Times* called Byrne's "offensive vanity in having his name put on the Meadowlands arena in five foot letters." I later learned that the governor's supporters did not consider my silence on the matter to be an act of kindness.

The charge that I devoted too much time and effort to criticism of President Reagan and the Republicans in Washington has some merit. I had spent a good part of 1981 fighting to keep the Reagan administration and

its congressional allies from cutting the budgets of environmental, transportation, health, and other federal agencies, thereby gutting critical
environmental, transportation, health, and other programs—including
programs like the Superfund in which I had a very deep, personal interest. I felt it was important to make voters aware of the many actions the
Reagan administration was taking that would have a direct, detrimental
impact on New Jersey. I also felt that by hammering away at the Reagan
administration, I was putting Tom Kean, the Republican gubernatorial
candidate, in the awkward position of trying to defend both his party's
very conservative president and his own, considerably more moderate record as an assemblyman.

In fact, there was very little in Tom Kean's record as an assemblyman
that I found particularly objectionable. We shared a deep commitment to
the environment. Kean was a sponsor of the bill that created the state
Department of Environmental Protection and was credited with being
a moving force behind passage of the Coastal Area Facility Review Act
(CAFRA), which limited development in the shore region. He also sponsored bills lowering the voting age from twenty-one to eighteen and creating the Division of Consumer Affairs—two measures I strongly supported.

And remember, this was 1981. These were the days before unlimited
sums of money came pouring into political campaigns. (In fact, both
the Kean campaign and mine accepted public financing, with limits on
both contributions and expenditures, for the general election.) This was
before "oppo research" became a common campaign tactic, with teams
of researchers gathering information that could be used to discredit or
weaken a political opponent. It was before campaigns became the domain
of specialized consultants, the high-priced hired guns who come in and
do polling, strategizing, focus groups, TV ads, fundraising, and, lately,
social networking. Before running campaigns became a full-time profession for consultants, these were the sorts of functions that used to be done
by the candidates themselves, along with a handful of trusted friends and
advisors.

Even if we could have run our 1981 campaigns the way campaigns are run today, I think both Tom Kean and I would prefer the race we ran. I would no more have wanted people scouring around for some intemperate language that might have shown up in the political columns he wrote as a teenager for the student newspaper at St. Mark's School than I would want people unearthing some inappropriate remark I may have made to an opponent in the Flatbush Boys Club boxing ring. I didn't bring up his deal with David Friedland, and he didn't comment on my past relationship with Angelo Errichetti.

⁂

After that narrow loss in 1981, I won re-election to Congress in 1982, 1984, 1986, and 1988, always receiving two to three times more votes than my opponent. Every weekend when I went back to my district or made an appearance elsewhere in the state, people would approach me and ask me when I was going to run for governor again. They all said they had enthusiastically supported me in 1981; suddenly I couldn't find anyone, anywhere who had voted against me.

I did give some thought to challenging Tom Kean in 1985. He had earned the distinction in 1982 of being the only governor in New Jersey history to raise all three of the state's major taxes—the income tax, the sales tax, and the business tax—in a single year. He did this despite having signed a campaign pledge not to raise taxes as governor. (I had refused to sign the same pledge, stating that I felt it would be fiscally irresponsible to make such a commitment.)

In addition, I believed that many of New Jersey's most pressing problems that we had discussed and debated in 1981—public school financing, solid waste management, low- and moderate-income housing, and auto insurance, among others—remained unsolved, and I felt that the Kean administration had been timid in addressing these issues.

But I also felt, after President Reagan's landslide re-election in 1984, that his policies posed a far greater danger to the nation as a whole than the Kean administration posed to New Jersey. After spending the latter part of the 1970s working in Congress for positive change during the Carter administration, I found myself throughout the 1980s playing defense—working with my fellow Democrats to protect what we had accomplished earlier from being undone by the Reagan administration.

I was already troubled about the approach that administration had taken to enforcement of environmental laws in its first term. After his re-election, I was even more concerned about the disruption his economic policies portended for his second term. Across-the-board budget cuts had states, cities, towns, school boards, and community organizations—groups that were traditionally allied in their efforts to provide essential public services—battling with each other over ever-smaller pieces of the federal budget pie.

In addition, there was considerable uncertainty in early 1985 about the spending limits that would be allowed under the state's public financing law. Under the existing law, candidates who accepted public financing would have a spending limit of $2.2 million in the general election. A Democratic bill vetoed by Governor Kean would have raised the spending limit to $3 million. Kean wanted it raised to $4 million, suggesting that anything less would result in candidates rejecting public financing, which would allow them to spend as much as they wanted.

I know a lot of members of Congress who spend more time on the telephone asking for money than they do on the floor of the House or Senate doing the public's business. Many of them actually enjoy fundraising. I don't. I hate it. I wish every election for every office could be financed publicly, relieving the people running from the degrading ritual of asking for money. The uncertainty surrounding the public financing of the 1985 election was a major factor in my decision not to run.

When I made the announcement that I wasn't running in March 1985, some of Kean's political operatives scoffed at the reasons I gave for passing up a rematch. They said the real reason I wasn't running was that I knew I would lose, that Kean was too popular to be defeated for re-election. The governor himself took the high road, telling an impromptu gathering of reporters, "'I'm disappointed any time a good candidate from either party drops out."

Those operatives were wrong to assume that fear of losing was more than a passing consideration in my decision. I lost my first bid for Congress in 1972 before winning it the second time around in 1974. I lost my first bid for the Democratic gubernatorial nomination in 1977 before winning it the second time around in 1981. I lost my first general election for governor in 1981 and had no reason to believe I couldn't win it the second time around in 1985.

Then again, Governor Kean did go on to win re-election in that year against the Democratic nominee, Essex County Executive Peter Shapiro, by nearly 800,000 votes, the largest margin in history. He carried 564 of the state's 567 municipalities. So even if those operatives were wrong in claiming that I wasn't running because I knew I would lose, they may have been right in their other assertion—that Kean really was too popular to be defeated for re-election.

So I spent the rest of the Reagan years and the first year of George H. W. Bush's presidency in Congress, where I concentrated on my committee and subcommittee work, defending Democratic values under assault by Republican administrations, attending to my constituent service, and mulling over the prospect of making a third run for governor in 1989.

And, then, along came Lucinda.

CHAPTER 6

Lucinda

Lighten up. You cannot always be so rational. There needs to be a place in your life for some emotion.

My life—public, private, and political—was changed by a soft-spoken elementary school teacher who had no experience at all in politics. Meeting her, getting to know her, and then marrying her made a profound difference in my life.

It was 1982. I had just lost the race for governor and had moved into the Chalet Apartments in Pine Hill. The complex was owned by Joe Maressa, who was retiring after serving three terms in the state senate (where he was succeeded by my former staffer, Dan Dalton). The apartment had been used by my district office staff. Now I had moved in and was using it when I was in the district on weekends or whenever the House wasn't in session.

Lucinda had the apartment just above mine. We would see each other every now and then, smile, and say hello. Then one day . . . well, I'll let Lucinda tell the story in her own words.

I went out one Sunday to do my grocery shopping. I stopped at a traffic light, and I looked over and saw this guy I recognized as my downstairs neighbor, who had come driving up to the light from the opposite direction. He looked at me. I looked at him. He smiled. I smiled back. As we drove away, I said to myself, "I think I'm going to invite him to dinner."

130

I knew he was a congressman. I remember voting for him. But I didn't know anything else about him. I would just see him coming and going, and we had said hello a couple of times, but that was it.

What I really liked was this guy's smile. So I just decided, on a whim, to invite him to dinner. After I got home from grocery shopping, I knocked on his door and said, "I'm making dinner. Would you like to have some dinner with me?" He said, "I'm on my way out. Can I have a rain check?" And I said, "OK."

He told me he was teaching at Rutgers University's Eagleton Institute of Politics in New Brunswick the next morning, and then he'd be going back to Washington. "I won't be back till Thursday," he said, which gave me a hint that he might be interested in seeing me after he got back. So the next morning before I went to work, not knowing if he even knew who I was, I wrote my name and phone number on a piece of paper and left it in his mailbox.

When he got back at the end of the week, he called me up. "Sorry, I was out of town," he said. "Would you like to share a bottle of wine?" Although I'm really a tea drinker, and definitely not a wine drinker, I said, "Sure."

And that's how it started.

He came over with his bottle of wine, and we talked. He told me he was separated from his wife. His children were all out of the house. One son, Gregory, was married. His other son, Christopher, had moved to Boston, and his daughter Cathy was going to Jefferson Medical School in Philadelphia.

He told me what was important to him at that point in his life was his children and his work, and I told him that was something we had in common. "My job is so important to me right now," I said. "I absolutely love what I do. And my son Mark is very important to me, so I'm in exactly the same place."

We talked a little more, and when he left, he said, "When I get back in town again, maybe we'll go to dinner." Sure enough, he called me the next weekend—and my first reaction was, "I don't even know what to wear.

What am I supposed to wear to dinner with a congressman? What's the expectation here?" What I ended up doing was throwing on a pair of slacks and a blouse that had a little bow on top.

He teased me unmercifully at dinner. "You look like a teacher," he said. "You're all buttoned up prim and proper." He said this with a smile, but I wasn't sure how to take it. I suspected it was just his strange sense of humor. So I told him, "You're lucky I don't have paint and grime all over myself after spending the day with a bunch of third-graders. You're lucky I could change my blouse and get here at all. I keep pretty busy." Of course, I said this with a smile too.

One of the things I learned during that dinner was that he likes to go to movies. So our next date was a movie. Neither of us remembers the name of it, but we both enjoyed the experience of sharing a movie, rather than going to the theater alone. (Remember, this was back in the early 1990s; if you wanted to see a movie, you had to leave the house and go to a theater.)

Our second dinner date didn't go so well. We went to a place in Deptford that had music and dancing, which wasn't exactly his style, nor was it mine. We were sitting at the bar and chatting, and for some reason, I don't remember what started it, he made a comment about how the only thing a lot of women wanted to do was get married. I just looked at him, and instead of contradicting him, I thought to myself, "He's not going to like me."

Later, when we were on our way back to Pine Hill he asked me, "Do you have hot water in your apartment?" I said, "Yes, I do," and he said, "Well, I don't." So I took a look at his hot water heater, and found that he didn't have the thermostat turned up. In fact, he had no idea where the thermostat was. He just figured the apartment only provided cold water, and that was fine with him.

"Now you should have hot water," I told him. He said he thought I was brilliant. I thought, "He's really not going to like me at all now."

From the very start, I wasn't sure what to call him. Just about everybody who knew him well called him Jim. Those who didn't called him "Congressman." I said to him, "You just don't seem like a Jim to me. You know, something about your mannerisms and everything." So I asked him, "Do you ever use James? Can I call you James? Did anybody call you James?" He said, "My mother once in a while would call me James, usually when she was mad at me." I said, "Well, you're never going to know me from everybody else who calls you Jim, so I'll call you James."

Years later, he took me to a reunion of his elementary school in Brooklyn, and a few of the people there called him Jimmy. Jimmy? No way. It's like when I was growing up, everybody called me Cindy.

My mother once saw the name Lucinda written in calligraphy on the doorbell next to a mailbox in an apartment building and she vowed that if she ever had daughters, one of them would be Lucinda. So I got my name off a doorbell. "When you grow up, you're not going to use Cindy," my mother told me. "You'll know when. You're going to use Lucinda." She was right.

Most people don't know that James has a great sense of humor. He always comes across as so serious, so unemotional, but if you really get to know him you discover that he has this Woody Allen–type sense of humor. In fact, our mutual love for Woody Allen may have been one of the things that turned our casual dating relationship into something a little more serious.

One weekend, we were in my apartment, and I happened to casually mention to him that I had these Woody Allen albums and asked him if he wanted me to put one on. "You like Woody Allen?" he asked. "I love Woody Allen," I said, and he said, "Well, I do, too. Not everyone does." I said, "Well, I think he's the greatest."

So I put an album on, and we started laughing. There we were, sitting on the couch, laughing at Woody Allen. We knew all the punch lines, and pretty soon we're saying them together and laughing and we're all snuggled up on the couch and we're laughing our heads off. I think we knew at that point that we were pretty much into each other.

It was, of necessity, a weekend romance. He spent the week in Congress in Washington. I spent the week in a third-grade classroom at the John H. Glenn Elementary School in Pine Hill. We had a nice long stretch of a couple years of just hanging out and having a great time together. I really liked him. He was a real guy. He was solid. He had a great smile and a wonderfully sardonic sense of humor.

In the summer of 1984, he went off to the Democratic National Convention in San Francisco and I went off to the Jersey Shore, where I shared a house with a girlfriend in Ocean City and got a job as a bartender at a place in Stone Harbor called the Rocking Chair. After the convention, he came down to see me. I told my roommate, "Go find something to do. I haven't seen him and he's coming to town. I want an evening with him."

It was quite an evening. We talked and talked and talked. And then, without warning, he blurted out something that sounded like it came straight out of the 1950s: "I want you to be my girl," he said. I stared at him. "I want you to be my girl," he repeated. So I told him, "I've been your girl."

When we got back to Pine Hill, he got rid of the apartment downstairs and moved in with me. His divorce had been finalized, but I asked him if this would pose any kind of a problem, with his kids, or his constituents, or anybody else. "No," he said. "It'll be fine." Later, I realized that's what he always tells me. Whatever comes up, whether it's political or personal, and I ask him if everything is going to be OK, he says, "It'll be fine."

One of the many things James and I have in common is our frugality. Both of us grew up in working-class families, and we learned early on the value of a dollar. When I was a kid, I never asked my mother for money for anything. I was the chief babysitter in our neighborhood, and I made pretty good money. I spent some of it on clothes and stuff, but I was always a good saver. When my marriage ended, I didn't ask my husband for anything. I left on my own. I kept on saving when I was teaching, because I wanted to be self-sufficient.

And James never spent any money on anything. In fact, when the secretary in his office was retiring, he asked me, "Do you know anything about checkbooks?" I stared at him in astonishment. "Of course I do," I said. "Well," he said, "I don't." Apparently, his secretary took care of all his deposits and payments (the few he had). He barely knew how to write a check, much less how to balance a checkbook.

After a couple of years of sharing the rent on our apartment, I had squirreled away a fair amount of money. I told James I was ready to move out of Pine Hill and buy a townhouse. He said, "Why don't we get one together?" I said, "Really? Are you sure? It's a big step." And he said, predictably, "It'll be fine."

And it was. We bought a nice little townhouse in the Blackwood section of Gloucester Township—and that would be our home until the state provided us with a somewhat larger place to live a few years later.

Throughout his time in Congress, James lived during the week in his apartment above the liquor store in Washington, where it was pretty obvious he never did anything more than sleep. He certainly didn't cook. And he certainly didn't clean.

I made one of my few visits to that apartment in 1986. Before James left on a congressional trip to Russia, he mentioned to me that the freezer in the apartment was all frosted up. I guess he remembered how I had "fixed" his hot water heater. So I asked him, "Would you like me to go down and look at it for you? I have a girlfriend. She'd love to go to D.C. We'll go down to D.C. I'll take a look at it." He said, "Sure."

So my girlfriend and I went down there, and the first thing we did was fluff the place up. It was a mess. He had all these old suits in the closet, polyester stuff, the kind of thing nobody would wear because it went out of style ten years ago. I said to my friend, "What the heck is all this stuff?"

Then we took a look at the freezer. Sure enough, he'd never defrosted it. I figured he probably didn't even know there was such a thing as a defroster.

Even when we had the two apartments in Pine Hill, upstairs and downstairs, he never did anything in his apartment. He didn't bring home groceries. He didn't cook. And the same thing was obviously true in Washington. "Well," I thought to myself, "that's just his personality. He's got other things to do."

I should have known then that James can't do a thing around the house. Don't let him carry anything in the door. Don't give him a hammer. If he tried to saw a piece of wood, he would probably saw off his hand. This is a brilliant guy, but please keep him away from tools. Don't have any expectation that he can do anything that pertains to a house, because all he really does is come in and go out.

Over the years, I've kept a scrapbook of all the places he went—he's always going off someplace—and there was this one event we went to together: a Willie Nelson concert. I cut out an article about the concert and put it in the scrapbook. Next to one of Willie Nelson's lyrics—"Mama, don't let your sons grow up to be cowboys"—I wrote, "Don't let them grow up to be congressmen."

<center>~~~</center>

One weekend in the fall of 1987, James said to me, "Come on, let's go out for a walk." So we went out for a walk, and he was very quiet, not saying a word. We walked and walked, and I thought to myself, "Where the heck are we going?"

Pretty soon we came to Highland Regional High School, and we walked all the way around it until we came to a cherry tree. Under that tree, he finally stopped and said, "The reason I'm taking you for this long walk is I have something to say. I want you to marry me. Would you marry me?" I said, "Really? Are you sure? You really want to take that step?" He said, "Yeah."

I told him there was one thing I insisted on. "Everybody in the state knows you," I said. "I want something just for us. I want it private, just for us." I knew, of course, that he would agree. "Oh, good," he said. "You don't want a wedding dress and all?" I said, "No, no, no. I don't want any of that. I want it local, as quiet as we can. I don't want all that hoopla around it. This is just for us."

I also kidded him that it wasn't surprising he had found his wife on his doorstep—because he didn't have time to look for one anywhere else.

We didn't set a date or anything. We got our blood tests and we signed some papers, but we weren't in any kind of hurry. I figured we might get married the following May, when there was some kind of conference James had agreed to go to in Bermuda, and that would be a nice place for us to honeymoon.

By this time, I had a pretty good sense of what made James tick. I knew how committed he was to his congressional responsibilities. I knew he was almost certainly going to run for governor again in 1989. I had met his kids, and I liked them. I was comfortable with the idea that they would accept me as their father's wife.

James hadn't met my son yet, but he had come to my school and met some of my students. I was very concerned about one particular problem child in my class. I think he may have been abused at home. James would ask me all the time how this particular child was doing. He was very interested in my professional life.

Knowing that James was always so serious, I felt like I needed to loosen him up a bit. So one Halloween, I pulled a good one on him. I went to school that day wearing a black wig, a black jacket, and a T-shirt with a lightning bolt and the words, "New Jersey, only the strong survive." After I got home, he called me from the office and said he'd be home around eight.

I kept my costume on, and just before he arrived, I slipped out the sliding glass door and went around the back. As soon as he let himself in, I came around front and rang the doorbell. He opened it, and I said,

"Trick or treat?"—and he didn't know what to do. It was like he had never confronted a trick-or-treater before in his life. And he obviously didn't recognize me. I finally said, "James, it's me." He asked, "What are you doing? You're such a kid." And I said, "Well, I hang around with kids all day. C'mon, you've got to lighten up and have a little fun."

On February 13, 1988, we went out to dinner with Dan and Suzanne Dalton. I had no idea (and neither did they, as it turned out) that James had already made plans for us to be married the following morning. I always make a big fuss on Valentine's Day. James knew that, of course, so he had gotten in touch with his law school friend, Carl Poplar, and asked if he and his wife Eleanor would host us for breakfast on Valentine's Day. He didn't tell me about it. He told Carl not to tell Eleanor about it until the day before, and not to tell anyone else—except to make sure also to invite Judge Isaiah Steinberg, a good friend.

On Valentine's Day morning, James said to me, "I have everything arranged. We're going over to Carl and Eleanor's house. The judge is going to be there, and we're going to get married." I said, "Perfect." So we got married.

Only later did James explain that the reason he chose Valentine's Day for our wedding was so he would never forget our anniversary. He would always remember it, he said, because it was the day of the Saint Valentine's Day Massacre. That's his sense of humor.

That summer, I went with him to the Democratic National Convention in Atlanta. That was my formal introduction to the world of politics. My informal introduction had occurred many years earlier.

Like James's mother, my mother was an avid reader—but her reading material of choice was the newspaper. She was also a news watcher, so politics was a regular topic of family conversation. Both my mother and my grandmother used to preach that democracy was important, voting was important, participating was important.

One of my earliest memories of politics came after President Eisenhower was elected in 1952. I was five years old. I remember my mother saying, "You know, we didn't vote for him. He's a Republican. We're Democrats, dyed-in-the-wool Democrats." But, she added, "Now he's our president and we should respect that." I pretty much accepted the fact, from that point on, that I was a dyed-in-the-wool Democrat.

We were living in Philadelphia at the time. My father, Tom Coleman, was a boilermaker in the Merchant Marines. His home was in Indiana, and that's where my older sister Maryjane and I were born. When my father started working on ships and heading out to sea for long stretches of time, we moved in with Aunt Mary in Philadelphia, where my sisters Barbara and Lily were born. Later, we moved to a rancher in Gloucester City. That's where my brother Tom Jr. and my little sister Joanne were born.

When James and I compare notes about our childhoods, a couple of things stand out. The first is that we were both pretty shy, quiet kids. We both enjoyed school, and we found role models in our teachers. I really loved all my teachers, but my favorites were two teachers, both named Mrs. Porch. They weren't related. One dressed in a beautiful suit every day, and her handwriting was gorgeous. The other was an older lady, and the nicest, kindest person I had ever met.

James and I both realized at an early age that we loved reading. My cousin had the entire series of Nancy Drew books, and I read every one of them. Then one day I picked up a book about Jane Addams, the founder of Hull House in Chicago. She was an inspirational figure, a Nobel Peace Prize winner who was appropriately nicknamed "the mother of social work" for her programs providing services to immigrants and poor people. She was a pioneer in early childhood education before anybody else was even thinking about it.

I knew after I read that book that I wanted to be a teacher. Nobody in our family had ever been to college (another thing I have in common with James), but I made up my mind that I was going to get my teaching degree. What I didn't expect, however, was how long it was going to take me to do it.

When James was finishing his junior year in high school, he decided he
needed some direction and structure to his life—so he joined the navy.
When I finished my freshman year at Gloucester City High School, I decided I needed some direction and structure to my life—so I transferred to
a Seventh Day Adventist high school in Plainfield, New Jersey.

I went there because I had been babysitting for one of our neighbors
who was a Seventh Day Adventist, and she used to take me to church with
her. My family was not particularly religious, so I guess I was attracted by
the idea of finding something to believe in. My neighbor told me about
the school in Plainfield and offered to sponsor me. Living with four sisters
and a brother was chaos as far as I was concerned, so I jumped at the
chance to get away from home.

It was a boarding school, so I spent weekdays there and sometimes
went home on the weekends to visit friends. But I also started forming
new friendships at the school. We would go to classes in the morning, and
then, after lunch, we had a work assignment. I was assigned to the laun-
dry, and after a while I was running it, supervising four or five other students and making new friends.

There was one particular friend, a boy, who was a couple of years older
than me. As I was finishing up my junior year, he was graduating. The
Vietnam War was heating up, and there was no doubt he was going to
be drafted. As a Seventh Day Adventist, he was committed to the religion's teaching of "noncombatancy," but he didn't want to be a conscien-
tious objector.

We talked a lot about what his options were. I knew I wanted to finish
high school, go on to college, and become a teacher. But I also knew (or at
least I thought I knew) that he and I would get married some day. If we
didn't wait, if we got married immediately, there was less chance he was
going to be drafted.

So I dropped out of high school and we got married. Within three months, I was pregnant, which meant there was almost no chance my husband would be drafted. It also meant that my dream of going to college and becoming a teacher would be deferred for a very long time.

James and I both made the same mistake: we married too young, before we had the chance to find out who we would really become as adults. I think we both realized our mistake fairly quickly, but he remained in his marriage because of his three kids and I remained in mine because of my son, Mark Rowe, who was born in 1965.

Like James, I earned my high school diploma by passing the GED. Then I got my associate's degree at Gloucester County Community College, and later my bachelor's degree at Glassboro State (now Rowan University) in early childhood education. Then I took additional courses to get accreditation as an elementary school teacher, because early childhood education jobs were so hard to find.

I finally landed my teaching job in Pine Hill. After I had been teaching there a couple of years, I moved to Pine Hill from Marlton. I was worried that my temperamental car, a big old brown Oldsmobile with a bad muffler, was on the verge of breaking down, and I wanted to be in a place where I could catch a school bus to work if I had to. Sure enough, the Oldsmobile died, and I went out and got a well-worn 1964 red Mustang, which I loved.

I was finally settled. I had a great job. I was comfortably self-sufficient. My mother had passed away and my father had retired to Florida, where he was happily remarried to a lovely widow. My life was finally calming down.

And then I met James.

⋘

It was an open secret when we went to the 1988 Democratic National Convention in Atlanta that James was going to run for governor the following year. When he formally announced his candidacy in April 1989, I told him I wanted to finish the school year before I became involved in the campaign. "You've got to give me till June to wrap this up," I said, "and then I'll go with you to every campaign event you want me to go to."

The first one I remember was a big rally at Cooper River Park in Camden. Everybody knew him there, of course, but nobody knew me—and I didn't know anybody. I had no clue what to expect. All of a sudden, I'm meeting all these people and I don't know their names. James told me, "Don't worry, you don't need to know anybody's name. You don't need to get into any conversations. You don't have time." So I just smiled a lot, and went along as best I could.

In one important respect, my personality is the opposite of James's. I'm more carefree and easygoing, but in a big crowd with a lot of strangers I can get a little intimidated. He's more serious and thoughtful, so in a big crowd he can come across as stiff and formal. I think that's why we always held hands at events like this. It made me feel more relaxed, and it made him feel more comfortable.

We had started holding hands almost from the moment we began dating. James was always very affectionate in private, but I think it also meant a lot for him to show some affection in public by holding my hand. He liked having me with him. Whenever we sat next to each other, he would hold my hand. I insisted on only one exception: when he was driving.

There's no other way to put this: James is a bad driver. I decided there was no way I was going to let him hold my hand while he was driving. I was going to sit in my own seat, far away, and he was just going to drive—with two hands on the wheel. One of the great things about the campaign, and later about the governorship, was that James never drove. He and I were always in the back seat. And there it was perfectly fine for us to hold hands.

Our hand-holding definitely caught the attention of the press. The weekend before the election, the *Asbury Park Press* began its profile of me with this sentence: "Lucinda Florio runs hand in hand with the man she married in 1988."

The campaign headquarters was in West Orange, so the staff got us an apartment in Montclair, which we used whenever we were going to be in North Jersey for more than a day at a time. The apartment was in an old school building, and I remember telling James how pleased I was that he had found a way for me to spend some time back in a classroom.

I missed teaching, but I really didn't have much time to think about it during the campaign. We were on the road 24/7. There was staff all over. Every morning, I just got in the car with him. I didn't always know where we were going. What I worried about most was what would happen if somebody came up and asked me a question. I was brand new to all this.

A woman named Kathleen Daley was working in the campaign, helping on media strategy and how to answer questions (and avoid others) when dealing with the press. She asked me to sit down with her and talk a little bit. It was very helpful. My "media training" focused primarily on what *not* to do.

Kathleen explained that if I was asked a question that was really rude or too personal, I should just look at the reporter nicely and not say anything. A reporter can't do much with an empty tape. I thought that was an easy trick to remember, though I very rarely had to use it. Another piece of advice she gave me, which I followed much more frequently, was not to say too much, to always give a quick reply or a very short statement. "Just be friendly," she said. "Be yourself."

Fortunately, the reporters were much more interested in James's campaign than they were in his wife. I had a few interviews with the press, but they were mostly about how we met, what my background was, and what kind of "first lady" I would be. I was happy to answer questions on the first two subjects and offered a smile and a shrug on the third one.

And the seniors, especially the women—the senior ladies—loved my husband. They would shove me aside to stand next to him and touch him and shake his hand and get a picture with him. I thought it was really great, and I'd just stand back and say to James, "Here come the ladies. I'm just going to step over here a little bit."

I was so naïve. I thought once the campaign was over, the press would go away, the crowds would go away, and everything would calm down. It didn't.

⋘⋙

After the election, I really wondered what I was going to do. I wasn't going to sit around. I had to do something. I just didn't know what. I said to James, "This is very difficult for me, not to think about being back in the classroom." And he said, "Don't worry. It'll be fine. You're going to have a bigger classroom."

The time between the November election and the January inauguration was a whirlwind. James spent most of his time lining up his staff and cabinet, and working on a smooth transition from the outgoing Kean administration to the incoming Florio administration. I spent most of my time trying to figure out how the two of us were going to live comfortably in this huge white elephant, the governor's mansion on Stockton Street (Route 206) in Princeton: Drumthwacket.

Drumthwacket (Scottish for "house on a wooden hill") sits on a piece of property that was once owned by William Penn. The original building dates back to the early nineteenth century; it was constructed by Charles Smith Olden, who later went on to become governor of New Jersey. In 1966, after the expanded structure had fallen into a state of considerable disrepair, it was sold to the state, to be used as the governor's mansion.

In the twenty-three years following that sale, no governor lived in Drumthwacket. Although Governors Hughes, Cahill, and Byrne all had large families, they lived in Morven, the much smaller governor's mansion a few blocks away. Governor Kean, who had a much smaller family, nevertheless chose to maintain his residence in Livingston, though he occasionally used a few rooms on the first floor of Drumthwacket for ceremonial occasions—and his chancellor of higher education occupied a couple of rooms on the second floor. The rest of the mansion could best be described as barely livable.

In the 1989 gubernatorial election, Congressmen Florio and Jim Courter spar in a televised debate.

Jim Florio's credentials for the 97th Congress, in which he would find himself fighting to save the Superfund and other environmental laws he sponsored from being undermined by the administration of incoming president Ronald Reagan.

An assortment of buttons and lapel pins were worn by supporters in the 1989 gubernatorial campaign and by visitors to Governor Florio's office after his election.

Boxes of "Florio's," dubbed "The Breakfast of Special Interests," were distributed by 1989 Democratic primary opponent Alan Karcher. Among the directions: "Add Milk & Watch 'em Waffle."

FLORIO'S A PEACH

After the NRA, Hands Across New Jersey, and other opponents started sporting "Impeach Florio" bumper stickers on their cars, the governor's supporters introduced their own variation on the theme.

Jim and Lucinda Florio show their optimism after casting their ballots in the 1989 gubernatorial election, which Congressman Florio would win by a margin of 62 to 38 percent.

Lucinda Florio holds the Bible as Supreme Court Chief Justice Robert Wilentz administers the oath of office to James J. Florio, the forty-ninth governor of New Jersey, on January 16, 1990.

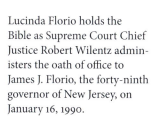

GOVERNOR'S INAUGURAL
SWEARING-IN
WAR MEMORIAL
TRENTON, N.J.
JANUARY 16,1990

Governor and Mrs. Florio on inauguration day

Governor Florio tours the site where a ruptured pipe spilled 567,000 gallons of heating oil into the Arthur Kill, and uses the occasion to announce the creation of the new post of Environmental Prosecutor.

GOVERNOR TOURS OIL SPILL
ARTHUR KILL
JANUARY 24,1990

PRESS CONFERENCE ASSAULT WEAPONS
NEWARK,N.J.
MARCH 19,1990

Governor Florio meets with members of the Essex County Sheriff's Office as part of a statewide campaign to generate support for a ban on assault weapons. Law enforcement agencies were among the strongest supporters of the ban.

At a Newark gymnasium, Governor Florio demonstrates the left jab that served him well as a 156-pound navy boxer—until a 172-pound opponent abruptly ended his career.

Governor Florio meets, but does not challenge, a boxer of considerably greater renown, Muhammad Ali.

Governor and Mrs. Florio are joined by U.S. Senator Frank Lautenberg and Vice President Al Gore.

To Jim Florio
With appreciation,
Bill Clinton

As he enters his final year in office, Governor Florio enjoys the opportunity to share thoughts and ideas with a kindred spirit, newly elected President Bill Clinton.

The holiday season at the State House finds the Florios celebrating the occasion with children of all ages.

Caroline Kennedy presents Governor Florio with the "Profile in Courage" award on May 24, 1993, joined by, from left, Senator Edward Kennedy, Mrs. Florio, John F. Kennedy Jr., and Jacqueline Kennedy Onassis.

At the New Jersey shore, Jim and Lucinda Florio enjoy the company of their ten grandchildren, who believe their Pop Pop's major claim to fame is bringing the dolphins back.

"If my philosophy of achieving political success can be summed up in a single phrase, it is to 'engage and inform' on the issues—to make sure that combatants and constituencies, the voters and the public, are engaged and informed in the decision-making process, and that they are provided with the information they need to make sound, rational decisions."

—JAMES J. FLORIO

The first time we did a walk-through of Drumthwacket, I turned to James and said, "How are we going to live here?" And he admitted, "I don't know." But he said, "We'll figure it out as we go. It'll be fine."

So we moved in. We lived out of boxes for the first couple of months. I turned on the kitchen tap one day and brown water came out. When James came home, I called him into the kitchen and said, "OK, Mr. Environmentalist, come here and explain this."

Some of the rooms had no heat. Others had too much heat, causing a buildup of mold in the pages of some old books that were supposed to be preserved. The kitchen wall needed shoring up. The attic floor was sinking. In one of the second-floor bedrooms, the heating vents were covered with chicken wire instead of screening. Outside, there was a tiered terrace leading down to the gardens. All the brickwork was crumbled and falling apart. A grotto area had collapsed. A pond was filled with slime. The gardens were dilapidated, filled with overgrown weeds, bushes, and briars.

On Inauguration Day, a bunch of my relatives and friends were in town, and we invited them back to the house for a reception in the downstairs area that was usable. After they all left, we went upstairs to a bedroom that had heat. The next day, James got up and went to work. And there I was, sitting in this big old house.

"OK," I said to myself, "I've got to figure this all out." The first thing I had to do was get a staff. Maria Rouco, who had worked in the campaign, said she would be my secretary. So I gave her some space of her own, and I said, "Now we have to find staff for the house." We had no one to cook. I couldn't even go out to buy groceries; I had given up my car because I had to have a state trooper drive me everywhere.

A good friend of mine, Carol Lampf, volunteered to help, along with another former campaign worker, Joanne Plumeri. Pretty soon, the staff started coming together. Carol found Camille Amadio to run the mansion. Then Camille brought on a couple of assistants, Hilda and Jackie, to run the kitchen—and from that point on everything started running a lot more smoothly. Thanks to my working-class roots, I felt less like their boss than a member of the team. We're all good friends to this day.

Now it was time to do something about the house. The Drumthwacket Foundation, created in 1982 to preserve and restore the mansion, was in no position to do anything. It was $30,000 in debt. Its board was inactive. Its executive director, Daphne Pontius, had a little office and a long list of needed repairs. I honestly don't know if she was still getting paid or was volunteering, but she made it clear that if we wanted to improve the condition of the governor's mansion, not to mention our own living situation, we would need to raise money—and get permission for just about anything else we wanted to do from the New Jersey Historical Society.

I didn't know the first thing about fundraising and very little about home improvement beyond setting thermostats on hot water heaters and freezers. But I did know how to make a lesson plan, and that's how I approached the challenge of fixing up Drumthwacket. I said to Daphne, "OK, let's figure out what our priorities are going to be. Then let's make a plan, like a lesson plan, and take it from there."

First, we revived the foundation board. Then, we got together with representatives of the Historical Society to discuss the work that needed to be done and how to pay for it. We needed at least $350,000 to start the project and another $250,000 to do the gardens. We sponsored tennis tournaments. We hosted receptions and cocktail parties. I went out and met the leaders of Johnson & Johnson and other major corporations. I received a lot of help from people like Bill Faherty at First Fidelity Bank, who was an unabashed cheerleader for the project.

What made me especially proud of our efforts was that it was my project, not James's. He had other matters to attend to. And besides, when it comes to his living conditions, James doesn't care. He just wants to know where his toothbrush is.

⚜

After the architects and engineers drew up plans, the construction people from the State House came over, looked at the plans and figured out what had to be done structurally, how much money we needed, who the workers were going to be, how they were going to schedule the project, and how quickly it could get done—recognizing that James and I were going to be living upstairs while they did everything else around us.

They hired the same company that had done beautiful work restoring the legislative chambers at the State House in Trenton to come over and fix up our house in Princeton. It took them eighteen months to turn Drumthwacket from an eyesore into a governor's mansion of which New Jersey could be truly proud.

The construction workers were a great bunch of guys—hard workers, solid people. They worked so hard all those months, and I got to know some of them. I wanted to show my appreciation when they finished by inviting them to a little reception in their honor. They could bring their families out and show them what they worked on. Some of them were so humble they didn't even think they should be asked, and several wouldn't even come. They did what they did, and that was it. Then they moved on to the next job.

I didn't know who would come, but I really wanted the workers to know that what they did was important, not only to us but also to the people of New Jersey. So we hosted the reception, and I think the workers who came had a really good time—and they were proud to show off their work to their wives and children.

Next came the garden. The rear of the house was transformed from an overgrown wasteland into a delightful backyard, thanks in large part to our gardener, Elizabeth Humes, a very pleasant lady who just loved her flowers. She created beautiful picking gardens near the house. Further back, the workers painstakingly restored the brickwork of the tiered terrace; rebuilt the collapsed grotto; removed the slime from the pond; and cleared out the weeds, bushes, and briars—and the entire backyard became a wonderful open space, whether to entertain a large group of visitors or a nice spot for just the two of us to sit back and relax.

While renovating Drumthwacket occupied much of my time and attention in the first couple of years of James's governorship, it was by no means my only activity. I spent many hours in what James had described as my "bigger classroom"—or, perhaps more accurately, a whole lot of smaller classrooms. I loved visiting schools all over New Jersey, whether it was a gifted and talented classroom in Bergen County or a special needs classroom in Cape May. Being together with kids was one of the great joys of my life, and I had many opportunities to pursue that joy as the state's First Lady.

And, of course, I accompanied James to as many events as I could. Although many days were divided between his schedule and my schedule, we tried as much as possible to combine them into our schedule. We went together to everything from groundbreakings for sewage treatment plants to senior-citizen center parking lot openings. From one day to the next, I didn't always remember where I was supposed to be. All I knew was I had to be dressed in heels all the time—but I always carried flats with me and changed into them whenever I could.

James and his staff scheduled events called "Capital for a Day," where we would spend an entire day in a different town, meeting with officials and community leaders, visiting hospitals and veterans homes, eating with local residents at a diner, and, my favorite, spending time in a classroom. I didn't appreciate seeing the "Dump Florio" yard signs we'd sometimes come across (James, on the other hand, joked that some people must have thought his first name was "Dump"), but I really enjoyed meeting people who wanted to share their concerns with us, and I think the people really appreciated the fact that James was taking the time to listen to them.

One event I will never forget was a dinner sponsored by the Italian-American Boxing Hall of Fame at Cameo Caterers in Garfield. The place was filled with a bunch of guys who looked like they were straight out of *The Sopranos*. I had never seen anything like that in my life.

I have a lot of fond memories from our time at Drumthwacket, our travels around the state (and occasionally across the country), our rides together in the back seat of a car that James wasn't driving, our visits to places I would never, ever have gone on my own. But I would be less than honest if I didn't also say I missed my privacy, our privacy. It was a difficult four years for James because of the many challenges he had as governor. It was also a difficult four years for me because of the toll it took on him and the lack of space in my own life.

When James lost the 1993 election, I was disappointed—and devastated for him. As governor, he had done what he thought was right. My heart broke for him; he was (and in many ways still is) a full-time public servant. The work he did, and what we did together, was important.

The people we worked with meant everything to us, and we learned so much from our experiences over those four years. It was a privilege to serve the citizens of New Jersey. To this day, people stop and say hello when we're at the beach, and it's always, "Thank you for what you did for the Jersey Shore; you were a good governor."

As 1993 was coming to an end, however, it was time for us to move on to the next chapter of our life.

⁓

On November 3, 1993, the morning after we learned that we would soon be moving out of Drumthwacket, James and I sat down at the kitchen table and started to map out our future. We had about $60,000 in the bank. We didn't have a car. We didn't have jobs. Soon we wouldn't have a place to live.

I told James I didn't think I could go back to teaching. People would treat me differently; they would know me from another role, and they would look at me and think of me in that role, instead of as a teacher.

I realized, too, that James faced an even starker reality. He had just had his whole professional career taken away from him, and he would be going through a period of time where I had to be there for him. All that he was about, and all he wanted to do, was to serve the public.

So the best I could do was just be there, and we would work together to figure out all the details. For the moment, he would concentrate on the transition to the administration of the new governor, Christine Todd Whitman, and start looking around for a job with a law firm. While he was putting together a plan for his future, I was focused on finding us a place to live.

After spending the last four years in a mansion, all we wanted was a nice little place we could call our own. I knew James would be spending a lot of time doing things for the Clinton administration in Washington, New York, and around the country. And that's exactly what he did. He was appointed chairman of the Federal Home Loan Bank in New York; he chaired a task force on labor relations for Labor Secretary Robert Reich; he served on the Energy Secretary's advisory board for Federico Peña and Bill Richardson.

We liked the Princeton area. So we put most of our things in storage and rented a nearby townhouse for a year while we looked for a more permanent residence.

We ended up in Metuchen, where we lived for more than twenty years before we decided to move to Moorestown to be closer to our grandchildren. I got very involved in civic activities, serving as board president of the local YMCA. Because of my background in early childhood education, I was especially proud of the partnership formed between the YMCA and the Jewish Community Center in Edison, which became the largest provider of children's services in Middlesex County. I also cochaired the mayor's wellness campaign and was an active board member for the Liberty Science Center in Jersey City. James used to kid me that when he went to the Metuchen library, they knew him as Lucinda's husband.

James likes to stay busy, and he hasn't slowed down much since his days as governor. He's still a fitness freak. I can't keep up with him. The only thing different is that now, instead of jogging four miles a day like he used to, he walks four miles a day—but he still does it carrying four-pound weights.

For the last twenty-five years, I've never known from one day to the next if he's teaching, going to a Pinelands Commission meeting, doing legal work, attending a business luncheon, giving a speech, receiving an award, campaigning for some candidate somewhere, or doing a magazine interview at the Metuchen Diner.

He doesn't know how to say no. "You act like you have to say yes to everything," I tell him. Sometimes he comes home after an event and complains that it was a waste of time because there wasn't enough substance to it. "You've got to pick and choose a little smarter," I say, but I know my advice is falling on deaf ears. James feels he has an obligation to take the time to meet with people, to speak to a group, or attend an event that interests him. He's very loyal to the people he has worked with and knows and supports. They have always been there for him, and he wants to be there for them.

He doesn't talk much about his work. His assistant, Susan O'Neill, brings order to his life. She tells him where he's going, what he's doing, where he has to be, and who he's going to talk to. So all I do is compare my schedule with his schedule and find out when he's going to be out of town or what time he's going to be home for dinner. Just like when he was governor, there's his schedule, my schedule, and our schedule.

And every now and then, maybe on a snowy evening when we're both home, we might put on a Woody Allen album—and with Margo, our Boston terrier, eagerly joining us for her own share of affection, cuddle up like a couple of teenagers on the couch.

CHAPTER 7

The Third Time Is a Charm

A genius learns from others' mistakes. The rest of us learn from our own mistakes. I am not a genius.

In 1974, I learned not to repeat the mistakes I made in my 1972 congressional campaign, and I won a seat in Congress. In 1981, I learned not to repeat the mistakes I made in my 1977 gubernatorial primary, and I won the Democratic nomination for governor. In 1989, I was determined to win the general election for governor by not repeating the mistakes I made in 1981.

At the 1988 Democratic National Convention in Atlanta, virtually all the attention was focused on the national ticket: Massachusetts governor Michael Dukakis for president and Texas senator Lloyd Bentsen for vice president. Within the New Jersey delegation, however, I did my very best to steer as much attention as I could to the following year's race for governor.

One of the mistakes I had made in my earlier campaigns was to start running too late, failing to lay the early groundwork—and thereby securing early support—for my candidacy. Another was to rely too heavily on my geographic base. Even in my statewide 1981 run, while I succeeded in garnering some support north of Trenton, both my campaign staff and my volunteers were made up largely of my supporters from Camden and Gloucester Counties.

This time around, I concentrated on picking up early endorsements from individuals and organizations from all parts of New Jersey. In the years leading up to the 1989 race, I made countless trips from Washington back to the state and spent countless hours meeting with people and speaking to groups far beyond the boundaries of my congressional district. I cemented relationships that would give me what I hoped would be an insurmountable lead in the race for the Democratic nomination and a comfortable head start in the general election campaign.

I didn't have an idle moment during the Atlanta convention. From early morning until late at night, I made the rounds of breakfast meetings, coffee breaks, receptions, dinners, and myriad meetings of delegates, alternates, committees, sponsors, and any other group that might be attended by more than a handful of potential New Jersey Democratic primary voters.

Having Lucinda by my side was an enormous benefit. She won a lot of people over with her warm and engaging personality. Very few people who had come to know me during my two decades in public office to that point would have described my own personality as warm and engaging. But if in my earlier campaigns I had come across as cold and aloof, Lucinda's presence had a calming effect on me. I felt more relaxed. I was told I was smiling a lot more. Many of the party regulars I encountered in Atlanta commented on how much more approachable I was. If my natural instinct in past campaign settings was to do a lot of talking, my countenance leading up to the 1989 campaign was to do a lot more listening.

By the time I made my formal announcement in April 1989, I had put together a professional campaign staff. Doug Berman, who was involved in Bill Bradley's successful 1978 and 1984 Senate campaigns, agreed to serve as my campaign manager. My press secretary in Washington, former *Bergen Record* reporter Jon Shure, left my congressional staff to become communications director for the campaign. David Applebaum took leave without pay from my congressional staff to serve as director of research and issues. Brenda Bacon, a health care professional, close confidante, and former Camden County freeholder, and Sharon Harrington, a veteran of several New Jersey Democratic campaigns, also came on board.

Washington-based media consultants Bob Squier and Carter Eskew, who had done great work for Senator Frank Lautenberg in his 1988 re-election victory over Pete Dawkins, put together our TV ad campaign. Joe Peritz & Associates, a Connecticut company, did our polling. On many Saturday mornings throughout the campaign, Rutgers political science professor Carl Van Horn brought together experts in health care, housing, labor, environment, and other policy areas to discuss the issues of the day.

I have always been more comfortable focusing on policy than on politics, and I was convinced that the issues in the 1989 gubernatorial election were going to favor my candidacy. I felt certain that my efforts on behalf of New Jersey—preserving the Pinelands, cleaning up hazardous waste sites, saving Amtrak, fighting back against Reagan administration attempts to dismantle social service programs—would be rewarded by the voters.

I also had the same advantage in 1989 that Tom Kean had in 1981: running to succeed a two-term governor of the opposite party. There were eight candidates in the Republican primary field. Regardless of which candidate the GOP selected, I was confident that history was on my side.

❦

Before I could devote my full attention to the general election contest, I had to win the Democratic primary. After competing in crowded primaries in both 1977 and 1981, I had the good fortune to be in a significantly smaller field in 1989. I faced only two primary challengers, Assemblyman (and former Speaker) Alan Karcher and Princeton mayor Barbara Boggs Sigmund.

Alan Karcher was a worthy adversary. Just ask Tom Kean. Alan was a thorn in the governor's side throughout his first term, leading assembly

Democrats in opposition to many of Kean's policy initiatives and pro-grams. It was the Karcher-led push for higher taxes that compelled Governor Kean to sign bills that increased income, sales, and corporate taxes after having promised in his 1981 campaign against me to reduce them.

After the 1985 Kean re-election landslide, the Democrats lost the majority in the assembly and Alan became the minority leader. From that position, he launched his own campaign for governor, and he shifted the target of his attacks from Kean to me. He knew that my refusal to sign a "no-tax" pledge had probably hurt me in the 1981 campaign, so he challenged me either to sign such a pledge in 1989 or to agree with him that the next governor was going to have to raise taxes. Knowing that the latter position wasn't going to win me any votes and the former wasn't one I could take in good conscience, I noted that the Kean administration was reporting a $300 million surplus in the current state budget, suggesting there would be no need in the immediate future for any kind of increase in taxes.

When he wasn't hammering away on the tax issue, what Alan mostly did was goad me. He made a point of always referring to me as "Jimmy," knowing I disliked the nickname (and Lucinda disliked it even more). He accused me of being the "boss" of Camden County, an ironic charge coming from the Middlesex County product of the powerful Wilentz organization. His best campaign gimmick was distributing little cereal boxes of "Florio's"—with instructions to "add milk and watch 'em waf-fle." Everybody, including me, got a good chuckle out of Alan's clever, if caustic, creativity, but in the end he finished a distant third in the primary with less than 15 percent of the vote.

Barbara Boggs Sigmund had a political pedigree bordering on Democratic royalty. Her father, Hale Boggs of Louisiana, served fourteen terms in the House of Representatives, rising to become majority leader in 1971. He would have become Speaker of the House had he not died in a plane crash in Alaska two years later. He was succeeded in Congress by his wife and Barbara's mother, Lindy, who served nine terms and later was named U.S. ambassador to the Vatican. Barbara's brother, Thomas, was a prominent Washington lobbyist. Her sister, Cokie Roberts, was a prominent broadcast journalist.

Barbara was charming and sophisticated. Her speech and mannerisms had a distinct New Orleans flavor. She was witty, energetic, and a boundless campaigner. In 1982, after launching a bid for Congress, she changed her mind and ran for the Senate instead; she finished fourth out of ten candidates in the primary won by Frank Lautenberg, carrying only her home county of Mercer. That same year, she lost an eye to cancer, and her eye patch became her signature, always color coordinated with her clothing.

Barbara finished second in the primary with 17 percent of the vote. I won 68 percent of the primary vote, and swept all twenty-one counties.

Although we were rivals for the Democratic gubernatorial nomination in 1989, I was saddened when Barbara lost her battle with cancer the following year at the age of fifty-one, and Alan passed away in 1999 at the age of fifty-six. Both were dedicated public servants who believed, as I do, that government has a fundamental responsibility to protect its most vulnerable citizens through policies that promote fairness and human dignity.

᷃᷄᷄

On the Republican side, things looked pretty much like my previous Democratic primaries: crowded. There were eight candidates, at least five of whom were reasonably well known and enjoyed a base of support.

Gerald Cardinale was a longtime state senator from Bergen County. Bill Gormley was a popular state senator from Atlantic County. Chuck Hardwick, the General Assembly Speaker in Governor Kean's second term, hailed from Union County. Cary Edwards had served in the legislature from Bergen County, but was counting on Kean loyalists across the state to support him after he had served first as chief counsel and then as attorney general in the Kean administration. Congressman Jim Courter was a six-term representative from a district that covered a large chunk of northwestern New Jersey.

In one important respect, Jim Courter's edge in the 1989 Republican primary was the same one I had in both the 1981 and 1989 Democratic races: his base was larger than everyone else's.

While each state legislative district in New Jersey had a population of approximately 218,000, congressional districts each had roughly 732,000 constituents. The state legislators—Cardinale, Gormley, and Hardwick—were therefore at a distinct disadvantage compared to Courter. Only Edwards had a real shot at overcoming Courter's geographic edge, but his 85,313 votes fell well short of Courter's 112,326. Courter rolled up big margins in the counties covered by his congressional district—Hunterdon, Morris, Somerset, Sussex, and Warren—and he finished with 40 percent of the GOP primary vote.

I did not know Jim Courter well. We said hello when we saw each other in the halls of Congress, but our interests and areas of specialty were decidedly different. He was devoted to his work on the Armed Services Committee and was intensely involved in issues like the Pentagon budget, military preparedness, base closings, and the Reagan administration's "Star Wars" missile defense system.

I had joined with him in support of keeping Fort Dix and Maguire Air Force Base open after a military base closure panel had recommended they be shuttered. I was disappointed when he was the only member of our state's congressional delegation not to vote for the creation of the Pinelands National Preserve.

By today's standards, given where his party has moved over the past two or three decades, Jim Courter would probably be considered a moderate Republican. But by 1989 standards, he was more conservative than his principal rivals for the Republican nomination and well to the right of most New Jersey voters.

The Republican Party hadn't learned its lesson. It shot itself in the foot in 1973, denying a second term to Governor Bill Cahill, the moderate incumbent, in favor of Congressman Charlie Sandman, a staunch conservative and unrepentant Nixon supporter. In the general election, Sandman was soundly defeated by Brendan Byrne. The following year, he lost his congressional seat to Bill Hughes.

In 1978, GOP primary voters rejected four-term incumbent U.S. Senator Clifford Case, a moderate who regularly attracted support from Democrats, and instead nominated arch-conservative Jeffrey Bell, whose foremost campaign issue, believe it or not, was a return to the gold standard. In the general election, Bell was trounced by Bill Bradley.

In Jim Courter, the GOP primary voters once again chose a candidate whose views placed him on the fringe of New Jersey's political landscape.

I entered the general election race with a clear vision of what I wanted to do—and what I *didn't* want to do. I wanted to emphasize broad themes that had resonance with voters: making automobile insurance affordable, taking forceful action against polluters, cleaning up the Jersey Shore. These were the issues that were on people's minds, and I made a point of addressing them throughout the campaign in speeches, in television advertisements, in campaign handouts, and in meetings with newspaper editorial boards. I disciplined myself to stay on message.

What I didn't want to do was fall into the same trap that had snared Michael Dukakis a year earlier in the 1988 presidential campaign. In that race, the Republican candidate, Vice President George H. W. Bush, repeatedly accused Dukakis, the governor of Massachusetts, of being "soft on crime." The Dukakis campaign cavalierly dismissed the accusation.

Then the infamous "Revolving Door" TV ad appeared, blaming Dukakis for a murder committed by convicted felon Willie Horton while Horton was on a weekend furlough from state prison. Instead of responding immediately that the prison furlough program under which Horton was released was instituted by his Republican predecessor—and that the federal prison furlough program under the Reagan-Bush administration was even more liberal than the Massachusetts program—Dukakis made the ill-advised decision not to respond at all.

THE THIRD TIME IS A CHARM

I wasn't about to let anything that the Courter campaign would throw at me go unanswered.

The Willie Horton TV ad had been produced by the Bush campaign's media advisor, Roger Ailes, who would later gain fame in some circles, and notoriety in others, as the head of Fox News. When Ailes signed on as Jim Courter's media advisor, I knew I had to be prepared for similar assaults to be lodged against me. If that happened, I was not only going to be ready for them; I was going to respond immediately.

Our campaign staff spent a lot of time anticipating the likely attacks the Courter campaign would launch and coming up with the counterattacks we would use to parry them. We also developed strategies for defusing the anticipated attacks before they even appeared.

We were pretty sure the likeliest line of attack the Courter campaign would pursue was the same one Alan Karcher had used in the primary: that I was the "boss" of Camden County. So even before the Courter campaign launched this attack (which, of course, it did), we released a position paper proposing a new ethics plan for the executive branch of state government. I promised to sign an executive order placing a two-year moratorium on former officials consulting or lobbying in areas connected with their former employment, putting an end to no-bid contracts, requiring full financial disclosure by all executive branch employees, and creating an independent ethics commission.

We were also confident that I would be accused, like all Democrats, of being a "tax-and-spend liberal." So we turned the tables, pointing out that the state budget had doubled in the eight years of the "tax-and-spend" Republican Kean administration. I promised a full-scale audit of state spending. And I reiterated the position I had taken in the primary: based on Governor Kean's assurance that the current state budget was running a healthy surplus, I saw no need to raise taxes if I was elected.

With Ailes on the Courter team, and with the image of Willie Horton still fresh in the public's mind, we were also certain that the Courter campaign would mimic the Bush campaign theme of "law and order." Early on, we reached out to organized police and law-enforcement groups and picked up their endorsements. To defuse what we anticipated would be Courter's enthusiastic embrace of the death penalty, I emphasized that I, too, favored the death penalty, but only in certain limited circumstances.

Although Bush had carried New Jersey over Dukakis (and was, in fact, the last Republican presidential candidate to carry the state), I felt certain that the implicit racism of the Willie Horton ad did not play well in New Jersey. I remember speaking at a church in Elizabeth, reminding the audience of the consent decree the Republicans had signed after the 1981 election, when the Ballot Security Task Force had tried to intimidate voters in minority neighborhoods from going to the polls. "They were in Newark, but not in Short Hills," I reminded them. "They were in Trenton, but not in Princeton. They were in Camden, but not in Cherry Hill." We were resolute that it wouldn't happen again in 1989.

While we were busy making our preparations for the upcoming general election campaign, the Courter team was rocked by the departure of some key members who were implicated in a congressional inquiry into influence peddling in connection with a Cumberland County housing rehabilitation project. One of the consultants who resigned from the Courter campaign was Greg Stevens, who had previously served as chief of staff to Governor Kean. The other was a secretive GOP operative named Roger Stone.

⨠

The scandal surrounded the renovation of housing units in the Upper Deerfield Township community of Seabrook Village, where frozen-vegetable magnate Charles F. Seabrook (with the help of his friend, Clarence Birdseye) had established a mammoth food-processing factory in the 1920s. In 1987, a group of investors purchased Seabrook Village. Without bothering to inform local officials or to seek the approval of the regional office of the federal Department of Housing and Urban Development, the investors, using Stevens's influence, went straight to the state Department of Community Affairs, which awarded them a $31 million HUD grant to rehabilitate 326 housing units.

The investors who purchased the property included Paul Manafort, a partner, along with Roger Stone, in the Washington political consulting firm of Black, Manafort, Stone & Kelly. In addition to owning part of the Seabrook Farms property, Manafort was paid a fee of $326,000—$1,000 per housing unit—for arranging the HUD grant. Manafort subsequently admitted to a congressional subcommittee that the way the deal was struck could be characterized as "influence peddling." Shortly thereafter, Stone and Stevens resigned as political consultants to the Courter campaign. Manafort and Stone would gain national prominence nearly three decades later, because of their involvement in Donald J. Trump's 2016 presidential campaign.

With Stevens and Stone gone, the Courter campaign relied primarily on media guru Ailes, campaign manager Ken Connolly, and spokesman Gordon Hensley. There were several attempts, mostly by Governor Kean and members of his inner circle, to involve more prominent Republicans in the campaign. Overtures were made to Roger Bodman, who had been Kean's transportation commissioner, and Assemblyman Bob Franks, chairman of the Republican State Committee, to run the Courter campaign.

Bodman declined. Franks, a very savvy political tactician who later served four terms in Congress, agreed to join the campaign—but Courter would not name him campaign manager, as Kean and others had hoped, because Franks had been aligned with Chuck Hardwick in the GOP primary. Moreover, Courter felt comfortable with Connolly, who had been recommended to him by Stevens and Stone. Franks campaigned for Courter, but was not an integral part of the campaign team.

Then, in September, just two months before the election, Hensley resigned as campaign spokesman, citing differences with Kean administration officials. Hensley had been a speechwriter in Pete Dawkins's 1988 Senate campaign and had been hired for the Courter campaign by Roger Stone. To succeed Hensley, Courter hired Don Sico, who went on to

On the campaign trail in 1989, Jim and Lucinda
Florio are joined by U.S. Senator Bill Bradley.

become the longtime chief of staff to Republican Assembly Speakers
Chuck Haytaian and Jack Collins—and, ironically, a close friend of mine
many years later.

By any measure, the Courter campaign was in disarray. There was
clearly a lot of tension between Kean's people and Courter's people—and
I took advantage of that. Governor Kean's office used to issue weekly recommendations on pending legislation in Washington that would affect New
Jersey. At a campaign appearance, my staff distributed a handout listing the
recommendations Kean had made in 1987. I had voted in accord with them
96 percent of the time; Courter had done so only 58 percent of the time.

Meanwhile, my campaign was running smoothly. I was very proud of
how organized we were. Appreciating the fact that there was no incumbent in the race, secure in the knowledge that I now enjoyed a broader

base of support than I had in previous campaigns, and confident that my opponent's conservative ideology was out of step with the New Jersey electorate, I worked hard to create an image of inevitability.

I spent a lot of time in the northern part of the state, primarily Bergen, Essex, and Hudson Counties. I was a regular patron at the Lyndhurst Diner in Bergen County, whose owner, John Sackellaris, was not only a loyal supporter but also an influential leader in the Greek community. Phil Keegan, whom I later appointed Democratic state chairman, helped organize the campaign in Essex County, where I also received support from Tony Carino, a city councilman from Newark's heavily Italian North Ward. In Hudson, I got the endorsement of Jersey City mayor Tony Cucci and a lot of help from Buddy Gangemi, whose father, Thomas, had served briefly as mayor of Jersey City in the early 1960s, before it was discovered that he wasn't a U.S. citizen.

Yes, that's yet another example of the kind of New Jersey political lore you just can't make up.

⁓

At most of my public appearances in the early part of the general election campaign, I avoided directing personal attacks against Jim Courter and instead emphasized our differences on policy. I wanted the tone of this campaign to rise above the level of the previous year's Senate campaign, in which Frank Lautenberg labeled Pete Dawkins a "carpetbagger" and Dawkins called Lautenberg a "swamp dog." I think Courter felt the same way, and for most of the summer we both steered clear of the kind of invective that had characterized the Senate race.

Then the TV ads started. They might be considered tame by today's standards, and none of them stooped to the level of a Willie Horton–type attack, but they were pretty hard-hitting on both sides. And many of them on both sides, truth be told, had at best a tangential connection to real issues of public policy.

On the environment, for example, one of my earliest ads highlighted my sponsorship of the Superfund law, and another pointed out that I enjoyed the highest environmental rating among members of the New Jersey congressional delegation, while Courter was ranked fourteenth and last. But the next ad went from comparative to negative, charging that Courter had failed to remove several barrels of home heating oil (which met the technical definition of what the ad termed "toxic waste") from property he owned with his brother.

On ethics, the Courter campaign released an ad claiming that I repeatedly accepted campaign contributions from a "corrupt" union, and another charging that I made a profit from investments in which I didn't put up any of my own money. My campaign came back with an ad attacking Courter for owning stock in defense contractors while serving on the Armed Services Committee and another accusing him of using his office to advance a real-estate transaction in which he had an interest.

On auto insurance, my campaign ridiculed Courter's reform plan as a "giveaway" to the insurance companies. On crime, his campaign accused me, along with my former law partner, Carl Poplar, of "fighting to keep drug dealers out of jail."

I can't say I'm especially proud of the tone and tenor of the TV ad campaign we ran. The 1989 New Jersey gubernatorial campaign was by no means the first race that featured a series of accusatory TV ads, but with the apparent success of the Willie Horton ad the year before, the media consultants to both my campaign and Jim Courter's argued that anything less than hard-hitting attack ads would fail to capture the public's attention. In retrospect, their involvement was an early indication of the outsized importance high-priced media consultants would come to play in our elections and the bare-knuckles tactics they would increasingly employ in the bitter and nasty campaigns we came to accept as commonplace over the next quarter-century.

There is one TV ad in particular that I regret approving. It was done in the form of a cartoon that depicted Courter as Pinocchio, with his nose growing every time he denied saying or doing something he had reportedly said or done. The ad didn't hurt me politically—and Courter came right back with a Pinocchio ad of his own, in which his nose shortened while mine grew—but to me the whole idea of turning a campaign that should be focused on serious policy issues into a battle of cartoonish attacks was really an insult to the voters.

There were, in fact, a number of substantive policy issues on which we had profound differences. In Congress, I had held hearings on the insurance industry and could speak with some knowledge and specificity about what I believed I could do as governor to bring down New Jersey's highest-in-the-nation auto insurance rates. Courter's plan reflected classic conservative orthodoxy. Deregulate the insurance industry, he said, and competition would bring down the high rates of insurance premiums—a claim that was disputed by Kean's own insurance commissioner.

We differed sharply on abortion. I had come down firmly on the side of a woman's right to choose, while Courter had been an outspoken abortion opponent in Congress. After the U.S. Supreme Court issued a ruling that summer declaring that states could place limits on legal abortions, I responded immediately, saying that I would not seek to impose limits as governor. Courter took days to respond, which surprised us—and when he did respond, he vacillated, which surprised us even more. From the staunch antiabortion position he had taken in Congress, he shifted to a hands-off approach, saying he would set aside his personal views and follow the lead of the legislature.

We also had differences on matters of law and order, not so much in substance as in degree. The death penalty was a hot-button issue, in part because of how badly Dukakis had handled a debate question about whether he would favor the death penalty if his wife were raped and murdered. (He gave a very unemotional response, saying who the victim was would have no bearing on how he felt the perpetrator should be punished.)

Courter touted his support for the death penalty at every opportunity and criticized me for saying it should be used more sparingly. But I had already garnered the support of most of the police and law-enforcement organizations in the state. And the Courter campaign made a big mistake late in the race, airing a pro-death penalty TV ad featuring video footage from the funeral of a slain state trooper. The trooper's parents were outraged. "They won't even let him rest in peace," his mother told the Associated Press. "That's all we want—for him to rest in peace. What kind of person could exploit a picture of a funeral?"

Courter also stumbled badly on the issue of gay rights, telling a reporter that he favored limiting the rights of homosexuals to work as teachers, foster parents, camp counselors, or in other positions that would put them in direct contact with children. After religious leaders and gay rights groups accused him of pandering to irrational fears and bigotry, he backtracked, saying this was his personal opinion, but that he wasn't advocating a written state policy barring homosexuals from particular jobs.

I responded that I didn't care if a teacher was gay; I cared only if he or she was a good teacher. This was long before the LGBTQ movement had gained the measure of public acceptance it now has, and more than a few conservative Democrats criticized me for taking such a libertarian position. But I felt very strongly that gays and lesbians should have no less protection against discrimination than all other Americans.

I think watching my brother Bill go through life as a gay man had a strong influence on my belief that homosexuals posed no threat to children or anyone else. Bill never told me, or our parents, that he was gay. I think my parents suspected he was, and I'm sure my father had a hard time accepting it, but Bill never spoke openly about his sexual preference. He was an art dealer, fairly prominent in the arts community in Manhattan, and when he started bringing his friend, an Iranian rug dealer, to family events, our suspicions were essentially confirmed.

Bill was widely respected in New York's arts and antiques world. There's no reason he wouldn't have been a really good teacher. I'm truly sorry he didn't live to see the day when he could have lived his life openly, instead of in the shadows.

*

There were two occasions during the campaign when I felt the Courter campaign took a step too far, making statements to which I took great offense. The first was an attack on my patriotism. The second was his assertion during one of our debates that his environmental record was at least as good as mine.

In September, the Courter campaign lodged the charge that Jim Florio does not stand up for America because he doesn't stand behind the American flag. The source of this absurd attack was a bill introduced in the state assembly two decades earlier that I (along with fellow Assemblyman Tom Kean) had declined to support. The bill would have increased penalties for burning the American flag.

This was one of those "gotcha" moments straight out of the Republican playbook. Find a purely symbolic vote somewhere in a candidate's past (and I had cast plenty of them over my twenty years in elective office) and then trot it out years later as evidence of some perceived failure to represent true American values.

I wasn't about to take this attack lying down. The very next day, I held a press conference at the War Memorial Building in Trenton, where I was flanked by representatives of the Veterans of Foreign Wars, Disabled American Veterans, and other veterans groups. I compared my twenty-two years of military service—four on active duty in the navy, eighteen in the Active Naval Reserve at Naval Air Station Lakehurst—with Jim Courter's two years in the Peace Corps.

I looked directly into the cameras and addressed Courter. "If you want to question my patriotism," I said, "do it to my face." That was the last anyone heard about my lack of patriotism.

The second incident occurred during our first debate, held at Monmouth College. We were lobbing a lot of charges back and forth when Courter started touting his environmental record. He said he had offered an amendment to ban offshore oil and gas drilling, and he boasted that he helped secure the first cleanup of a toxic waste dump in New Jersey, which was in his congressional district. The clear implication was that he was a champion for the environment.

I am not, by nature, a spontaneous person. When I was a kid, I used to lie in bed at night thinking about, and planning for, everything that was going to happen the next day. Like a good Boy Scout, I always wanted to Be Prepared. Even as an adult, I have a strong preference for preparedness over spontaneity. And I pride myself on almost always managing to keep calm in moments of stress.

But that night, at that moment, I was so astonished that I blurted out on impulse, "Cut me a break!"—which drew an equally impulsive outburst of cheers and applause from my supporters in the audience. When they quieted down, I went on to claim that the people in Courter's district had to call me to get action on the dumpsite he mentioned.

It turned out I was wrong: Courter had, in fact, been instrumental in getting that hazardous waste site in his district cleaned up. But what everyone talked about the next day was my spur-of-the-moment outburst, reflecting my umbrage that Jim Courter would dare compare his record on the environment with mine. Most of the follow-up stories highlighted this exchange and went on to report that environmental legislation was the hallmark of my congressional career while Courter's expertise lay in issues related to national defense and the armed services.

Organized environmental groups also weighed in, criticizing Courter for touting a "Clean Air Champion" award he had earned from the Sierra Club. The organization noted that more than 200 members of Congress had received the same award as Courter and emphasized that its membership, like that of every other major environmental organization, strongly endorsed my candidacy.

On Election Day, I was confident of victory. The leading newspapers in the state had endorsed me. Our polling showed me with a double-digit lead beginning in late summer, and there was no evidence of slippage as the election approached. Former state senate majority leader Steve Perskie, whom Governor Kean had appointed as a judge on the Superior Court, resigned from the bench to join my team, quietly planning how we would make the transition, if I won, from campaigning to governing. Carl Van Horn started delving more deeply into the policy issues we would be addressing, if I won, as soon as I took office.

Election night ended early. I swept Bergen, Essex, and Hudson Counties by a combined margin of nearly 200,000 votes. I carried every county in South Jersey, including rock-ribbed Republican Ocean County. Courter outpolled me in his base counties of Hunterdon, Morris, Sussex, and Warren, but by a combined total of only 16,000 votes. I carried the other seventeen counties by more than 300,000 votes and swept to statewide victory by a margin of 62 percent to 38 percent.

The transition period was a very interesting time. Most of the public and media attention during a transition tends to focus on personnel. Who's going to get what job in the new administration? Steve Perskie and others were deeply involved in the process of gathering and vetting resumes, and I certainly focused a good deal of my attention on the cabinet and staff appointments I would be making.

But I was at least equally attentive to the detailed list of agenda issues Carl Van Horn and his Saturday morning policy group had been developing. I spent a lot of time during the transition reviewing detailed policy documents that not only analyzed the problems we would face on entering office but also identified the range of solutions that could be put into effect in a relatively short period of time.

On education, for example, we knew the state Supreme Court would soon release a decision in the highly contentious *Abbott v. Burke* case. It had ruled in 1985 that the formula used to fund public education violated the state constitution's guarantee of a "thorough and efficient system of free public schools." Now, the Supreme Court was poised to declare whether the revised formula the legislature had adopted pursuant to that ruling passed constitutional muster.

Given the consensus among education experts that the court would reject the revised formula, we needed to prepare for the likelihood that the state would be ordered, as it had been in the past, to increase its level of financial support for the public schools. There were myriad ways in which this could be done, but if we were to choose the best way to accomplish this—which in my view meant the fairest way—we needed to get started well in advance of the anticipated court ruling.

I asked Carl Van Horn to join my administration as the director of policy. Several people who were involved in his Saturday policy discussion group came on board as well. One of the first to join the staff was Tom Corcoran, an educational consultant with a broad knowledge of public school financing issues. Another was Henry Coleman, who had headed up a comprehensive review of state fiscal policy as executive director of the State and Local Revenue and Expenditure Policy Commission. Tom and Henry would play key roles in the development of our school funding initiative.

Greg Lawler, who had so ably directed my congressional subcommittee staff, came up from Washington to serve as legislative counsel, a position from which he would play a leading role in the development of our auto insurance reform package. Brenda Bacon brought her expertise in health care to the position of chief of management and planning. Two of my former congressional staffers also took key posts in the governor's office: Jon Shure as communications director and David Applebaum as executive assistant.

I appointed Steve Perskie to be my chief of staff. I had initially thought that Doug Berman, having run my campaign, would be interested in that position, but I believe he was strongly influenced by Dick Leone to opt instead for the post of state treasurer. Leone had run Brendan Byrne's first gubernatorial campaign and used the office of the state treasurer to wield considerable power in the Byrne administration.

As the inauguration approached, I felt we were well positioned to hit the ground running. We would reform auto insurance. We would clean up the Jersey Shore, introducing the Clean Water Enforcement Act and appointing an environmental prosecutor to take aggressive action against polluters. We would take aim against assault weapons. We would meet whatever mandate the Supreme Court gave us to provide a "thorough and efficient" system of public education.

And then the outgoing Kean administration hit us with a one-two punch. A sharp downturn in the U.S. economy in the last two quarters of 1989 had turned what had been a $300 million surplus in the state budget for the current fiscal year into a $600 million deficit. Worse, the projected deficit for the fiscal year that would begin in July 1990 was $1.4 billion. On top of the revenue we would need to meet the anticipated Supreme Court mandate, we now had six months—in a national economy plunging into recession—to fill a budget gap of $2 billion.

As much as I was looking forward to taking the oath of office as governor, I wondered if my timing could possibly have been any worse. In my quest to win election to New Jersey's highest office, was the third time really a charm—or would it be the kiss of political death?

CHAPTER 8

Meeting the Challenges
in Trenton

*In public life, criticism of policy is unavoidable. But when the criticism
turns personal, it hurts.*

Our administration got out of the gate quickly, engaging in an unprecedented level of legislative and administrative activity within the first few
months that produced the following results: creation of the office of the
State Environmental Prosecutor, introduction and passage of the Clean
Water Enforcement Act, reform of automobile insurance, formulation of
a strict new ethics code for executive branch employees and appointees,
and the ban on assault weapons—all very popular measures.

Then, in preparation for the new fiscal year that would begin July 1,
1990, came the budget measures: dramatic cuts in the current year's budget; a freeze on new spending and hiring; a one-cent increase in the sales
tax and extension of the tax to some previously untaxed items, including
paper products; a more graduated income tax with a substantial increase,
from 3.5 to 7 percent, on income of more than $70,000 a year; and a
new Quality Education Act to meet the state Supreme Court's mandate,
requiring among other things that the cost of teacher pensions, paid by
the state, be included when calculating a local district's entitlement to
state aid.

The total package of $2.8 billion would also return a substantial por-
tion of income tax revenues to municipalities and school districts in the

form of property tax relief. But the immediate tax increases brought an outcry from the public, spurred by a new, populist radio station (101.5 FM) and the emergence of a grassroots anti-tax organization, Hands Across New Jersey. Changes in the school aid formula and pension calculation brought opposition from the powerful teachers' union, the New Jersey Education Association (NJEA). The assault weapons ban infuriated (and mobilized) the National Rifle Association. And the extension of the sales tax to paper products came to be dubbed the "toilet paper tax."

By September 1990, my approval rating, which stood at an already perilous 42 percent in March, after the budget crisis had made it apparent that higher taxes and cuts in popular programs and services lay ahead, dropped to an anemic 18 percent.

The greatest difficulty I faced in the ensuing months was trying to remain stoic, so I could engage and inform the public in a reasoned discussion of the need for the new taxes and the improved services (and more level playing field) they would provide. The mood in the state, however, was not conducive to reasoned discussion. People were angry, and their anger was fueled by 101.5, Hands Across New Jersey, the NJEA, the NRA, and Republicans in the legislature who saw opportunity in the unpopularity of my actions.

For the first time in my political life, I faced opposition that was based less on policy differences than on personal attacks. The harshness and vulgarity of the public discourse from the summer of 1990 through the fall of 1991 were like nothing I had ever experienced during my first two decades in public office. In the years since then, we have come to accept such uncivil behavior as a fact of political life; for its time, however, the discourse was uncommonly malevolent.

How we went from a solid victory in the November 1989 gubernatorial election to a much-maligned governorship in the span of eight short months can be explained in any number of ways. To some, it was the predictable result of trying to do too much too soon. To others, it was the unavoidable consequence of raising taxes in the midst of a recession. To still others, it was a perfect storm of tempestuous grassroots outrage and intense special-interest hostility, fueled by a media maelstrom that swept across New Jersey with unprecedented ferocity.

I think it was all of these and more. When I look back at all the things we did in those first few months in office, I recognize and appreciate the criticism directed at the way we did them. I am unmoved, however, by criticism directed at what we did. I felt at the time that cleaning up our beaches, enforcing our environmental laws, reforming our auto insurance system, raising ethical standards for executive branch employees and appointees, banning assault weapons, fixing the state's finances, reducing property taxes, and properly funding public education were the right things to do.

And I still feel that way today.

In 1988 and 1989 alone, the New Jersey shore—the lifeblood of our tourism industry and a major economic force in the state—experienced more than 800 beach closures. State and local health officials were forced to close down beaches that were contaminated by medical waste, fecal bacteria, and sewage sludge. Television accounts of hypodermic needles and empty prescription vials with New York addresses washing up on New Jersey beaches offered visual testimony to this assault on our shoreline.

Businesses from Sandy Hook to Cape May reported $1 billion in lost revenue in the summer of 1988. Hotels, motels, and bed-and-breakfasts, usually booked for the entire summer, posted vacancy signs. Restaurants closed. Despite near-record temperatures in late August and early September, visitors stayed away. What should have been a booming Labor Day weekend turned out to be a bust.

The summer of 1989 wasn't much better. Although there were fewer reports of medical waste washing ashore, beach closures caused by combined sewer overflows and other sources of contamination were still happening with alarming frequency. The economic fallout was still being felt from the previous year; families who used to spend summers at the shore up until 1988 opted to go elsewhere in 1989.

I campaigned as the environmental guy from Washington who was going to fix things. And immediately on taking office in January 1990, I initiated action aimed not only at cleaning up pollution at the shore but also at finding and punishing the polluters. Just two weeks before I was sworn in, a ruptured Exxon pipe had spilled 567,000 gallons of heating oil into the Arthur Kill, the waterway that separates New Jersey from Staten Island. I chose the setting of a nearby marina dock to announce that I was creating the new office of State Environmental Prosecutor and appointing Steve Madonna, a former deputy state attorney general, to the position.

"We in New Jersey consider anyone who destroys our ecosystem or who poisons our air and water has committed one of our greatest crimes," I said. "Let Steve's appointment send a message to all potential polluters, large or small, that they will pay for their actions."

The creation of the environmental prosecutor position was the most visible sign of our commitment to take aim against polluters and clean up the environment. But it was by no means the only one. I realized, from the years I spent in Congress researching and analyzing environmental issues, that what grabs the most headlines isn't always the biggest problem. Hypodermic needles on the beaches and oil spills in the Arthur Kill may have been on the six o'clock news and the front pages of newspapers, but what really demanded attention was the flow of inadequately treated sewage that was fouling our waterways and beaches.

New Jersey desperately needed a dramatic upgrade to our sewer treatment plants, many of which were discharging raw sewage into pipelines that led directly into the ocean. This is not the kind of issue that fascinates the press and the public. It appeals instead to policy wonks like me, who are always looking for the most effective and efficient ways that government can do what it's supposed to do: solve people's problems. Sometimes, the best solutions don't make headlines; they just make sense.

On Asbury Park's boardwalk in May 1990, Governor Florio signs the Clean Water Enforcement Act following its passage by a unanimous vote of both houses of the legislature.

Our interest in reducing the environmental damage done by the discharge of raw sewage happened to coincide with the interests of the Alliance for Action, a coalition of New Jersey business, labor, professional, academic, and governmental representatives promoting economic development through capital construction and infrastructure investment. With the strong support of the Alliance and its founding president, Ellis Vieser, we took decisive action, issuing $1.5 billion in bonds to upgrade sewage treatment plants across the state.

A corollary step was the introduction and passage of the Clean Water Enforcement Act, which set strict discharge limits on sewage treatment plants and levied automatic fines against plants that exceeded their permitted limits. This important legislation won unanimous approval in both houses of the legislature, and I was pleased to sign it into law.

My grandchildren were young when all this was happening. They don't remember the hypodermic needles on the beaches. They aren't especially interested in government bond issues or sewage treatment plants. But when I took them to the shore a few years later and saw brown pelicans perched on the pier poles at fishing docks, or when we went out on a boat to look at humpback whales and dolphins in the ocean, they knew it was because the water was cleaner than it used to be—and they appreciated that I had something to do with that.

As far as they're concerned, Pop Pop's major claim to fame is bringing the dolphins back.

If taking action to clean up the beaches and otherwise protect human health and the environment was among the highest priorities of the voters who elected me governor, doing something about the outrageous cost of auto insurance wasn't far behind.

In the mid-1980s, the Kean administration and the legislature created something called the Joint Underwriters Association (JUA), a state-run pool that provided auto insurance coverage to "high-risk" drivers—which basically meant anyone the insurance companies weren't willing to cover voluntarily. By the time I took office in 1990, more than half the state's drivers were covered by the JUA, including many with clean driving records. For no other reason than to boost their profits, auto insurance companies were unwilling to write policies for an estimated 2.4 million of New Jersey's 4.3 million licensed drivers.

To make matters worse, the JUA had racked up a deficit of more than $3 billion. Every insured New Jersey car owner was paying an annual surcharge of $225 just to support the program, and the fee was scheduled to go up another $80 in a few months.

Throughout my campaign, I promised audiences, "The JUA is DOA." During the transition, I announced that I would present a plan shortly after taking office to restore fairness to the auto insurance system and reduce rates. In my inaugural address, I vowed, "We will bring back fairness to a system that has abused the drivers of New Jersey for too long."

I had learned quite a lot about insurance while serving in Congress. The subcommittee I chaired held a number of hearings, bringing people down from New Jersey to talk about auto insurance, so I felt I had a pretty good understanding of what needed to be done. For starters, we needed to give the state Department of Insurance both the tools and the front-office backing it needed to stand up to the insurance industry.

One thing I have always thought about insurance—not just during our efforts to reform auto insurance in New Jersey in the 1990s, but right up through the congressional battles over health insurance a quarter-century later—is that the insurance industry has always benefited from one indisputable fact: very few people outside the industry really understand it. In New Jersey, the Department of Insurance was typically over-matched by insurance company lawyers, actuaries, accountants, and other self-described experts. I came into office determined to fill key positions in my administration with people who would stand up to the industry.

My insurance commissioner, Sam Fortunato, understood the industry completely; he was a longtime executive at Metropolitan Life Insurance Co. Sam's deputy commissioner, Jasper Jackson, had considerable experience and expertise in auto insurance regulation. My public advocate, Fred Caraballo, was an experienced litigator. My legislative counsel, Greg Lawler, who had served as staff counsel to my congressional subcommittee, devoted his immediate attention almost exclusively to the auto insurance issue.

Together, they formed a team that had real authority—and knew what to do with it. Working with key legislators, they put together a bill with the appropriate acronym FAIR: the Fair Automobile Insurance Reform Act of 1990. It reformed the whole system. It got rid of the JUA, eliminated the surcharge, and allowed medical claims to be shifted from auto policies to health coverage. It also included a number of less radical provisions, including auto theft and antifraud initiatives, as well as mandatory fee schedules for towing and storage costs.

Flanked by legislative leaders, Governor Florio signs the Fair Automobile Insurance Reform Act into law on March 12, 1990.

I distinctly remember sitting in meetings with insurance industry executives on one side of the table and Sam Fortunato on the other. The executives were predicting dire consequences, ranging from market chaos to bankruptcy, if the FAIR bill became law. They told us the law would be declared unconstitutional. They threatened to stop writing policies in New Jersey. With every argument they raised, Sam calmly and coolly challenged their facts, disputed their reasoning, and put them in their place in a very authoritative way.

After the bill was passed and I signed it into law, Allstate Insurance Company indeed sued us. "They call themselves the 'good hands' people," I noted the next day. "The question is: which part of our anatomy do they have their good hands around?"

I had now created two groups of enemies. The first was a fairly small number of public utilities, businesses, and industries that were affected—in their view adversely—by the Clean Water Enforcement Act. The stricter discharge limits and stiffer fines for exceeding these limits meant they either had to make substantial capital improvements to their factories and treatment plants or pay a steep price for their failure to do so.

The second group was the insurance industry. Many of the companies doing business in New Jersey did a lot of grumbling after the FAIR Act was signed into law. Their applications for rate increases were subjected to more rigorous scrutiny and more frequent adjustments than their previous submissions to the Department of Insurance. A few of the smaller insurance companies simply stopped writing policies and left New Jersey.

I was very comfortable in the belief that, while I had earned the wrath of some special interests, I had successfully advanced the public interest. I realized that stricter discharge limits and stiffer fines would increase the costs to some utilities and companies, which they would pass on in whole or in part to their customers. In other words, both the private and corporate citizens of New Jersey would pay marginally higher utility and sewer bills. But in return they would get unpolluted waterways, cleaner beaches, and a healthier environment.

Auto insurance rates saw a steady decline after the FAIR Act took effect. Allstate lost its lawsuit against the state. The Department of Insurance then denied the company's request for a 28 percent rate increase. Allstate promptly declared that it would stop writing auto policies in New Jersey.

Under state law, any insurance company that stops writing policies for one type of coverage is not permitted to write policies for any other type of coverage, with the single exception of life insurance. If Allstate was going to stop covering drivers in New Jersey, it was also going to have to give up writing policies for homeowners, renters, landlords, businesses, and other customers. Furthermore, any insurance company that left New Jersey was obliged by law to find replacement coverage for the policyholders it was abandoning.

I wasn't about to be bullied. "We could have kept Allstate in New Jersey by agreeing to the 28 percent rate increase they wanted to charge our drivers," I said. "That wouldn't be fair, and we won't be blackmailed into agreeing." Later, I added, "When I was growing up in Brooklyn, there was always one guy who would say that if you didn't play by his rules he would take his bat and ball and go home. If that's what an insurance company wants to do, we won't back down from our commitment to fairness for drivers and reasonable rates."

Allstate did not stop writing policies in New Jersey. After threatening for two years to leave, the company agreed to drop its legal challenges against the FAIR Act and to pay $75 million toward its share of the debt that had been run up by the JUA. In return, Allstate received an average 6.5 percent rate increase—less than one-quarter of what it had requested a year earlier.

Soon, a number of other companies that had stopped selling policies in New Jersey long before I became governor, including GEICO, Kemper, and Nationwide, returned to the auto insurance market. And auto insurance rates continued to drop.

I had acquired another, smaller group of enemies when I issued Executive Order No. 1, subjecting more than one thousand executive branch employees—and, for the first time, appointees to independent state authorities, boards, and commissions—to a detailed set of financial disclosure regulations. Making good on a campaign promise, I ordered officials, their spouses, and their dependent children to report all sources of income; all assets valued at more than $1,000; any interest in a state contract, real estate holding, or business subject to state regulation; and the names of companies in which they held stock, outstanding loans, and other liabilities. Anyone refusing to comply with these regulations, I said, would "have the choice of resigning or being fired."

A number of highly qualified and competent people chose to withdraw their applications for executive branch positions or to step down from appointed positions they already held, rather than comply with this executive order. Some of them didn't state a reason, but I suspect it was because they had conflicts of interest. Others, for whom I had greater sympathy, told me they feared that if they disclosed how much they were worth, they would put themselves and their families in danger.

A lot of politicians spend a lot of time talking about "win-win" situations. It has been my experience, however, that most decisions on major public policy issues involve winners and losers. More often than not, the best solution to a public policy problem maximizes the benefits for the winners while minimizing the costs for the losers.

When those on the losing side are corporations, they are usually better able to absorb the loss than citizens. In some cases, such as the utilities and industries affected by the Clean Water Enforcement Act, they can pass the added cost of compliance on to customers. In other cases, as in passage of the FAIR Act, insurance companies may have to live with less profit, reduced executive compensation, or smaller dividends for stockholders. In both these cases, the public benefited—from a cleaner environment and more affordable auto insurance rates.

And in the case of the executive order applying a more stringent code of ethics to executive branch employees and appointees, the price paid by those who either removed their resumes from consideration or chose to give up the positions they already held has to be weighed against the value to the public of having a government free from conflicts of interest.

In my view, what the winners won in all these instances was much greater than what the losers lost.

Now it was time to tackle the budget—or, to be more precise, the budgets. New Jersey's state budget operates on a fiscal year running from July 1 to June 30. When I took office, we were already halfway through the current fiscal year, and we had less than six months to prepare a budget for the upcoming one.

From day one, I knew we were going to have to make deep cuts in the current budget, and it was pretty clear that these cuts alone wouldn't be sufficient to bring the budget into balance by the end of the fiscal year on

June 30. I also knew that the budget for the upcoming fiscal year would be even more problematic.

Unlike the federal government, the New Jersey state government is constitutionally prohibited from operating at a deficit. By law, the state's revenues for the fiscal year must equal or exceed its expenditures. (This is actually the law in every state except Vermont; for this reason, people should never be impressed by governors who boast that they balanced their state's budget.)

Shortly before leaving office, Governor Kean approved a 5 percent increase in the pensions of retired police officers and firefighters, which had the effect of increasing the size of the deficit we were about to inherit. The following week, with the severity of the looming budget crisis now fully evident, I urged the governor to impose a freeze on spending and hiring. Later, our team encouraged the outgoing administration to help balance the current budget by asking the lame-duck legislature for a one-cent increase in the sales tax. Governor Kean agreed to the spending and hiring freeze, but rejected the sales tax hike.

When my administration took office, we filled essential positions, but with the exception of the environmental prosecutor, we didn't create new ones. We honored the contractual obligations the state had made to its employees, but we put a temporary hold on salary increases. We cut back on the number and use of state vehicles. We limited out-of-state travel. We deferred all but the most essential maintenance.

All this scrimping and saving barely put a dent in the $600 million shortfall in the current $12.1 billion budget, not to mention the projected $1.2 billion shortfall in the coming year's budget. We needed to make more severe spending cuts, and we needed to raise more revenue.

We also had to consider the potential impact of the imminent New Jersey Supreme Court decision on the constitutionality of the state's system of financing public education. As mentioned, it had ruled, years earlier, in the case of *Robinson v. Cahill*, that the state had a constitutional obligation to correct the fiscal disparities that existed between poor, mostly urban school districts and wealthier, mostly suburban districts. The revised funding formula adopted by the legislature pursuant to this ruling spawned another case, *Abbott v. Burke*, which the court would soon decide.

The Kean administration had stridently defended the revised funding formula in court filings and hearings, but the evidence was so plainly on the side of the plaintiffs (twenty public schoolchildren in Camden, East Orange, Irvington, and Jersey City) that we were certain the high court would order the state to provide additional aid to underfunded school districts. Thus, in addition to our mounting budget woes, we had little doubt we would soon confront another daunting fiscal challenge.

We had three fiscal issues to deal with. We had to balance the budget in the six months remaining in the current fiscal year. We had to present a balanced budget for the following fiscal year. And we knew we would soon have to come up with a new funding formula for the public schools. The big question before us was whether we should deal with each of these issues separately and distinctly or come up with a plan to combine all of them into a single legislative initiative.

Opinions varied sharply over which strategy to employ. Within the administration, however, there was consensus to go with the latter approach: to present the legislature with a package that balanced both budgets with a combination of spending cuts and tax increases and that put forward a new public school financing scheme aimed at equalizing spending between poor and wealthy districts. State Treasurer Doug Berman was a leading proponent of this strategy. His reasoning, with which I agreed, was that if difficult decisions had to be made, we should make them right away. Whatever wounds we would cause would then have time to heal.

Legislative leaders had deeply opposing views of the wisdom of this strategy. Assembly Speaker Joe Doria, who had so enthusiastically embraced the assault weapons ban, was just as supportive of our preference for a comprehensive budget/school aid initiative. Senate President John Lynch, who had warned me about the political repercussions of the assault weapons ban, took the opposite view. The experience of recent governors supported his cautious position.

Governor Brendan Byrne failed in his efforts to convince the legislature to revise the public school financing system and to enact the state's first income tax to pay for it, until the state Supreme Court took the unprecedented step in 1976 of ordering the public schools closed unless the legislature acted. Governor Kean refused to raise taxes to balance the state budget in 1982 until the legislature presented him with a spending plan that included hikes in income, sales, and corporate taxes.

The Lynch strategy was to heed the lessons of these experiences and move slowly—patch together a short-term mix of budget cuts and tax hikes to get through the current fiscal year and then put the onus on the legislature, as Governor Kean had done, to present the administration with a longer-term fiscal plan. Don't rush to adopt a new school funding formula, but wait until the state Supreme Court applied pressure, as it did during the Byrne administration, to put forward a fiscal remedy.

Just as he had accurately anticipated the political fallout from the assault weapons ban, John Lynch had a keen sense of the likely public reaction to our budget and school aid strategy. I appreciated his advice, but I rejected it for two reasons. First, I felt I couldn't in good conscience let kids in underfunded school districts go through another year receiving a substandard education. Second, I had spent two decades in public life preparing for this moment, crisscrossing the state, gathering support, and accumulating political capital. I believe there's no reason to accumulate political capital unless you intend to use it.

The agenda we put together combined budget cuts that were painful to many constituencies with tax increases that were painful to many constituents. It also included a new school-aid formula that increased state support to all public school districts, with the lion's share going to those districts that were least able to raise funds locally.

The budget cuts hit hard and pretty much across the board, affecting everything from agricultural assistance to mass transit subsidies, from higher education aid to senior citizen programs to funding for the arts. As soon as we unveiled our budget proposal, the range of demonstrators who descended on the State House included farmers, commuters, college students, health care workers, arts patrons, and others representing individuals and groups facing sharp reductions in state financial support.

One of the tax increases we proposed was likewise across the board: the one-cent increase in the sales tax. In and of itself, this increase would probably have aroused a lot of opposition, coming as it did in the midst of a national recession. But what really angered taxpayers was the extension of the sales tax to items that had previously been exempt. New Jersey had traditionally applied the sales tax only to items that were not considered necessities, exempting most food items, clothing, and other essential products. We felt we needed to broaden the base.

Our first instinct was to take a slightly different approach: to raise the additional revenue primarily by hiking excise taxes on cigarettes and alcohol, imposing a new excise tax on petroleum products refined and distributed in the state, and extending the sales tax to telecommunications, janitorial, and cable television services. However, the revenue raised from all these sources would still not be enough to balance the budget. And we had to shelve the cable TV tax when it met with resistance in the legislature—which we were later to learn was organized by a prominent lawmaker who, as an attorney in private practice, happened to represent the cable industry.

At that point, we felt we had no choice but to expand the list of previously exempted items subject to the sales tax. These items included goods like soap, detergents, and paper products—but the singular product that came to represent the resultant public outrage was toilet paper. The visual aids favored by the next group of demonstrators who gathered in Trenton were rolls after rolls of toilet paper, which they hurled with great fanfare onto the steps of the State House. It was a very effective use of symbolism to drive home a political message.

Altogether, the sales and excise tax increases would raise about $1.5 billion. We still needed an additional $1.3 billion to balance the 1991 budget and to meet the anticipated Supreme Court order to increase the state's share of funding for the public schools. To raise this revenue, we proposed another tax increase. But this one, unlike the sales tax hike, was *not* across the board. It was an increase, from 3.5 to 7 percent, in the state income tax rate applicable to taxpayers earning more than $70,000 a year. This may not seem like a huge amount of money today, but in 1990, only about 17 percent of New Jersey taxpayers met this threshold. The other 83 percent would see no change in their income tax rate.

Because the state constitution mandates that revenue raised through the income tax is used only to provide relief from property taxes, we proposed that the proceeds from the higher income taxes to be paid by the top 17 percent of wage earners be used to lower property taxes for all homeowners. We would accomplish this by meeting the Supreme Court mandate to increase the state's share of the cost of providing what the state constitution defined as a "thorough and efficient system of free public schools." The result would be a corresponding decrease in the amount local school districts would need to raise through the only means available to them: the property tax.

Accompanying the budget proposals we presented to the legislature was the new Quality Education Act, a complex piece of legislation aimed at substantially increasing state aid to school districts that were limited in their ability to fund public education locally. Most but not all of these districts were in the state's depressed urban centers, and they lagged far behind wealthier suburban districts in the resources they were able to devote to the public schools.

The funding formula we put forward was designed to close the gap between those poorer districts and their wealthier counterparts, but in a way that the educational improvement we wanted to advance in

Legislative leaders applaud as Governor Florio signs the Quality Education Act, setting forth a new school-aid formula that increases state support to all public school districts in order to comply with a landmark state Supreme Court ruling.

low-achieving districts didn't come at the expense of high-achieving districts. This is always the delicate balance in education funding: the last thing you want to do as you lift the quality of education for students in the poorest schools is condemn to mediocrity the performance of students in the best schools.

One of the keys to achieving this balance was to include the cost of teachers' pensions in the calculation of state aid to local districts. The state, not the school district, paid into these pensions, so there was little incentive for the local district to control this cost. Because the state's pension contribution was a percentage of each teacher's salary, any salary increase approved by the district automatically increased the pension cost to the state.

We proposed that the state continue to bear this cost, but factor it into the formula for distributing aid to local school districts. Every New Jersey school district receives state aid based on a number of financial and educational factors, and we felt that the cost of teachers' pensions should be one of them. A wealthy school district that doled out large salary increases to its teachers would have the increased pension cost to the state added to its existing allocation of state aid. This, in turn, would have the effect of reducing aid for other purposes, which would serve as an incentive for local districts to rein in salaries.

Needless to say, this change in the funding formula enraged teachers. I thus acquired another formidable enemy: the New Jersey Education Association.

I have always had a pretty thick skin, both literally and figuratively. As a boxer, I was pretty good at taking a punch—until I got my jaw broken. As an assemblyman and a congressman, I was pretty good at taking criticism. If a competitor, a colleague, or a constituent took me to task—on the campaign trail, in a committee hearing, or at a town hall meeting—over a policy position I had taken or a vote I had cast, I would defend my actions as best I could. If my defense was not convincing, I would observe, respectfully, that we could agree to disagree.

As governor, however, I quickly came under fire that was far more intense than anything I had ever experienced in the boxing ring or the political arena. Some of it was to be expected; individuals and groups affected by our deep budget cuts had good reason to be angry, and some of the enemies we had acquired—the polluters, the insurance industry, the NRA, and the NJEA, to name a few—weren't about to surrender to our policy initiatives without a fight.

What I did not anticipate, however, was the outpouring of anger by the general public about both the tax increases and the Quality Education Act. In years past, unpopular actions by a governor of New Jersey might generate a flurry of angry letters to the editor or a critical editorial or two in the state's daily and weekly newspapers. They might even provoke the occasional rally outside the State House.

As Benjamin Franklin once observed, "New Jersey is like a barrel tapped at both ends." (Others have called the state "a valley of humility between two mountains of conceit.") In modern times, this characteristic has manifested itself in an almost total lack of coverage of New Jersey issues by the New York and Philadelphia media, the absence in New Jersey of a statewide commercial television station, and a newspaper landscape dominated by dailies and weeklies focused on local rather than state coverage. This has usually meant that whatever happened in Trenton rarely generated much interest beyond Mercer County.

But this was all about to change. On March 1, 1990, a struggling Trenton-based FM radio station with a powerful signal, WKXW, rebranded itself as "New Jersey 101.5." Its announcers launched an advertising campaign proclaiming the station's new image: "Not New York. Not Philadelphia. Proud to be New Jersey." It featured regular New Jersey traffic reports and New Jersey weather forecasts. Its morning and afternoon programming switched from oldies music to a talk and news format. Much of the news focused on what was happening at the State House. And virtually all the talk focused on what a horrible governor I was.

At the same time, Trenton's tabloid newspaper, *The Trentonian*, known mostly for its coverage of local sports, took aim in its news and editorial pages at my administration's "liberal tax and spend" policies. Every morning featured a new front-page salvo against actions my administration was taking, both real and imagined, for the evident purpose of turning Trenton into Moscow on the Delaware.

Together, 101.5 and *The Trentonian* carried the anti-tax, anti-Florio message day in, day out. I was annoyed by the coverage, much of which I thought was unfair, but I couldn't allow myself to be overly bothered by one particular radio station or one particular newspaper that exposed its listeners and readers to an unflattering portrayal of my administration and me.

What this media onslaught spawned, however, was a movement that extended far beyond the listenership of 101.5 and the readership of *The*

Trentonian. A postal worker from Jackson Township named John Budzash called into 101.5 one afternoon, launched into an anti-tax tirade, and urged like-minded New Jersey residents and taxpayers to join him in protest. In short order, Hands Across New Jersey, a grassroots anti-tax organization, was up and running.

In many ways, 101.5 was a forerunner of antigovernment talk radio, and Hands Across New Jersey was a forerunner of the Tea Party, which would arise two decades later. Hands Across America grew out of the public distrust of government, and it spread, with both the overt and covert support of interests that might benefit from this distrust, into a movement. Both the opposition Republican Party and the NRA had a vested interest in fueling the anti-Florio fire.

Soon, John Budzash and other Hands Across New Jersey principals became daily guests on 101.5. After they organized a massive State House rally featuring, among other things, several Florio dummies hanging in effigy, I invited the organization to bring a representative group to my office to discuss their grievances. In addition to Budzash the postal worker, a man who worked as a mechanic and a woman who was a real estate broker came to meet with me.

I told them I wanted to hear their arguments and understand their concerns. I expected to get an earful about the tax on toilet paper, but instead they told me that, by increasing the income tax I was essentially putting a limit on how much money they could make. I was incredulous. "How many people here make more than $70,000?" I asked. They all laughed. "None of us," they said. "Well, then," I explained, "the income tax increase doesn't apply to you at all."

I continued, "How many of you got money back from your insurance company after we repealed the JUA?" They all said they got back about $400. "Then why are you here?" I asked. "You are exactly the people we're doing these things for." And that is when I learned what we were up against.

"I'm not a communist," one of the visitors explained. "I want to be a millionaire someday. And I don't want to pay more income tax when I am.

That's why I'm against what you're doing." I thought to myself: How do you deal with this? Here's a person who is benefiting directly from our policies, and he's out there leading the charge against these policies. My faith in the doctrine that engaging and informing the public would lead to reasoned discourse and consensus-driven public policy was truly being put to the test.

My town hall meetings were no less adversarial. I remember facing a fairly hostile crowd in Washington Township, a Gloucester County community that knew me well and generally supported me during my years in Congress. They wanted to know why I was doing what I was doing in Trenton. I patiently explained why I felt the budget cuts and tax increases were necessary, and I could sense the crowd beginning to come around. But one member of the audience was unmoved. "I don't know," he said. "Out of all these things you're telling us, I don't even know if they make any sense. You're the worst governor since Pontius Pilate."

I told him I appreciated the biblical reference. What else could I say?

⋘

If the public reacted with anger to the pocketbook issues of budget cuts and tax increases, there was a distinctly uglier undercurrent in the opposition to the Quality Education Act. At virtually every town hall meeting where public school financing was the main subject, I witnessed what I can only call out-and-out racism. Sometimes it was latent, other times it was blatant—but it was almost always there.

I was often asked by people in affluent suburban towns why I was so intent on giving money to *them*—meaning schoolchildren in poor urban areas. Depending on the level of hostility I sensed in the audience, I would sometimes appeal to their humanity, their sense of fairness, their commitment to the constitutional guarantee of "equal protection under the law." In other cases I would explain that what I thought was in the public interest was also in their self-interest.

"Whatever reason you have for opposing this," I would tell them, "all of you look very affluent, very comfortable. You look like you've made a success out of your lives. You ask me why I want to give money to *them*. Well, your workforce in the future, if you want to continue your affluence, is going to be *them*. *Them* is going to be working for you in your company. In fact, you want *them* to get a decent education that will enable *them* to become productive people."

Most of the time, my argument that the state had a moral obligation to improve the educational opportunities afforded to children in low-achieving school districts struck a responsive chord. The argument that it was in their enlightened self-interest to provide financial support to students in poor districts also resonated with many in the audience.

But in too many other instances, the response was less charitable. "They can't learn," someone would yell at me when I explained that poor kids in the cities were just as entitled to a quality education as rich kids in the suburbs. "They'll always be animals," another person would cry out. I think many people who found my arguments unconvincing may have been offended by these bigoted outbursts by their neighbors, but that wasn't enough to make them converts to the cause of closing the education gap between rich and poor.

In my view, this was a classic example of the resistance most people have to change. I don't think bigotry was the main cause of opposition to the Quality Education Act. I think it was the threat of having a system people knew replaced by a system they didn't know. People become accustomed to the status quo. It may not be perfect, it may not even be fair, but it's what they know. It's predictable. Change is unpredictable. Change is threatening. Any legislator can tell you an immutable fact of political life: it is almost always easier to defend the status quo than to advocate change.

Nevertheless, we tried. At town hall meetings, in radio and TV interviews, in speeches and op-ed pieces, and in meetings with editorial boards up and down the state, I did my best to explain both what we were doing and why we were doing it. For the most part, the media were supportive. The newspapers, focused as they were on local and regional coverage, tended in their editorials to find fault with budget cuts that hurt particular programs, services, or school districts in their circulation area, but otherwise generally approved of our policies.

Interestingly, the company that owned 101.5, the radio station that was subjecting me to a daily onslaught of condemnation, also owned the *Asbury Park Press,* the state's third-largest daily newspaper. The *Press's* State House reporters provided generally fair and accurate coverage of my administration, and its editorial page was a fairly reliable supporter of my policies. That made it pretty clear that programming at the radio station was being driven not by ideology but by ratings—and Florio-bashing was obviously good for ratings.

While the backlash against the tax increases continued, we tried to mitigate, as best we could, some of the damage done by the budget cuts. For example, I took no pleasure in cutting funding for the arts. One casualty of these cuts was Waterloo Village, a restored canal house in Sussex County that had been transformed into a popular open-air museum and performing arts center by a dedicated, indefatigable patron, Percy Leach. Percy came to see me one day and said he had an idea for raising revenue. "What's the idea?" I asked. "Boxing," he said.

"You have a background in boxing," he continued. "I've done some research on boxing and found that in the 1880s and 1890s, around the time of the history we're re-creating at Waterloo Village, people in high society would conduct very fancy boxing matches. I want to do that at Waterloo Village." So he did. He put up a boxing ring and got a contract with ESPN. Then he invited the "high society" of New Jersey to dress up in tuxedos and gowns and, for a substantial charitable contribution that would offset the loss of state funding, enjoy an evening of boxing.

I was pleased to offer my support and to attend one of the matches—comfortably seated outside the ring.

One of the more satisfying aspects of governing is taking pride and plea-sure in successful initiatives and programs that do not necessarily cap-ture a lot of public attention, but do improve the lives of many of the people you are sworn to serve. Even as controversy swirled around assault weapons, the budget, school aid, and other headline-grabbing issues, several programs we initiated were providing meaningful assis-tance to students, workers, commuters, and many others without cap-turing widespread public attention or generating much in the way of news coverage.

One example is a program called the New Jersey College Loan Assis-tance for State Students, or NJ CLASS. Established in 1990, this program provides assistance for students who fall between the gaps; they don't qualify for the federally subsidized Pell Grant program for low-income students but can't afford to take on debt at the higher interest rates charged by private loan programs.

NJ CLASS offers low-interest loans to these students, allowing them to receive a higher education without taking on an unsustainable level of debt. It provides a choice of repayment options and doesn't charge a pen-alty for prepayment. It can be used by New Jersey residents attending in-state or out-of-state schools and by out-of-state residents attending New Jersey schools.

No taxpayer funds are used to support this program. It is a national model, and it continues to function today. Over the years I have met scores of young people—and, nowadays, not-so-young people—who thank me for the NJ CLASS program and tell me that, without it, they would not have been able to complete their college education.

Another example—also a national model that remains largely in place today—is the Workforce Development Partnership Program. Enacted with bipartisan support, this program provides training for dislocated

The governor of New Jersey meets the future governor of California, as Arnold Schwarzenegger, chairman of President George H. W. Bush's Council on Physical Fitness and Sports, visits the Garden State.

workers while they are collecting unemployment insurance. Without this training, many workers would likely remain unemployed for a much longer period of time than they do.

The program, run by the New Jersey Department of Labor, also provides training for employed workers to increase their skills so that they will be able to retain their jobs—and the companies they work for will enjoy greater productivity.

We also undertook a significant number of large infrastructure projects, designed not only to improve the movement of people and goods around our congested state but also to stimulate the state's economy during a period of recession. Although one of our earliest initiatives, the Clean Water Enforcement Act, got a lot of press coverage because of the public outcry over hypodermic needles washing up on our beaches, its importance as an infrastructure project went largely unreported, despite the fact that it financed multimillion-dollar improvements to aging sewage treatment plants.

Transportation was a major focus of our infrastructure efforts. Thousands of construction workers who would otherwise have been jobless were put to work connecting the Newark Airport Monorail with the Northeast Corridor rail line, putting new rail cars in service for NJ Transit, widening the New Jersey Turnpike, and numerous other projects.

All of these projects resulted in necessary—and in some cases long overdue—improvements to our transportation network. All were creatively financed with toll revenues from the roads and bridges in the region and in coordination with the Port Authority of New York and New Jersey. They are illustrative of how state and bi-state authorities can and should be used for their intended purposes.

⁓

The greatest frustration I felt during the many months of criticism of and protests against our budget and school-aid initiatives was the response I would get to the one question I asked over and over again: What's the alternative?

Much of the time, the response was silence. Sometimes someone would say, "Don't ask us. You're the governor. That's your job." And I would answer, "That's right. It's my job—and I'm doing it."

Then there was the usual litany of suggestions. Do an audit of state government. Cut waste, inefficiency, fraud, and abuse. Reduce the state workforce. Get rid of all those state cars. Stop throwing money down the rat hole of inner-city schools.

To each of these I offered a response. My Government Management Review Commission did an audit of state government. It found $70 million in savings in the Fiscal Year 1992 budget and identified another $140 million in waste and inefficiency that could be cut from the following year's budget. It also targeted ninety-seven boards and commissions for elimination and another fifty for consolidation.

My first executive order outlawed all conflicts of interest, and there hadn't been even a hint of corruption in my administration. We reduced the state payroll for the first time in years and cut back on the use of state cars, long-distance phone bills, and expense accounts. If you want to reduce school aid to the cities, take it up with the state Supreme Court or start a movement to amend the state constitution. My job is to obey the law and uphold the constitution.

Nobody likes to pay taxes. I understand that. I also understand that any politician who raises taxes does so at his or her political peril. President George H. W. Bush enjoyed a 90 percent approval rating after he launched Operation Desert Storm in January 1991. Less than two years later, he lost his bid for re-election when his most widely quoted campaign pledge—"Read my lips. No new taxes."—turned out to be an empty promise.

I was told repeatedly by legislators, lobbyists, political operatives, and others that the smart way to deal with the budget crisis was not to raise taxes but to cut spending to the bone. This would provoke such an outcry that legislators would have no choice but to increase revenues, allowing me to shift the responsibility to them for raising taxes. To me, this tactic would be worse than an abdication of gubernatorial leadership; it would reduce the serious business of governing to a silly blame game.

Once we had made the decision to seek legislative approval for both the sales tax increase and the more graduated income tax, I faced a difficult choice. The Fiscal Year 1991 budget—which had to be proposed, presented to the legislature, and adopted, all in less than six months—included severe cuts to nearly every department of state government. I knew that many of these cuts would be difficult for the departments' commissioners to defend. I also realized that several of the commissioners had been on the job for only a few weeks, and it wouldn't be fair to ask them to present and defend their budget requests before the legislature's Joint Appropriations Committee.

State Treasurer Doug Berman, who understood the details of the budget better than anyone in the administration, suggested that he should represent all of the departments in the legislative hearings. This would ensure that the administration would speak with one voice and that no cabinet officer would be caught flat-footed by a question he or she couldn't answer. This made sense to me, and I approved this approach.

In retrospect, I believe this was a mistake—not because Doug didn't do a commendable job representing the administration and our budget priorities, but because it sent the unintended message that I didn't trust my own cabinet. I don't think it harmed my personal relationship with my cabinet members, but it did prevent them from establishing their own credibility and developing their own personal relationships with legislators. I should have realized, from my own experience in Congress, that personal connections forged between representatives of the legislative and executive branches are often the key to formulating sound public policy.

This episode also reinforced the belief that there were only a handful of people empowered to make decisions in my administration—which, I have since found, is a common complaint heard in the early days of virtually every administration at every level of government. To a certain extent, I believe it was probably true of mine. Though I don't consider myself a control freak, I felt that on the most pressing issues we faced— environmental legislation, auto insurance reform, the assault weapons ban, the budget, and education funding—I needed to be fully informed and involved in structuring the policy details. And these issues pretty much consumed my first year in office.

As we moved into our second year, I acknowledged in my State of the State address that "1990, to say the least, wasn't a year for the fainthearted." But I had a very optimistic outlook for 1991. In the budget message I presented to the legislature at the end of January, I proposed the largest property tax relief program in the state's history and the largest reduction in government spending in forty years.

It was the investments we had made in 1990, in the form of increased sales and income tax revenues, that allowed us to provide returns on these investments in 1991. Throughout the spring, municipalities and school districts were reporting, for the first time in anyone's memory, real reductions in local property tax bills. By the end of the year, property taxes had gone down or been stabilized in 85 percent of the state's municipalities.

This was due, in part, to changes in the Quality Education Act pushed by legislators representing rural and suburban districts. They offered amendments to shift $360 million in school aid to property tax relief. In addition, in a bid to regain support from the powerful NJEA, they voted to delay for two years the inclusion of the cost of teachers' pensions in the calculation of state aid to school districts. I was not enamored of these changes (and, as it turned out, neither were the courts), but I recognized the pressure felt by legislators who would be up for re-election in November, and I signed the changes into law.

It didn't matter. The passage of time didn't matter. Lower property taxes didn't matter. Slashing state spending didn't matter. Mollifying the teachers' union didn't matter. None of these could make up for eighteen months of voter fury. The midterm election of 1991 was, to put it plainly, a disaster.

There was never much doubt in anyone's mind that 1991 was going to be a Republican year in New Jersey. The first indication that Democrats were in trouble came in the 1990 U.S. Senate election, when a little-known Republican challenger, Christine Todd Whitman, came within 60,000 votes of unseating the incumbent, Bill Bradley. Most observers credited Whitman's unexpectedly strong showing to the voters' discontent with Democrats in general and with me in particular.

Historically, the party that controls the seat of executive power loses legislative seats in the midterm election. It happens to presidents, and it happens to governors—and the larger the size of their presidential or gubernatorial victory, the greater the number of legislative seats their party loses two years later.

In the 1978 congressional election midway through President Carter's presidency, the Democrats lost fifteen seats in the House of Representatives. In the 1982 congressional election midway through President Reagan's first term, Republicans lost twenty-seven House seats. At the state level, in the 1975 election midway through Brendan Byrne's first term, Democrats lost seventeen seats in the assembly. In the 1987 election, midway through Tom Kean's second term, Republicans lost eight seats in the assembly.

The size of my victory in the 1989 election had carried a number of Democratic legislators into office on my coattails, turning the assembly from having a two-seat Republican majority (41–39) to an eight-seat Democratic majority (44–36). If history were to repeat itself, several of the lawmakers elected with me in 1989 would be vulnerable in 1991 even under the best of circumstances.

And the circumstances in 1991 were anything but the best for Democrats. The national recession continued to hit hard at New Jersey's economy, heightening the already angry public response to the sales and income tax increases. President George H. W. Bush's approval rating had slipped from the stratospheric 90 percent he enjoyed early in the year, but it was still above 60 percent at the time of the November election.

Democrats were also victimized by the calendar. Members of the New Jersey General Assembly are elected to two-year terms, but for the state senate there is a different system. A senate term is usually for four years. But in the election immediately preceding the decennial census (in this case the 1989 election) members of both houses are elected to two-year terms.

After the census, the boundaries of legislative districts are redrawn to reflect population shifts that have taken place over the past decade. After redistricting, all 120 seats in the legislature are contested in the new districts: senators have four-year terms and those in the assembly have two-year terms. In the 1991 midterm election, this meant all forty senate seats and all eighty assembly seats were on the ballot.

So it wasn't just assembly members whose seats were in jeopardy; senators were likewise vulnerable. And the new district boundaries, which reflected the movement of New Jersey residents between 1980 and 1990, made matters even more difficult for Democrats. The predominant shift in the population over the past decade had been away from Democratic cities toward more Republican suburbs.

All of these factors contributed to the devastating defeat we suffered on November 5, 1991. There is no escaping my culpability; Democrats who were defeated for re-election to the senate and assembly, especially those who lost by narrow margins, quite rightly blamed me for their defeat. Nearly all of them had supported my agenda, controversial as it was, and I was deeply appreciative of their loyalty.

Now, however, I faced the prospect of governing with a legislature that would be overwhelmingly Republican—27–13 in the senate and 58–22 in the assembly: this meant that both houses met the two-thirds majority necessary to override my vetoes. I spent a lot of time over the next couple of months reading up on divided government, of how presidents and governors had managed to achieve success, either because of or despite dealing with legislatures controlled by the opposing party.

I had a bit of experience from the other side of this equation, having seen how Speaker of the House Tip O'Neill and President Reagan, who could not have been more ideologically different, found common ground on a number of issues, including tax reform. I also knew how to play defense when common ground was beyond reach, as I did in protecting the Superfund and other environmental programs from the opposing party's attempts to undermine or destroy them.

Now the shoe would be on the other foot. I would be playing defense from the executive side, not the legislative, and I would be defending the record I had built over the previous two years. I would also work hard to find common ground with the Republican legislature on issues that transcended ideology or partisanship. It would be a daunting task, but not, I thought, an impossible one.

As I prepared to deal with the new Republican majority in the legislature, one of the public perceptions I had to dispel was that I had ignored the Republican minority during the first two years of my governorship. I expected this kind of criticism from Republicans. It's a common complaint, whether true or not, from the minority party. But I didn't expect it from the press, and I bristled as this charge appeared regularly in print.

My administration sought Republican ideas and Republican votes in formulating several of our policy initiatives. One of our earliest bills, the Clean Water Enforcement Act, was passed unanimously by both houses of the legislature. The auto insurance reform package, vigorously fought by the insurance industry and opposed by Republican legislative leaders, nevertheless earned a smattering of support from GOP members in both houses.

We presented the assault weapons ban to the legislature and sought both Republican and Democratic input. We presented our budget and tax plans to legislators of both parties and asked Democrats and Republicans alike if they had any constructive suggestions for avoiding the spending cuts and revenue increases we foresaw. The Quality Education Act and the proposed school funding formula to meet the Supreme Court mandate were subjected to numerous legislative hearings—and were amended along the way in response to comments from members of both parties.

It was clear, however, that we would receive no Republican support for the sales and income tax increases or for the Quality Education Act. With the single exception of Senator Bill Gormley, the proudly moderate, independent-minded legislator from Atlantic County, no Republican supported the assault weapons ban. But it wasn't for our lack of trying. It was a calculated decision on the part of Republicans to place the blame for these controversial initiatives squarely on my fellow Democrats and me.

Early on in my governorship, I issued a challenge to Republicans to join us in crafting a bipartisan response to the state's pressing fiscal issues. "If they don't want to help us solve this problem," I said of the Republicans, "they risk being irrelevant." For the next two years, assembly minority leader Chuck Haytaian declared at every opportunity that I had dismissed Republicans as irrelevant. It didn't bother me so much that he distorted my statement; that kind of thing happens all the time in politics. As mentioned earlier, what bothered me was that the press reported this distortion as fact.

It also bothers me that this sort of obstructionism seems now to have become a guiding principle of the Republican Party, as evidenced by U.S. Senate Minority Leader Mitch McConnell's declaration in early 2009 that "the single most important thing we want to achieve is for President Obama to be a one-term president." Chuck Haytaian wasn't as blunt in his determination to make me a one-term governor, but he didn't hide his resolve to fulfill the ambition so clearly expressed in the rallying cry of the anti-tax protest marchers: to make New Jersey "Florio-free in '93."

What I was facing for the next two years wasn't just a clash of ideas or conflicting ideologies. It was a strategic challenge to coexist with a Republican majority that hoped I would be irrelevant to its pursuit of competing policy and electoral goals. But, of much greater concern, I was confronting a deepening divide between the parties, a decline in the spirit of bipartisanship that had once energized government and was now threatening to debilitate it. I was determined to fight this trend for as long as I was in public office. I am saddened that the divisiveness I feared would debilitate government in the early 1990s has only widened in the years since and, for the moment at least, has effectively rendered government all but dysfunctional a quarter-century later.

CHAPTER 9

Bridging the Partisan Divide

Divided government can be messy—but it can also get things done.

The morning after the 1991 legislative election, I got a call from former governor and former New Jersey Supreme Court chief justice Richard J. Hughes. In 1963, he had suffered as I just had through a midterm election that turned the legislature from Democratic to Republican control—and the Republican majority he had to contend with was even more lopsided than the one I was about to face.

"I'll give you some advice," Hughes told me. "You should accommodate them as much as possible—but never compromise on principle."

For the next two years, this is exactly what I tried to do. But we didn't get off to an especially accommodating start.

The Republicans who took control of the legislature in January 1992 had campaigned vigorously against much, though not all, of the record I had compiled in my first two years as governor. They promised to repeal the sales tax increase and cut government spending. They assured the NRA and its supporters they would overturn the assault weapons ban. They told insurance companies they would amend our auto insurance reform package to their liking. They told suburban school board members they would change the Quality Education Act, and they told teachers they would protect their pensions.

They made good on their first promise. They repealed the sales tax increase, returning it to 6 percent from 7 percent, and restored the exemption for paper products, effective July 1. The timing of the repeal's implementation was important; it meant the revenue from the higher sales tax would continue to come in through the end of the current fiscal year, allowing us to balance the current budget.

But putting the one-cent reduction in the sales tax into effect July 1 created an immediate $600 million hole in the budget I had proposed for the fiscal year that would begin that day. I thought the repeal was irresponsible and I vetoed it, but both houses of the legislature overrode my veto. At about the same time, the federal government announced that it was denying New Jersey's request for $450 million in retroactive Medicaid payments, bumping up the projected shortfall in the upcoming budget to more than $1 billion.

This set the stage for a bruising budget battle. The $16 billion budget I proposed for the coming fiscal year called for no new taxes and no layoffs of state employees. The Republicans countered with a $14.7 billion budget that called for slashing property tax rebates, laying off thousands of state employees (and firing all management-level staff earning $50,000 or more annually), and either eliminating or substantially reducing a host of health and social service programs.

I met with the Republican legislative leaders—Don DiFrancesco, president of the senate, and Assembly Speaker Chuck Haytaian, in the hope that we might forge some kind of compromise. In this, our first attempt to find common ground, we failed.

Although the governor of New Jersey has the power to remove expenditures from the budget through the line-item veto, he or she is not empowered to add revenue to the budget—and there was simply no way the Republicans were going to back down from their commitment to cut the sales tax.

So I vetoed the entire budget—the first governor in New Jersey history to do so. And the legislature promptly overrode my veto—another first in New Jersey history.

What followed was the largest layoff of state workers in New Jersey history, and it created turmoil throughout the agencies of state government. New Jersey's rigorous civil service system often prevented department heads from identifying their least productive employees as the people to lose their jobs. Instead, workers in senior positions moved down a step by "bumping" workers with less seniority, who in turn "bumped" workers a step below them, and so on, until the workers who ultimately lost their jobs were those with the least seniority, occupying the lowest-paying positions.

State employees were not the only casualties of this budget. A $35 million reduction in support for NJ Transit forced cuts in services and eliminated scores of management jobs at the state's public transit agency. Another $10 million came out of funding for federally mandated compliance with the Americans with Disabilities Act and the Clean Air Act. Homestead rebates—one of the means by which the state used income tax revenues to provide property tax relief—were slashed.

But after the dust from the budget and tax skirmishes settled, things began to change. The legislature did some modest tinkering with the public school funding formula, primarily to benefit wealthier suburban districts, but it did not rewrite the Quality Education Act that was implemented during the first half of my term. Nor did it repeal the income tax increase, eliminate the office of the Environmental Prosecutor, or scale back the auto insurance reforms. And when lawmakers did vote to repeal the assault weapons ban, I vetoed it—and the senate sustained the veto (see chapter 1).

By the time the following year's budget came before the legislature, for the fiscal year beginning July 1, 1993, economic conditions had improved, the rhetoric had cooled down, and the budget was adopted with only minor use of my line-item veto power.

In the meantime, I developed a particularly cordial working relationship with Senate President DiFrancesco. I appointed Bob Hughey, who had served as Republican governor Kean's commissioner of environmental protection, to be chief of economic recovery, a newly created cabinet-level post. I instituted an open-door policy, encouraging GOP legislative leaders to sit down with me in the governor's office to discuss policy areas where the executive and legislative branches might overcome their partisan differences and find common cause in advancing the public interest.

Despite our differences, we found a surprising number of such policy areas, allowing us to work cooperatively and collaboratively to forge agreement on several important initiatives. Some of these initiatives were already under way before the legislature changed hands, but all required bipartisan support to succeed. Three in particular stood out: welfare reform, expansion of health care benefits, and economic development.

⋘⋙

In 1976, the *Chicago Tribune* ran an article about a woman who had managed to con the federal government into paying her benefits to which she was not entitled. At a campaign rally that year, California governor and Republican presidential hopeful Ronald Reagan complained, "She used 80 names, 30 addresses, 15 telephone numbers to collect food stamps, Social Security and veterans' benefits for four nonexistent deceased veteran husbands, as well as welfare. Her tax-free cash income alone has been running $150,000 a year."

Reagan did not unseat Gerald Ford that year in his bid to become the Republican presidential nominee, but he did win the presidency four years later—and his disparagement of the so-called welfare queen continued, becoming one of the hallmarks of his two terms in the White House.

My own experience representing Camden, first in the state assembly and later in Congress, brought me into contact with a very different kind of welfare recipient. All of the people I met on the streets of one of the nation's poorest cities had only one name and, if they were lucky, an address they could call their own. Many of them didn't have a phone number because they couldn't afford a phone. They weren't receiving

Social Security or VA benefits. They were stricken by poverty, and their lifeblood was welfare.

As Brenda Bacon, my chief of management and planning and a former member of the Camden County Board of Chosen Freeholders, was fond of pointing out, "People on welfare have more challenges by noon than most of us have all day long."

Regrettably, "welfare" is one of those loaded words, something that connotes much more than just another government program. What some people see as a safety net, a humanitarian offering to our less fortunate fellow citizens, others see as a cash cow milked by undeserving recipients, a generous handout that encourages government dependency. One fascinating finding in survey research is that when Americans are asked if they think government should do more to relieve poverty, most people say yes. But when asked whether the government should expand welfare programs to relieve poverty, most say no.

I was always troubled by the Reagan rhetoric on welfare, how he seized on one egregious example of abuse and turned it into an indictment of the entire structure of federal assistance and antipoverty programs. At the same time, there was some validity to the argument that government benefits shouldn't be used as a crutch by citizens who are perfectly capable of standing on their own two feet. I felt that meaningful welfare reform shouldn't be patronizing and punitive; it should be rehabilitative and empowering.

Transforming our welfare system meant providing assistance to people who truly needed it, encouraging people to break the vicious cycle of poverty, and providing opportunity to people who were inspired to rise above it.

Despite the Reagan administration's disdain for welfare, there was no meaningful reform effort undertaken at the federal level throughout the 1980s. So in 1991, we set out to reform the welfare system in New Jersey. And in 1992, we succeeded.

The six-bill package that made its way through the legislature included a mix of proverbial sticks and carrots—incentives for welfare recipients to improve their lot in life and penalties for those who chose not to do so.

It was spearheaded by Assemblyman Wayne Bryant, whose district included Camden, the state's most welfare-dependent city. Because the bills included some punitive provisions that were highly controversial, many observers felt that only an African American legislator representing Camden could successfully shepherd this package through the legislature.

To my mind, the process of putting the welfare reform package together was almost as important as the outcome. Hearings were held all over the state and in the most unlikely settings: a public housing project in Newark, a drug rehabilitation center in Atlantic City, a day care center for welfare mothers in Camden. Welfare recipients were invited to express their views on job opportunities, affordable health care, child care, and obstacles they encountered in their efforts to lift themselves out of poverty.

The legislation that emerged from this process created a new approach to welfare. It was called the Family Development Program. It required all welfare recipients to take part in job training, education, or employment-related activities. It ensured that each member of a welfare family would attain, at a minimum, either a high school education or a vocational skill. While family members were being educated or trained, the state would provide support services such as day care, family counseling, and, if needed, substance abuse counseling and treatment.

The most controversial component of the package was the imposition of a cap on additional cash benefits for women who conceived a child while receiving benefits from the Aid to Families with Dependent Children (AFDC), the main federal-state welfare program. This provision was vigorously opposed by many progressive organizations, especially women's groups, who argued that it unfairly penalized vulnerable and needy children for their parents' behavior.

Assemblyman Bryant wanted inclusion of this provision to send a message to recipients that welfare must be temporary, not a way of life. He contended that the cap would encourage welfare mothers to take advantage of the other features of the welfare reform package—job training, day care, counseling, etc.—that were designed to strengthen families and facilitate their entry into mainstream society. (The courts subsequently upheld the provision, noting that while it withheld AFDC benefits, women who conceived additional children retained eligibility for Medicaid, food stamps, and other benefits.)

Republicans were happy to let Wayne Bryant take the lead on welfare reform, and he took a tremendous amount of heat for it from many of his fellow Democrats. But in the end, both parties embraced the reforms. Working across the aisle, a strong bipartisan agreement was reached on the entire welfare reform package.

New Jersey's Family Development Program later served as a model for Congress, which passed similar legislation, the Personal Responsibility and Work Opportunity Reconciliation Act of 1996, at the national level. When President Bill Clinton signed that bill into law, he fulfilled his campaign pledge "to end welfare as we have come to know it"—a pledge he had made shortly after I signed New Jersey's welfare reform package into law four years earlier.

Midway through his administration's efforts in 2017 to repeal and replace the Affordable Care Act, more widely known as "Obamacare," President Donald Trump famously quipped, "Nobody knew health care was so complicated."

I did. So did everyone else who had ever tried, at both the federal and state levels, to make any significant changes in the extraordinarily costly, inequitable, and inefficient way health care is practiced, delivered, and paid for in the United States.

My years representing Camden in Congress had already left me disillusioned about the ability of the state to plan adequately for hospital care in New Jersey. The city had three hospitals—Cooper, Our Lady of Lourdes, and West Jersey—all competing with each other. Cooper was a trauma center providing high-end tertiary care. Our Lady of Lourdes was a solid community hospital with a strong program in vascular and cardiac care. West Jersey was also a community hospital, which had a specialty in behavioral health.

On paper, the state required an extensive planning process by and for hospitals. For example, before it could provide a new program or service, every hospital had to demonstrate that there was a compelling need for that service in its region and then obtain a certificate of need from the state to that effect. But there was no overarching plan that identified which hospitals should specialize in which services. Every hospital wanted the latest equipment and technology, even though that would mean expensive duplication of services.

Trying to get hospitals to share services was every bit as hard as trying to get municipalities to consolidate. We had more municipalities in New Jersey per square mile than any other state in the country, but none wanted to give up its own mayor, its own police chief, its own public works department, and certainly not its own name, even though economies of scale would bring down the nation's highest property taxes. Likewise, no hospital wanted to give up its own emergency room, its own maternity ward, its own CAT scanner or MRI machine, even though doing so might help bring down the cost of hospital care.

The stratification of the medical profession was another barrier to health care planning. For instance, there was a huge controversy between the osteopathic physicians at Kennedy Hospital in Stratford and the allopathic physicians at Cooper Hospital in Camden. Dr. Stanley Bergen, president of the University of Medicine and Dentistry, asked me to join him for a dinner meeting, where representatives of the competing sides would try to resolve their differences. Instead, they almost came to blows. Dr. Bergen stood up, threw his napkin down on the table, and stormed out of the room.

Meanwhile, the health insurance market was in turmoil. The market for individuals was drying up. It got so bad that Blue Cross-Blue Shield, the state's largest insurer, was threatening to stop writing individual health insurance policies.

Between the fractious medical practitioners, the ultra-competitive hospitals, and the unstable insurance industry, I knew long before I became governor that bringing order to our chaotic health care system would be a tall order.

〰〰〰

I was fortunate to have three talented staff members—Brenda Bacon, Amy Mansue, and Betsy Ryan—who not only understood what was wrong with our health care delivery system but also had a keen sense of what needed to be done about it. Our primary goal was to improve people's access to health care. And that meant changing the way health care was funded.

People with pre-existing conditions couldn't get insurance. Most insurance policies didn't cover preventive care. Too many people were receiving their primary health care in emergency rooms. We needed more community health centers. We needed more primary care doctors in underserved areas, both urban and rural.

In March 1990, shortly after I took office, the Pepper Commission, a bipartisan federal commission on national health care reform headed by Florida congressman Claude Pepper (with whom I had served on the House Committee on Aging), released a report detailing a plan to reform the nation's health care system. The commission stopped short of calling for universal health insurance, but recommended a public health program for the uninsured, a long-term care program for the elderly, and a requirement that employers provide insurance to employees.

After the legislature passes a bill put forward by the Florio administration to establish an Office of Emergency Medical Services for Children in the state Department of Health, the governor signs the measure at a school in Montclair.

A month later, I appointed a blue-ribbon Commission on Health Care Costs to determine the causes and potential cures for the spiraling costs of health care in New Jersey. The commission came back with ninety recommendations, many of them similar to the ones the Pepper Commission had offered at the federal level.

These recommendations formed the core of a ninety-six-page bill, the Health Care Cost Reduction Act, which I signed in July 1991. It was a sweeping piece of legislation. Among many other provisions, it mandated that insurance companies offer five standard individual health insurance policy options and greatly expanded medical services for the poor.

All of this happened before the 1991 midterm election. It didn't draw the same level of public and press attention as budget and taxes, auto insurance, or assault weapons. But it certainly attracted the attention of

the entrenched interests: hospitals, doctors, nurses, health insurance companies, pharmaceutical companies, labor unions, and businesses—all of
which were actively engaged in the process, though some more willingly
than others.

Six months after the election, a new challenge arose. In May 1992, a
federal judge ruled in favor of a lawsuit brought by the Carpenters Fund,
striking down New Jersey's Uncompensated Care Fund, which paid for
hospital care provided to uninsured and indigent patients through a
19 percent surcharge on the hospital bills of insured patients. Many hospitals throughout the state depended on these payments just to keep their
doors open. New Jersey law requires that all hospitals provide care for all
patients who require it, regardless of whether or not they have insurance.
The judge gave the state six months to come up with a new program.

Throughout the fall of 1992, the Republican legislature and my administration grappled with myriad options to meet the court's deadline. Some
labor groups and business organizations lobbied to kick the sales tax back
up to 7 percent to help pay for hospital care for the poor. Others favored
increasing the "sin" taxes on tobacco products, liquor, and beer.

With an eye toward the 1993 election, which was now just a year
away, the Republicans were in no mood to vote for any tax increase,
much less a hike in the very tax they had so gleefully cut a few months
earlier. Nor, to be honest, was I particularly enthusiastic about revisit-
ing this matter.

I met frequently with Don DiFrancesco and Chuck Haytaian throughout this period. We found that, despite our differences over fiscal issues,
we had a common interest not only in resolving the uncompensated care
crisis but also in fixing other systemic problems that plagued our health
care delivery system. Years later, many of these same issues translated into
an intense, combative relationship between the Obama administration

and Republicans in Congress in the debate over the Affordable Care Act of 2010. In New Jersey, we dealt with them in a more collaborative way in crafting the Health Care Reform Act of 1992.

Our effort was spearheaded on the policy side by Chief of Management and Planning Brenda Bacon and on the legislative tactics and strategy side by Chief Counsel Bob DiCotiis. Both Brenda and Bob were in contact every day, either on the phone or in person, with health care professionals, legislative leaders and staff, and a host of other interested parties. Brenda was widely respected for her knowledge and expertise, while Bob's open, friendly style earned him the friendship of Don DiFrancesco and Chuck Haytaian, who would frequently tell me how skillful Bob had been in finding consensus on matters that might otherwise have led to conflict.

Despite passage of the Health Care Cost Reduction Act a year earlier, our chief concern in health care was still access. Too many people in New Jersey still did not have health insurance in 1992—and they weren't just the unemployed, the indigent, or the poor. Some were workers who couldn't get insurance from their employers. When those without insurance tried to get coverage in the individual or small-group market, the insurance companies, fearful of taking on big medical risks, either charged them exorbitant premiums or denied them coverage outright.

"Insurance companies make their money not by being efficient or managing care," I noted at the time, "but by weeding out the sick and insuring only the healthy."

There was one exception to this industry model. Blue Cross-Blue Shield of New Jersey, in exchange for its tax-exempt status, was required to write coverage for all applicants, including those with pre-existing conditions. In return, hospitals had to charge less for care they delivered to Blue Cross-Blue Shield patients. This put a strain on the hospitals, particularly in a recession, when the number of people without insurance and seeking charity care rose. Meanwhile, Blue Cross-Blue Shield kept asking the state for larger and larger premium increases.

The four-bill package we came up with relieved Blue Cross-Blue Shield of its obligation to be the "insurer of last resort." Instead, we created the Individual Health Coverage Program, applicable to all insurers wishing to sell coverage to individual customers. The program provided "guaranteed issue" and "community rating"—meaning that insurance companies had to offer health coverage within a given territory at the same price to all applicants, regardless of their health status. Similar rules were applied to insurers that sold to small businesses.

In effect, we were trying to force insurance companies to balance their policyholders between older, sicker people who would cost them more and younger, healthier people who would cost them less. It was not a radical concept. In my view, it is essentially what the whole concept of insurance is all about. In 1992, most Republicans in the New Jersey legislature felt the same way—in stark contrast to what their congressional counterparts were to profess two decades later.

The final bill in the package addressed the court's mandate by transferring $1.6 billion over the next three years from the state's Unemployment Trust Fund to the Uncompensated Care Fund. It was not an especially artful resolution to this chronic problem. "The new method of paying for the care of those who can't afford it is far from perfect," I admitted as I signed the bill. "But it was the only option that the legislative process made available."

In fact, nobody was totally pleased with the Health Care Reform Act of 1992. Labor and management—represented by the state AFL-CIO and the New Jersey State Chamber of Commerce—both opposed the package. Urban hospitals claimed it would put them out of business. With the exception of Blue Cross-Blue Shield, the insurance industry foresaw lower profitability, and many providers were still smarting from the auto insurance reforms we had instituted two years earlier.

There was one other group that steadfastly opposed the legislation: senate and assembly Democrats. The measure that passed the upper house by a vote of 21–18, and the lower house by a vote of 48–23, did not receive a single Democratic vote. The irony that I was solidly aligned on this issue with the veto-proof Republican majority in the legislature was not lost on me—or anyone else, for that matter.

⚜

If there is one issue on which Democrats and Republicans almost always agree, at least in principle, it is economic development. We don't always advocate the same strategies for achieving it, but I've never encountered a politician who doesn't support generating economic activity that creates jobs, stimulates investment, encourages entrepreneurship, helps small business, and otherwise promotes development that contributes to a healthy, vibrant economy.

In recent years, the favored economic development strategy in many states has been to shower private enterprise with public subsidies—usually in the form of tax incentives—either to attract companies to relocate from other states or to keep companies from moving to another state. This has effectively created an "arms race" between states, with each adding to its arsenal of incentives to lure (or keep) the targeted company. It also has the effect of reducing the state's tax revenue—which, it seems to me, is the very antithesis of what economic development is supposed to do.

Our approach was different. We believed in investing in enterprises that would not only create jobs and generate economic activity in their own right but would also stimulate significant economic development in their surrounding community. We did this not by giving away public money but by committing it to projects that leveraged private investment. Then we used these public-private partnerships to build the attractions and infrastructure that created centers of vibrant economic activity around the state.

We also made sure that decision making was centralized in the state Treasury Department. Too often, competing economic development projects are championed by competing developers, who pitch them to whatever office or agency of government they think will be most receptive. One developer might go to a mayor, another to a county freeholder board, and still another to any of a number of city, county, or state agencies (and there are many) that offer some form of financing for economic development projects. I felt it was critically important that we avoid having different levels and agencies of government competing with each other over these projects.

We assembled a talented and creative group of individuals—an economic development "SWAT team"—that worked under the guidance of Associate State Treasurer Rick Wright, who reported directly to me. Later, when Rick became my chief of staff, he retained this portfolio.

We invested all over the state. In downtown New Brunswick we invested in the development of Civic Square. We invested in the expansion of the Rutgers football stadium in neighboring Piscataway. We invested in the restoration of the Strand Theater in Lakewood. In Trenton, we invested in the construction of a Marriott Hotel and a new minor league baseball stadium and supported the fledgling Roebling Center by supplying an important new tenant, the state's Housing and Mortgage Finance Agency.

These were the kinds of economic development projects I had in mind when I delivered my 1992 State of the State message to the new legislature. Its centerpiece was my proposal for an Economic Recovery Fund, to be administered by the state Economic Development Authority (EDA). Because the economy was still in recession, banks and other financial institutions were reluctant to provide financing for the kinds of projects we needed to jump-start New Jersey's economy. I proposed that the state set up a fund that would invest directly in these projects and leverage additional money through public-private partnerships, grants, guarantees, and direct loans.

Five months later, the Republican legislature approved the Economic Recovery Act of 1992. In addition to giving the state EDA authority to make direct investments and enter into public-private partnerships, the legislation directed that the funds generated be used for infrastructure and transportation improvements, such as airports, ports, and terminal facilities; cultural, recreational, and tourism facilities and improvements; an environmental cleanup business assistance pilot program; and capital improvements to primary and secondary school facilities.

Having an extremely professional and highly regarded staff at the EDA was one of the keys to gaining strong bipartisan support for the new law. Tony Coscia, who had been recommended to me by Commerce Commissioner George Zoffinger to head the EDA, won praise for his directive that the authority stop behaving like a state agency and start operating more like a bank. Tony was with the EDA for eight years, four as CEO and four more as chair of the board. His obvious talent and competence later earned him appointments to two of the toughest jobs in the country: chair of the Port Authority of New York and New Jersey and chair of Amtrak.

Tony's deputy, Caren Franzini, was a registered Republican who had worked in the Kean administration, but so impressed us that we asked her to stay on. On my last day in office, when Tony moved up to become chair of the EDA board, I appointed Caren to succeed him as CEO—a position she held through Democratic and Republican administrations for the next twenty years. New Jersey lost a visionary and inspirational leader— and a genuinely nice person—when Caren passed away at age fifty-seven in January 2017.

The Economic Recovery Fund was capitalized by an initial appropriation of only $7 million in state funds, but we were able to add another $200 million in bond funds, obtained through a novel leveraging of annual lease payments owed to the state by the Port Authority of New York and New Jersey. These bonds were issued, on a taxable basis, because we knew from the start that the Economic Recovery Fund would be used to leverage private investment, not merely to finance public spending.

The creation of this fund enabled us to undertake—or, in the case of one major project, breathe new life into—a number of important economic development initiatives. Three in particular stand out: the New

Jersey Performing Arts Center in Newark, the Atlantic City Convention Center, and several interrelated projects in Camden.

⫘

The New Jersey Performing Arts Center, widely known as NJPAC, was the brainchild of Governor Kean. He envisioned it as the catalyst for redevelopment of downtown Newark, an entertainment venue that would attract world-class performers, who would draw large audiences, who would in turn create a demand for restaurants, bars, convenience stores, and other neighborhood businesses.

When I took office, the law creating NJPAC was already on the books. The funding would come from a combination of public and private contributions. So far, a number of New Jersey's largest companies (and more than a few wealthy individuals) had pledged contributions, but the state's ability to contribute was severely hampered by economic conditions.

Larry Goldman, the president and CEO of NJPAC, was a relentless fundraiser and tireless advocate for the project. He knew that Governor Kean supported it, but he didn't know whether I would do the same. On the one hand, he knew that my son Christopher was a composer (in fact one of his original pieces had been performed at my inaugural), but he had also heard that I wasn't the kind of guy who would sit through a symphony or an opera.

Larry spent a lot of time in Trenton trying to convince Tony Coscia, State Treasurer Doug Berman, Associate State Treasurer Rick Wright, and me that NJPAC was a good investment. But we didn't really need much convincing. Larry wasn't wrong in thinking that Tom Kean's appreciation for classical music far exceeded mine, but I definitely shared my predecessor's vision of NJPAC as a catalyst for the economic revitalization of downtown Newark. I was determined to get the project moving.

Because the project needed a large upfront infusion of cash, the EDA issued bonds, backed by a lease to the state of the future NJPAC facility.

The state then sublet its leasehold to NJPAC. The EDA assembled the land, importantly buying more than just the footprint of the NJPAC facility, so that both the state and the performing arts center would be able to control and prosper from future adjacent economic development. Direct grants from the Economic Recovery Fund supplemented the bond funds.

In October 1993, seven years after Governor Kean introduced the idea of building a performing arts center in Newark, a combination of private philanthropy and public bonds finally led to the official groundbreaking of the NJPAC. It opened four years later.

Today, NJPAC is not only one of the largest performing arts centers in the United States but also has one of the largest arts education programs in the country. It has featured 2,600 artists and hosted more than 10 million patrons, including 1.5 million children.

Just as important, NJPAC has been an economic catalyst. Neighborhood restaurants and a Whole Foods have opened, property owners have renovated buildings in the area, and corporations and professionals have moved in. One Theater Square, a 22-story, 245-unit apartment building, is under construction across the street from NJPAC—on the additional land we had the foresight to buy. The Prudential Center, home of the New Jersey Devils hockey team, was built nearby. Prudential has built a new world headquarters and Panasonic a North American headquarters in Newark. Cablevision is building a headquarters, and Military Park is being renovated.

None of this would have happened without NJPAC blazing the trail for redevelopment in New Jersey's largest city.

᠅

There is one immutable truth about convention centers in this country that most politicians won't tell you: convention centers don't make money. In fact, their purpose isn't to make money. Their purpose is to generate the kind of economic activity that will bring improvements and income to the surrounding neighborhood and the larger community.

A modern, attractive, well-located convention center should do what NJPAC has done in Newark—lead to the creation of nearby restaurants, shops, and other attractions that create jobs and provide revenue to the community. If the state or any other public entity is going to put its money into a convention center, it has to make sure that money isn't just going down the black hole of operating the facility. Instead, it has to come back to the treasury in the form of revenue from the economic activity that the facility generates.

This is what we wanted to accomplish in Atlantic City. In 1964, the city had hosted a major national convention when the Democrats came to town. Three decades later, despite a casino industry that attracted millions of visitors annually and a new rail line offering direct train service from Philadelphia, few organizations other than two state stalwarts—the NJEA and the State League of Municipalities—were bringing large numbers of conventioneers to Atlantic City.

Atlantic City Convention Hall, famous for hosting every Miss America Pageant since 1940 (and the nation's first indoor football game ten years earlier), had outlived its usefulness as a convention center. Its location on the Boardwalk was iconic. Its architecture made it a prime candidate for designation as a National Historic Landmark, which it received in 1987. Despite renovations in 1959 and 1984, however, it was not a suitable venue for the conventions of the 1990s.

Caren Franzini, who happened to be an Atlantic City native, wasn't the only holdover from the Kean administration who played a prominent role in our economic development efforts. Laura Sanders had served as the State Treasury's liaison to the Casino Reinvestment Development Authority. We kept her on as assistant state treasurer (she later served as my deputy chief of staff), and she became our point person on matters related to Atlantic City.

In August 1990, I signed an executive order creating a coordinating committee to offer recommendations on handling five issues in the Atlantic City area: the Atlantic City International Airport, general transportation improvements, housing development, revitalization of retail areas, and whether to build a new convention center at the site where both the Atlantic City Expressway and the new rail line terminated.

The recommendation regarding the convention center that the committee gave to me some months later contained a very sage piece of advice. The convention center, the committee advised, should not be thought of as a single project, but rather as a piece of a much bigger project, one that included the convention center, a hotel, and a retail corridor that connected these facilities to the Boardwalk. Instead of thinking of it as a $200 million handout for a convention center project that would never pay for itself, I was advised to think of it as a $600 million infrastructure investment that would generate broader economic activity.

I agreed with this assessment, but wondered how the state could possibly meet the price tag. Between our bonding capacity and our prospects for leveraging private investment, I was confident we could make a substantial down payment on the project—but $600 million was out of our price range. What we needed was a brainstorm of creative financing.

We actually came up with three creative financing options. The first was Doug Berman's idea. The New Jersey Sports and Exposition Authority was experiencing some financial problems because revenue from horse racing in the Meadowlands was declining—in part because of competition from casino gambling in Atlantic City. But Atlantic City itself was declining because casino revenues weren't going back into the community.

Doug put these problems together to come up with the suggestion that the Sports Authority take over the Atlantic City construction project. The funding would come from bonds issued by the Sports Authority, with the state covering the debt service on the bonds.

Neither the Sports Authority nor the Atlantic County Improvement Authority, under whose auspices the convention center was to be built, greeted this arrangement with enthusiasm. It took a lot of cajoling, but both entities eventually came to recognize that without such an arrangement, neither the Atlantic City Convention Center nor the accompanying infrastructure would likely be built. And the Sports Authority wasn't likely to find a better deal to put it back on solid financial footing.

The second piece of creative financing was the imposition of a $2 fee on parking in casino facilities, of which the casinos got 50 cents and the Casino Reinvestment Development Authority, or CRDA, got $1.50. The proceeds were to be used to finance construction of a sufficient number of hotel rooms in Atlantic City to support the convention center. And that's exactly what happened. The number of hotel rooms doubled in the next four years, adding 2,000 permanent jobs. Meanwhile, construction of the Atlantic City Convention Center began in October 1992. It opened in May 1997, along with 1,747 new hotel rooms.

The third element was to use the CRDA, which was focused on housing, as an "EDA South" to organize and finance the rest of the puzzle pieces. The new convention center was sited next to the train station, but between the convention center and the Boardwalk casinos was the unattractive hulk of NJ Transit's aging bus station, several poorly tended parking lots, some vacant or semi-abandoned buildings, and a few courageous small businesses. The convention center was within strolling distance of the Boardwalk, but there was nothing in between to encourage visitors to take that stroll.

For the convention center to succeed, it needed to have a hotel built next to it and the corridor to the Boardwalk needed to be redeveloped. The CRDA was able to use revenue from a separate investment tax on casinos to attract a developer to build the hotel, Doubletree-Caesars (now a Sheraton), which opened in time to support the convention center. NJ Transit built a new bus center several blocks away, removing the worst eyesore. Finally, the CRDA adopted a plan to acquire land, market Atlantic City to retail developers, and turn the corridor into a retail area called "The Walk." Today it features more than 100 stores and restaurants, operated by Tanger Outlets.

As proud as I am of our team's creativity, and of the benefits our economic development efforts brought to Atlantic City, I cannot ignore the fact that Atlantic City faced—and continues to face—extraordinarily difficult problems. In the late 1970s, when Atlantic City was the exclusive venue for casino gambling on the East Coast, the crowds and the money came pouring in. But as legalized gaming spread to neighboring states, the crowds in Atlantic City disappeared. So did the money and, ultimately, so did five of the city's twelve casinos.

Casino gambling offered Atlantic City a spectacular but brief rebirth. The convention center, the adjacent hotel, and "The Walk" reflected the state's commitment to make the infrastructure investment the city desperately needed in the early 1990s. The same or greater level of commitment may be even more necessary today than it was a quarter-century ago.

⟪⟫

When I moved to Camden in the early 1960s, there was a sarcastic joke going around that Philadelphia wasn't really as boring a city as its reputation suggested. It just seemed that way because it was across the river from exciting Camden.

Or, to put it another way, if Newark mayor Ken Gibson was right when he declared that wherever American cities were going, Newark would get there first, there were plenty of folks in South Jersey who would argue that Camden ranked a very close second.

In many ways, Camden reminded me of the Brooklyn of my youth. It was a gritty, working-class city. Philadelphia may not have been considered an especially glamorous place back then, but Camden definitely lay in its shadow, just as Brooklyn lay in Manhattan's. The unrest that swept through many American cities in the late 1960s left a deep scar on Camden. Entire neighborhoods were abandoned. Large sections of the city were blighted.

Fortunately for Brooklyn, the gentrification of Manhattan has spilled across the East River. Unfortunately for Camden, the rebirth of Philadelphia didn't flow as easily across the Delaware.

Governor Florio confers with his predecessor, Tom Kean, shortly before a
ceremony naming the newly opened New Jersey State Aquarium in Camden
in the former governor's honor.

Bringing economic development to Camden has been a multistep process, involving a number of related projects and initiatives. In 1988, the
Kean administration took the first major step in Camden's comeback,
breaking ground for a $42 million state aquarium on the Camden water-
front south of the Ben Franklin Bridge. Even before the aquarium opened
in February 1992, my administration was pursuing a number of additional
economic development activities in Camden.

The first was fulfillment of an understanding reached early on with the
city's largest employer, Campbell Soup. Gordon McGovern, the company
CEO, told us point-blank, "You build the aquarium; we'll build our world
headquarters." The situation was not unlike what was going on in Newark
with NJPAC. The aquarium was a project the Kean administration had
started, but when my new administration arrived, its future was uncertain.

As with NJPAC, I needed no convincing that the aquarium was a worthy project—and Campbell Soup's commitment to build its world headquarters was icing on the cake. It took almost twenty years, but the opening of Campbell Soup's gleaming, 80,000-square-foot headquarters in Camden's Gateway District in 2010 can trace its roots directly back to the Republican Kean administration's decision to begin the aquarium project in Camden and my decision, as a Democrat, to complete it.

Camden's steady deterioration had an adverse impact on another of the city's major employers, GE/RCA Aerospace. RCA had a long and storied history in Camden. The "Nipper Tower" atop the old RCA Victor building near the foot of Market Street has long been a Camden landmark. Inside what was once the Victor Talking Machine Company's Building 17, recorded music had its origins, produced on flat disks that came to be known as "records." When the Radio Corporation of America purchased the Victor company in 1929, Camden was a national leader in the new broadcast medium, and RCA Victor became the world's largest manufacturer of radio sets.

In 1985, General Electric bought RCA, and the new company, GE/RCA, was much more than a titan of the broadcast industry and a purveyor of household appliances. GE/RCA Aerospace was one of the nation's largest defense and aerospace companies and, along with Campbell Soup, one of Camden's largest employers.

By the early 1990s, GE/RCA was saddled with more than one million square feet of old industrial facilities, far more than the company needed. If the company was to stay in Camden and to stay competitive in the industry, it had to find a way to get out from under these old facilities that it owned and find new space it could lease. An estimated 2,500 jobs were dependent on GE/RCA's ability to continue operating in Camden.

Our economic development "SWAT team" negotiated with GE/RCA representatives for several months before we struck a deal. In March 1991, I signed what was probably the longest letter of intent I ever laid eyes on. It described, in meticulous detail, the terms of an arrangement in which

After his economic development "SWAT team" negotiated a public-private partnership to keep 2,500 GE Aerospace jobs in Camden, Governor Florio joins company officials, key legislators, and Commerce and Economic Development Commissioner George Zoffinger (right) to announce the agreement.

the state EDA would purchase and own the site of the new facility, which would be developed through a public-private partnership with GE/RCA, with the company agreeing to occupy the facility under a long-term lease. In the spring of 1993, GE/RCA Aerospace (now owned by Lockheed Martin) moved into its new building on Camden's waterfront.

Again, this was an example of the state taking an equity position in a collaborative deal with a company, rather than simply giving money away, either in the form of direct payments or tax incentives, to a private enterprise. It ensured that in addition to saving jobs, the state would receive a steady return on its investment over an extended period of time.

Two more projects in Camden merit attention. The first is the LEAP (Leadership, Education and Partnership) Academy University Charter School. In 1993, working with the Delaware River Port Authority, we provided a $1.5 million strategic planning grant to the Rutgers-Camden Community Leadership Center to study the feasibility of establishing a new community school in Camden.

I am not what you would call an enthusiastic supporter of charter schools. In too many cases, I believe they drain funding from traditional public schools without showing any measurable benefit. But a carefully crafted charter school program that offers a unique educational setting and enhances learning opportunities for inner-city children in a city like Camden can serve as a model, and I was impressed by the knowledge, commitment, and dedication of the LEAP Academy advocates, chief among them Gloria Bonilla-Santiago.

Dr. Bonilla-Santiago is the visionary who transformed the LEAP Academy from a concept on a drawing board in 1993 into an enormously successful and widely acclaimed K–12 four-school academy today, with an enrollment of more than 1,500 inner-city students who routinely exceed state averages on standardized tests. Every LEAP Academy senior class since 2005 has achieved not only a 100 percent graduation rate but also a 100 percent college placement rate.

I was in office only long enough to see the seed of the LEAP Academy planted, but I take a small measure of pride in its growth and achievement. It is not just an educational success story; it is also part of an economic development success story. From its humble origins in a temporary modular classroom building, LEAP Academy now occupies five buildings on Cooper Street along what has become Camden's "Education Corridor," which also features the campuses of Rutgers and Rowan Universities, Camden County College, and the Rutgers Early Learning Research Academy.

The second project worthy of note is the Camden amphitheater. Three separate companies—Sony Music, PACE Entertainment, and Blockbuster Video—were interested in developing an entertainment venue in the Philadelphia area, and we were keen to work with them on a plan to build it on the Camden waterfront.

Like Campbell Soup, PACE Entertainment delivered a blunt message to the state. Its leaders told us, "We'd like to build a shed amphitheater. We have $12 million. You bring the dirt."

What PACE wanted to build would need an enormous amount of dirt. The company envisioned an indoor-outdoor facility where people could sit and listen to music under the stars on a gently sloping grass bowl. The site chosen was a flat plain, with soil so starved of nutrients that even weeds were scarce.

I personally did not make the commitment for the dirt; the economic development team did that in my name. They told me about it and assured me it would be met. Their problem, I later learned, was that at the moment they were making this commitment, they lacked the resources to assure state title to a 20-pound bag of topsoil, much less the 500,000 cubic yards the amphitheater required.

Then Bobby Rand, a member of our "SWAT team" who commuted to Trenton every day from Camden, found the dirt—under the Tacony-Palmyra Bridge. The Army Corps of Engineers was deepening the Delaware River channel so that larger ships could access the ports of Philadelphia and Camden, and the dredged spoils were being deposited under the bridge. The topmost layer of the dredged material was contaminated, but what was underneath was clean.

Recognizing the potential value of reusing the uncontaminated dirt to create the sloping grass bowl for the amphitheater, Bobby went to the state Department of Environmental Protection (DEP), which had regulatory authority over the material as solid waste. The DEP agreed to have the material tested and, based on the results, changed the designation of the uncontaminated material from solid waste to recycled clean fill. (This change, incidentally, led to a statewide initiative for dredged material reclamation and reuse and a regional, national, and worldwide change in dredged material policies that ultimately turned uncontaminated dredged material from a liability requiring disposal into an asset for construction projects.)

The rest of the project had its own complications. But after we came up with the dirt, we worked out the site issues; the environmental issues; and the access, parking, security, and funding issues. We then hammered out an agreement that ensured a steady flow of revenue to the state and the city, through payments in lieu of taxes. To her credit, Governor Whitman gave the green light to the Sony/PACE amphitheater, a unique year-round $56 million, 25,000-seat facility that opened in 1995. It has changed hands several times since then, but over the past twenty years, what is now the BB&T Pavilion has been one of the top amphitheaters in the country.

On the other hand, I was disappointed when Governor Whitman rejected what I considered the most ambitious project we had in the works for Camden: a new home for the Philadelphia 76ers basketball team. Harold Katz, the owner of the 76ers, had been pressuring Philadelphia officials for years, without success, to build a new arena for his NBA team. He contacted us about moving the 76ers across the Delaware, just as the NFL Giants (later joined by the Jets) had moved across the Hudson to take up residence in the Meadowlands. We worked out all the financial details, identified a site, signed a letter of intent, and were all set to construct a temporary facility for the several years it would take to build the new arena in Camden.

After I lost the election, Harold Katz made multiple visits to Trenton to try to get the incoming administration to commit to continuing the project. His appeal fell on deaf ears. A few days before she took office, Governor-elect Whitman announced that she would kill the deal: Camden would not be the new home of the 76ers.

It took another twenty-two years for Philadelphia's NBA team to become a part-time resident of Camden. In September 2016, the 76ers opened a 125,000-square-foot training facility, which will also house the team's corporate offices, on the Camden waterfront. It was financed, as so many projects are these days, by an enormous tax break: $82 million over ten years.

All of our economic development efforts—in Newark, Atlantic City, Camden, and elsewhere—represented an investment in New Jersey's future. They cost a lot of money, and many of the projects required extensive cooperation between a Republican legislature and a Democratic governor. But they created a lot of jobs, and they were structured in such a way that money would flow to the state for years to come.

They were all part of a concerted effort to put our state's financial house in order. Despite the ups and downs of the economy, the tax battles I fought with the Republican legislature, and the difficult choices we had to make each year to balance the state budget, our standing in the financial community never wavered. New Jersey enjoyed a triple-A bond rating from Moody's throughout my term as governor.

⋘

Back in 1967, just after I passed the bar, my father told me about an advertisement he had seen in a magazine for a great deal on land in Florida. For a down payment of $2,500 and another $50 a month for the next couple of years, he could buy a piece of property in a place called Lehigh Acres, outside Fort Myers, and build a little home where he and my mother could live.

I told him I thought he was crazy. He said, "What do you know? You've only been a lawyer for two weeks." He bought the property. My parents moved to Florida.

They lived there for twenty-five years, in a little house in a secluded part of Lehigh Acres, so far back in the tract that it never really got fully developed. My mother liked it that way; she was reclusive. My father was happy because he found some houses to paint, which brought in some money, and plenty of places to gamble, which sometimes had the opposite effect.

Then my father got sick. He had always had stomach problems, and they started to get worse. In his late seventies, he developed heart trouble as well. As his illnesses became more debilitating, he couldn't work as much. He was also spending a great deal of money on prescription drugs, which was steadily draining his bank account.

When my brother Bill was dying of AIDS in the summer of 1991, my parents came up from Florida to visit him in the hospital. For the first time in my life, I thought my father looked really old. A few months later, he reached the point where he was diagnosed as terminally ill. In retrospect, knowing how deeply my father cared about my mother, I probably shouldn't have been surprised that, rather than digging any deeper into the savings he knew she would need to live on after he died, he then chose to take his own life.

I sometimes wonder how different the end of my father's life would have been if Medicare had started offering Part D prescription drug coverage long before 2006. I can't imagine having to make the choice my father faced: paying for the medication he needed to sustain his life or safeguarding his wife's financial security by shortening his life. That's a choice nobody should ever have to make.

I am glad that my father was there to see me sworn in as governor of New Jersey on January 16, 1990. I am sad that he didn't get to see me complete my four-year term.

≪≪≪≫

As the 1993 gubernatorial election approached, I wasn't really thinking of it so much as a traditional campaign, filled with promises about what I planned to accomplish over the next four years. Instead I saw it as an opportunity to explain what my administration had already achieved, and was continuing to achieve, in the way of responsible public policy.

I spent a lot of time campaigning at the Jersey Shore. I reminded people what the beaches had looked like the summer before I took office and described what we had done to make subsequent summers measurably better, both environmentally and economically.

I also visited cities—Newark, Atlantic City, Camden—the places where our economic development efforts were bearing real, visible fruit. Many of the ribbon cuttings and groundbreakings I attended throughout 1993 may have been thought of by others as campaign events, but I considered them very much a part of my gubernatorial responsibilities. I believed the best campaign I could run was to highlight the positive things I was doing as governor.

Budget and tax issues were still perceived, quite correctly, as my political Achilles heel, but the polls showed that my popularity had pretty much bottomed out in the summer of 1991, rising slowly but steadily since then. Our polling through the summer and early fall of 1993 showed me gaining momentum—never quite enough to make me overconfident, but definitely enough to ease my apprehension about the outcome of the election.

The economy was also helping. Things had started to pick up from the recession. In January 1993, the Bureau of Labor Statistics (BLS) calculated the nation's inflation rate at 3.3 percent; by October it had dropped to 2.7 percent. Between November 1992 and November 1993, the BLS reported that the national unemployment rate decreased by 0.9 percent, from 7.4 percent to 6.5 percent. Over the same time period, the unemployment rate in New Jersey fell 2.5 percent, from 8.4 percent to 5.9 percent—by far the strongest showing of any state in the country.

In 1992, property taxes levied by New Jersey municipalities and school districts had risen by just 1.9 percent, the smallest increase in anybody's memory. I knew there was still deep resentment about the 1990 tax increases, even though the sales tax hike had since been repealed and the income tax increase affected only the wealthiest 17 percent of the state's taxpayers. But I was cautiously optimistic that the combination of property tax relief and the dramatic drop in unemployment would help restore a healthy portion of the political capital I spent three years earlier.

There was one more factor that I felt was in my favor. This would be my fourth gubernatorial campaign, but the first in which I faced no primary opposition and had a unified Democratic Party behind me. In 1977, I was one of four candidates who ran against the incumbent, Brendan Byrne, in the primary. In 1981, I was one of ten candidates on the Democratic primary ballot. In 1989, I was one of three. In 1993, although my popularity wasn't much better than Brendan Byrne's had been in 1977, nobody challenged me for the Democratic nomination.

The Republican primary was slightly more competitive. There were only three candidates: Christine Todd Whitman, who had come surprisingly close to unseating Bill Bradley in the 1990 U.S. Senate race; Cary Edwards, who had finished second to Jim Courter in the 1989 Republican gubernatorial primary; and Jim Wallwork, a conservative state senator from Essex County.

The main contest was between Whitman and Edwards, and it was spirited. Edwards chided Whitman for hiring a couple as domestic help and failing to pay their taxes. (Earlier that year, President Bill Clinton's first nominee for attorney general, Zoe Baird, had been forced to remove herself from consideration for the same reason.) Later, Edwards admitted that he, too, had hired a housekeeper and failed to pay her taxes. Eyebrows were raised when it was revealed that the Whitmans were getting a tax break on a 300-acre property used for raising livestock, allowing it to be classified as agricultural land. With a net worth in excess of $1 million, they were criticized for receiving a tax benefit that could have gone to people in greater need.

Whitman, however, prevailed, gathering 41 percent of the Republican primary vote to Edwards's 34 percent and Wallwork's 25 percent. While there was speculation that she might be vulnerable in the general election because of the taxes she didn't pay, she clearly felt that I was more vulnerable because of the taxes everybody else was paying.

❧

The Whitman campaign was managed by Ed Rollins, the bombastic consultant who had run Ronald Reagan's hugely successful "Morning in America" campaign in 1984. My campaign hired James Carville, the equally bombastic "Ragin' Cajun" who had run Bill Clinton's successful presidential campaign in 1992.

What made the campaign interesting, for those who enjoy following politics as a spectator sport, was the role reversal of these two high-powered consultants in the 1993 race. In the 1984 campaign, Rollins was defending the record of the incumbent president; now he would be challenging the record of the incumbent governor. In the 1992 campaign, Carville was challenging the record of the incumbent president, George H. W. Bush; now he would be defending the record of the incumbent governor.

"The (Whitman) message will be very much like the Clinton message," Rollins told the *New York Times* in April, even before she won the GOP primary. "The message is change." Describing the task facing Carville, Rollins said, "He is one of the hottest political consultants in the country. He has never failed to keep his thumb on the pulse; he understands blue-collar people and values. But now he is the Establishment; he has to defend the record of the incumbent. Christie (Whitman) gets to be like Bill Clinton, attack the record."

That is exactly what she did. Throughout the campaign, she hammered away at taxes and spending. Although my administration had reduced the state payroll by 10,000 jobs and the state's unemployment rate had plummeted in the last year, she charged that the tax increases we had implemented in 1990 cost New Jersey 280,000 jobs. Although my administration had performed a thorough audit of state spending, which showed millions of dollars in savings, she promised a "performance audit" that would lead to deep cuts in the state budget.

What she did not do, for months after her win in the June primary, was offer a specific plan for how she was going to create jobs, cut taxes, and reduce state spending. Polling during this four-month period showed support for my candidacy hardening, while hers remained soft. I repeatedly challenged the Whitman campaign to offer a detailed plan for achieving her "pie in the sky" dream of lower taxes.

She unveiled her plan in late September. Had she released it a week or so later, I might have termed it the proverbial "October surprise"—if I had taken it seriously. Instead, I was incredulous. What her campaign issued was a two-page proposal, calling for a 30 percent reduction in the state income tax, to be phased in over three years. There was no explanation of how she would pay for the proposed tax cuts, no explanation of how the state budget would be balanced in the face of such a drastic cut in revenue, and no explanation of what would happen to property-tax relief programs, which were paid for by income tax revenues.

Initially, the press and the public agreed with my assessment that the Whitman tax plan was an empty promise, nothing more than a political ploy. A steady stream of editorials in the state's leading newspapers called the Whitman proposal vague and unrealistic. Even *The Trentonian*, which heaped unrelenting hostility on virtually everything I did as governor, criticized Whitman for doing a poor job of defending her plan.

A CBS/*New York Times* poll taken a week after the Whitman plan was unveiled found that only 10 percent of respondents believed she could make good on her promise to reduce taxes. The poll showed me with a 21-point lead: 51 percent to 30 percent. My own campaign polling never showed as large a margin, but it was tracking a steady majority of voters saying they were likely to vote for me.

There were, however, a couple of troubling signs. For one thing, the New Jersey Education Association, still angered over the teacher pension issue, chose not to make an endorsement in the election—and Republicans actively sought support for Whitman and GOP legislative candidates from local teachers' union affiliates, particularly in suburban districts. At the same time, we were counting on urban educators to be supportive of our efforts under the Quality Education Act, which pumped more money into their districts, but we weren't seeing the level of enthusiasm we thought we had earned.

Then there was the NRA. On the campaign trail, Whitman offered some tepid criticism of the severity of the assault weapons ban, but the NRA was under no illusions that she would undo the ban in its entirety if elected. The gun lobby's intent, pure and simple, was to punish me for

what I still considered to be the signature achievement of my governorship, and the means of accomplishing this was to pump money and man-
power into Hands Across New Jersey. What had started as a grassroots
movement was now, in effect, an arm of the NRA, and the anti-tax activists maintained their singular focus on attacking my record on taxes. The
Whitman plan was nothing less than music to their ears.

Our biggest concern was the significant number of undecided voters
that kept showing up in the polls. The 51–30 result in the CBS/*New York
Times* poll was an outlier; most other polls showed that the race was not
only closer but was also steadily tightening as Election Day neared. And
a large percentage of voters remained undecided right down to the final
weekend.

If that group had broken 50–50 on November 2, 1993, I would have won
re-election. It didn't—and I wasn't.

⋘

In 1981, I had the dubious distinction of losing the closest gubernatorial
election in New Jersey history—a margin of 1,797 votes out of 2,290,201
votes cast. In 1993, I earned a special place in history by losing the second-
closest gubernatorial election ever in New Jersey—a margin of 26,093
votes out of 2,446,155 votes cast.

An exit poll on Election Day 1993 found that 59 percent of voters had
made up their minds by Labor Day, and I won this group by 53 percent to
47 percent. But 30 percent said they didn't decide until the last two weeks
of the campaign, and I lost that group by 58 percent to 42 percent. To put
it another way, Whitman picked up about 120,000 votes in the last couple
of weeks of the race, nearly five times her final margin of victory.

Ironically, my record of cutting the state payroll by 10,000 jobs, which
probably won me some votes around the state, cost me dearly in the place
where most state employees live: Mercer County. In 1989, I carried Mercer by a margin of 69 percent to 31 percent; in 1993, I lost it by 53 percent
to 47 percent. I also lost two other counties I had won four years earlier,

Monmouth and Ocean, where Hands Across New Jersey was particularly active. I lost Passaic County, which I carried in 1989, largely because of a lower-than-expected turnout in Paterson, the state's third-largest city. And although I won Essex County, the turnout in Newark was very disappointing.

There may have been a reason for that. A week after the election, the *New York Times* reported that Whitman's campaign manager, Ed Rollins, boasted that the state Republican Party funneled $500,000 in "walking around money" to suppress the vote in urban Democratic areas. The money was used, Rollins was quoted as saying, to make payments to black ministers who agreed not to urge congregants to vote for me, as well as to Democratic Party workers who agreed not to participate in get-out-the-vote activity on Election Day.

Rollins later recanted, saying he fabricated the voter-suppression story just to get in a dig at James Carville, his rival political strategist in the race. He was evidently able to convince a federal grand jury two weeks later that the Whitman campaign did nothing more than respectfully request restraint by black ministers who were supporting my re-election. In other words, Rollins went before a grand jury and swore under oath that he was a liar. The echoes of the Voter Suppression Task Force from the 1981 election were hard to ignore.

In the end, though, I believe the election really did come down to two issues: guns and taxes. I thought the voters would agree with me that Whitman's promise late in the campaign to cut income tax rates by 30 percent was fiscally irresponsible, that it would be impossible to achieve without massive borrowing or deferring payments into the state pension fund. (In fact, this is exactly what happened.) But the popular sentiment in the fall of 1993 can be summed up simply: Florio raised taxes; Whitman said she won't.

There is little sense in reexamining what I might have done differently, either in my four years as governor or in my re-election campaign, to change the minds of about 13,000 voters. And I will leave to others the task of analyzing the eventual fiscal consequences of the Whitman administration's 30 percent income tax cut. I'm not the kind of person who indulges in a lot of second-guessing, nor do I wish to re-engage in an argument I lost a quarter-century ago.

In my last week as governor, however, I was heartened to read an editorial in the *Bergen Record* commenting on my four years in office. "In a day when most government leaders look to opinion polls for guidance," the editorial observed, "Mr. Florio is a politician with backbone. As a result of his hard work and political courage, he leaves the state in better shape than he found it."

Those kind words aside, I didn't really have a lot of time in the aftermath of the 1993 election to dwell on my accomplishments, my shortcomings, my legacy, my regrets, or any of the other products of my time in public office. After twenty-four years as an elected official—five years in the state Assembly, fifteen years in Congress, and four years as governor—I now had to decide what to do with the rest of my life.

From Public Life
to Private Citizen

A new job, a new home, and a new career—in law, in academia and,
for the first time in my life, in business.

On November 3, 1993, Lucinda and I were sitting at the kitchen table in Drumthwacket, the governor's mansion in Princeton, contemplating our future. In a little more than two months, I would be unemployed. We would have no car, no house of our own, and about $60,000 in the bank. For the first time in the twenty-six years since I had graduated from law school, I had to go out and find a job.

After spending virtually my entire adult life in government, I definitely wanted to stay involved in public policy. After enjoying a couple of part-time teaching stints at the Eagleton Institute of Politics and Rutgers-Camden Law School, I definitely wanted to teach. And after surviving for thirty years on the public payroll, I definitely wanted for the first time in my life to actually make some money.

Fortunately, opportunities arose that eventually allowed me to do all three.

The first opportunity that came my way was a job. Mike Perrucci, who had been one of my earliest and most loyal North Jersey supporters as the

Democratic chairman in Warren County, contacted me and encouraged me to join his law firm: Mudge Rose Guthrie Alexander & Ferdon, headquartered in New York City. Although I found it vaguely troubling that Mike was asking me to join the same firm Richard Nixon joined after losing the race for governor of California in 1962, it was an attractive offer, and I said yes.

Lucinda and I moved into a furnished townhouse at Canal Pointe, a condominium complex off Route 1 in West Windsor Township, just across the border from Princeton. Mike's office was in Morristown, forty miles away. My first day on the job was January 26, 1994—eight days after I left the governorship.

There's a great punch line often attributed to Brendan Byrne, but it may have originated with Richard Hughes: you know you aren't governor anymore when you get into the back seat of a car and it doesn't go anywhere. Fortunately, outgoing governors in New Jersey have a state trooper assigned to drive them for a period of time after leaving office, so when I got in the car that day, it did go from West Windsor to Morristown—through a blizzard of snow and ice.

When I got to the office, nobody was there. We turned around, and I went back home. That was my introduction to the private sector.

Working for Mudge Rose was an interesting—if brief—experience. After enduring governmental bureaucracies at the city, state, and federal levels, I now found myself in a massive private bureaucracy: a 126-year-old law firm populated by 190 lawyers. Every partners' meeting was a battle between the bond lawyers and the trial lawyers, a clash of monstrous egos.

Mike and I were able to avoid a lot of the contentiousness by staying in New Jersey, where we managed the Morristown office, attracted several young associates, and were well positioned to spin off our own firm— Florio & Perrucci—when Mudge Rose dissolved in October 1995.

Two years later, we got a very attractive offer from another big (and politically connected) New York law firm: Fischbein Badillo Wagner &

Harding. We joined up with that firm, but kept our office in New Jersey in order to retain a certain amount of independence. This allowed us to avoid the kinds of internal fights that seem to break out with alarming regularity when more than a couple of dozen lawyers are in the same room.

Sure enough, Fischbein Badillo lost its attraction after about three years, and we were back to being Florio & Perrucci again. But this time we decided to expand our own firm, rather than team up with another behemoth. Doug Steinhardt, the Warren County Republican chairman, joined the firm and gave us a bipartisan presence. Then Paul Fader signed on after serving as chief counsel to Governors Jim McGreevey and Dick Codey.

Now we were Florio Perrucci Steinhardt & Fader, a full-service law firm with a growing number of partners and associates in six offices: three in New Jersey (Phillipsburg, Rochelle Park, and Cherry Hill), two in Pennsylvania (Bethlehem and Harrisburg), and one in New York City.

Let me make it clear I am not what you might think of as a traditional lawyer. The British draw a distinction between a barrister, who represents clients in court, and a solicitor, who advises clients and undertakes negotiations. I have essentially functioned as a solicitor.

My practice of law draws on the knowledge I acquired by writing laws as a legislator and executing laws as governor. I have advised clients in subject areas I know something about—environment, energy, transportation, and health care—and I have tried to help them understand, comply with, and, where appropriate, work to modify the laws that govern their activities.

In this respect, my legal career has been more or less an extension of my political career. I am still, at heart, a policy wonk.

Much of my legal representation involves converting public issues into private opportunities. For example, one of my clients was Rollins Environmental, which operates landfills and incinerators, including incinerators licensed to burn hazardous waste.

Rollins retained me because a provision in the federal law allowed cement kilns to burn hazardous waste without using the same safety-improvement technology that regulated hazardous waste companies were required to have. This put Rollins at a competitive disadvantage.

We created an organization called ART, the Association for Responsible Treatment. We went out and recruited other companies that, like Rollins, were being disadvantaged by the loophole in the federal law. The organization took its case to Congress and succeeded in getting the law changed—not to grant the regulated companies the same exemption enjoyed by the cement kilns, but instead to subject the cement kilns to the same technology required of the regulated companies.

This change served two important purposes. It leveled the playing field, eliminating a provision that had created unfair competition. And it advanced public policy, holding all companies involved in hazardous waste incineration to the same high standard of safety-improvement technology. It was a good outcome, and it was good business.

More recently, I was retained by a town in Burlington County to fight a hazardous waste incinerator a company was proposing to build across the river in Bristol, Pennsylvania. If the company had done all the necessary preparatory studies, including air monitoring, to show that the facility would not adversely affect public health and the environment on the New Jersey side of the Delaware, I would not have taken the case. But the company didn't. So I did.

There was one distinct difference between this case and most of my legal work: I made a personal appearance on behalf of my client before an adjudicatory body.

Hazardous waste incineration is regulated under the Resource Conservation and Recovery Act, the landmark 1976 law of which I happened to be a principal congressional sponsor. I used my personal knowledge of the details of the law in my appearance before the Bristol Planning Board, arguing that the zoning variance sought by the company ran counter to the spirit of the legislation and violated the regulatory provisions established to uphold the law. My argument carried the day, and the incinerator proposal died an appropriate death.

Not all of my legal representation has been in the field of hazardous waste incineration. In fact, a great deal of it has been in the areas of health care and energy. During the first term of the Clinton administration, when health care reform was a particularly hot national issue, I was retained by several pharmaceutical companies seeking advice on how to deal with the changes being contemplated in Washington. I was also consulted regularly by officials in the administration, as well as members of Congress, on the health care and welfare reforms we had put in place in New Jersey.

Energy has been a particular interest of mine. There is such a close connection between both the production and consumption of energy and the quality of the environment that the fields are really interrelated. That's one of the reasons we combined the Board of Public Utilities and its Energy Office with the Department of Environmental Protection in my administration. It became the DEPE—the Department of Environmental Protection and Energy—with overlapping jurisdiction that reflected the synergy between energy and the environment. Regrettably, this logical marriage was broken up shortly after I left office.

For the first few months of my life after government, I concentrated most of my attention on my law practice. In September 1994, however, I started teaching at Rutgers. It was a source of relatively modest income, but brought rich intellectual rewards. It also meant dividing my time (and driving myself) between a townhouse outside Princeton, a law office in Morristown, and a classroom in New Brunswick.

It was time to find a new place to live.

⤜⤛

Lucinda and I started looking for a house in a town that would be more convenient to my two workplaces. Highland Park met that specification, and some new homes were being built there on a bluff overlooking the

Raritan River. So we went to look at a very nice house in our price range. We liked it and gave serious consideration to buying it—until someone suggested we come back and check it out at around 5:00 on a weekday afternoon.

Unless you live in or near Middlesex County, you might not be aware of what Route 18 looks like—and sounds like—at rush hour. But if you're thinking about buying a house that overlooks Route 18, you'd be well advised to acquaint yourself with the sights and sounds the highway produces at rush hour. Lucinda and I availed ourselves of the 5 o'clock experience and promptly decided to start looking for a quieter spot a few miles away in Metuchen.

Our Dutch colonial in a lovely residential neighborhood in Metuchen was a perfect fit for us. For fifteen years, I spent my weeknights in an apartment over a liquor store in Washington, D.C. For about five of those years, I lived with Lucinda on the weekends, first at our Pine Hill apartment and later in our Gloucester Township townhouse. Then, for four years, we lived in the governor's mansion that was in an almost constant state of renovation and repair. After that, for a year, we lived in a rented furnished townhouse. Now, for the first time in our lives, we had our own permanent home.

I became perhaps the most regular and loyal customer of the Metuchen Municipal Library. Lucinda threw herself into a host of civic activities. I was known by most people around town simply as Lucinda's husband—except when I led a community revolt against a zoning change that would have taken down two houses and put up five in a lovely wooded area right across the street from our house.

Call me a NIMBY (Not In My Back Yard) if you like, but I prefer to think that I was, as one of the local newspapers described me, a "citizen activist," mobilizing our neighbors to fight the zoning change. And we won. Instead of replacing two houses with five, the developer took down one old house, put up a new one in its place, and left the rest of the wooded area intact. I drew almost as much satisfaction from this outcome as I did from some of my legislative and gubernatorial accomplishments.

I also drew enormous satisfaction from teaching. I think teaching was always in my blood. When I enrolled at Trenton State College in 1958, the school had just changed its name from the New Jersey State Teachers College at Trenton. Most of my classmates and virtually everyone who had attended the college before I arrived planned to become teachers. When I spent the year after graduation at Columbia University, I was on a Woodrow Wilson Fellowship designed to prepare people for teaching at the college level.

I have tried to approach teaching in much the same way as I approached lawmaking and governing. It's all about engaging and informing your audience, whether you're dealing with a class of a dozen undergraduate or graduate students or a congressional district of hundreds of thousands or a state of eight million. At the college level, the goal is to turn passive students into active thinkers, challenging them not to simply accept and regurgitate what *I* think, but to figure out for themselves and explain to me what *they* think.

In some classes, this is easy. Especially at the graduate level, the students aren't intimidated by having a former governor as their teacher, and they welcome the opportunity to express their own views on a wide variety of subjects. Undergraduate classes can be more difficult. The students are less accustomed to the idea that their professor doesn't want them to submit papers repeating what he or she said in class, but rather to present a reasoned analysis of their own conclusions.

In many of my classes I played the devil's advocate. The subject of my course, which I taught for more than twenty years, was the formulation of public policy, and as I would introduce a particular issue—say, environment or energy or health care—I would purposely say something provocative or even totally outrageous just to get a response. Sometimes it took a lot of prodding, but eventually one of the students would react and another student would present a different view, and then we could truly begin a robust discussion of the issue.

This was the process of engagement, and from this process the students gathered the information they needed to formulate reasonable and responsible positions on public policy issues.

~~~

One of the most eye-opening conclusions I drew from my two decades of teaching is how much—and how quickly—things change.

I separated my public policy course into three units. The first two were always environment and energy; the third might be health care, education, transportation, or another subject area, depending on what issue happened to be of particular relevance or urgency. I look back now on the notes I used in my classes twenty or ten or even five years ago, and I marvel at how totally outdated they have become.

I vividly remember the class discussions we had when First Lady Hillary Clinton was heading up the effort to reform health care during my first year of teaching. They could not have been more different from the discussions we had fifteen years later during the debate over Obamacare. Many of the core issues were the same—quality, access, and affordability chief among them—but the public conversation had changed radically, from an emphasis on policy to a preoccupation with politics.

In the 1990s, nobody had ever heard of the process of hydraulic fracturing to extract natural gas from shale. Today you can't have a meaningful discussion about energy (or the environment, for that matter) without devoting a lot of attention to fracking.

I have found that students are, for the most part, very receptive to new ideas and concepts. In this respect, they are more amenable and adaptable to change than the voters at large. They are easier to engage and inform. They give me hope for the future—because their ability to accept and adapt to change, which is happening all around them at an ever-increasing pace, will be critically important to our state, our nation, and our world.

Today's younger generation strikes me as being much more interested in civic affairs than in politics. In fact, they seem to think so poorly of politics (and politicians) that they shy away from engaging in anything that smacks of political activism. I have suggested they should think of politics as the means to an end, not as an end in itself. Like it or not, politics is the vehicle for getting directly involved—and, ultimately, having the ability to effect change—in civic life. When students would tell me they found the practice of politics distasteful, I would offer a simple solution. It's up to you, I said, to change it.

In addition to the pleasure I took from energizing and challenging students, one of the joys of my affiliation with Rutgers was having an office on the third floor of the Heldrich Center for Workforce Development, part of the Edward J. Bloustein School of Planning and Public Policy. There I was surrounded by academic experts in many different fields, including my former policy director, Carl Van Horn. The Heldrich Center was a virtual think tank for discussing and analyzing new government, business, and labor policies. Sharing ideas with Carl and others, exploring new ways to deal with increasingly complex public policy issues, was as intellectually satisfying as it was stimulating.

I also served for a time as a public service professor in residence at Monmouth University. This was a very different kind of teaching for me. Instead of generating and moderating give-and-take sessions with small groups of students, I prepared and delivered lectures to much larger audiences. If my Rutgers classes were a lot like the town hall meetings I used to hold as a member of Congress, my Monmouth appearances were more like the speeches I gave as governor.

The main point I have tried to make in all the classes, lectures, and speeches I have given in recent years is that the change we're experiencing now is unprecedented. It is dramatic. It is rapid. It is complex.

The dilemma of our time—and the challenge that confronts the next generation of leaders in our country and around the world—is that change is occurring far more rapidly than it ever has in the past, and it is outpacing our ability to formulate the policies needed to deal with its consequences. We are behind the curve.

We have to find ways to get ahead of the curve and confront this change. Applying old policies, old laws, and old rules and regulations to new issues and new problems is just not going to work. We need to develop new policies, new laws, and new rules and regulations—in other words, a whole new strategic approach to problem solving—if we are going to adapt effectively to change.

The first step is to become engaged and informed. The second step, for those students I hope to have inspired in my Rutgers classes and my Monmouth lectures, is to get involved in the development and implementation of public policy that acknowledges and adapts to change.

Whether they run for office themselves or advise someone else who does, whether they serve in the executive, legislative, or judicial branch at the municipal, county, state, or federal level, it is their commitment to managing and directing the forces of change in the public interest that will allow our participatory democracy to survive and flourish.

⟪⟫

In 1982, after I lost the gubernatorial race to Tom Kean, I gave a passing thought to running for the U.S. Senate. I think I could have won that race. The seat was open, having been vacated by Harrison Williams in the wake of the Abscam scandal. Governor Kean had appointed Nicholas Brady to serve as a caretaker until the next election.

The Democratic primary field that year was as crowded as ever—ten candidates, including my fellow congressman, Andy Maguire of Bergen County; my former congressional colleague, Joe LeFante of Hudson County; my future gubernatorial primary competitor, Barbara Sigmund of Princeton; and a businessman and political newcomer named Frank Lautenberg.

On the Republican side were Congresswoman Millicent Fenwick and Jeffrey Bell, who had lost the 1978 Senate race to Bill Bradley.

I chose not to run that year, in part because I had just lost a statewide race by a razor-thin margin and didn't look kindly on the prospect of spending back-to-back years campaigning from one end of New Jersey to the other. In addition, some of my most prized pieces of legislation, in particular the Superfund law, were under attack by the Reagan adminis- tration, and I felt I was better positioned to save them as a veteran mem- ber of the House of Representatives than I would have been as a freshman senator.

Lautenberg wound up winning the Democratic primary with 25 percent of the vote and in the general election upset Fenwick to win the Senate seat. He won re-election in 1988 and 1994 before announcing he would not run again in 2000.

When the 2000 Senate race was approaching, there was growing senti- ment around South Jersey that someone with roots south of the Raritan River should occupy one of New Jersey's two seats in the U.S. Senate. The seat Bill Bradley had held for three terms after his 1978 victory was then occupied by Bob Torricelli of Bergen County. The seat that was now open had been held for eighteen years by Senator Lautenberg, a native of Pater- son who maintained a residence in Secaucus.

I was approached by a number of people from South Jersey who felt enough time had passed since my narrow re-election loss in the 1993 gubernatorial race to make me a viable candidate in the 2000 U.S. Sen- ate race. There were no other prominent Democrats lining up to run. At the top of the ticket, the early polling gave Al Gore a commanding lead over George W. Bush in New Jersey. It was a race that certainly looked winnable.

I was very comfortable with the idea of returning to Washington. I knew from my fifteen years in the House of Representatives how the pro- cess worked. I was confident I knew the substance of most of the issues. I felt I had a good understanding of New Jersey and what its citizens wanted their senators to do for them.

There was one striking similarity and one glaring difference between the 1982 U.S. Senate race and the 2000 contest. The similarity was the presence in both Democratic primaries of a wealthy political novice. In 1982, it was Frank Lautenberg. In 2000, it was Jon Corzine. The difference was the size of the Democratic primary field. In 1982, ten candidates were running. In 2000, there were only two.

I started out feeling I could win the Democratic nomination by running my campaign on the issues. After our first debate, I felt even more confident that my knowledge and experience would carry the day. Here's how *Bergen Record* columnist Mike Kelly summed up the debate:

> It's always dangerous for journalists to name winners and losers in political debates; ultimately the voters decide. But naming Jim Florio the winner of this debate is an easy call. After just 30 minutes of watching the meticulous Florio verbally pound his opponent, you almost wished a referee had intervened and rescued Corzine. For all his Wall Street money and talk about "bold ideas," Corzine came off just as many Democratic strategists silently fear—a rookie who needs to passionately tell voters what he stands for and why.

By the time primary day came around, however, it was evident that the strategy of running my campaign on the issues couldn't make up for the reality of running my campaign on a shoestring.

In my three general election campaigns for governor, I accepted the limits on both contributions and spending imposed by the state's public financing law. After my very able fundraisers, Lewis Katz and Karen Kessler, had collected enough contributions to reach a specified threshold of individual donations, the state provided matching funds up to a statutory limit established by the legislature and enforced by the Election Law Enforcement Commission. Both the size of individual contributions and the total amount spent on the campaign were limited by law.

The 2000 Senate primary bore no resemblance at all to my gubernatorial general election campaigns. I raised and spent about $2.5 million, nearly all of it in the form of individual donations. Jon Corzine spent $35 million, nearly all of it his own money. A headline in *The Hill* just a few days before the June primary pretty much summed up the race: "Florio vs. Corzine Pits Experience vs. Money."

The *New York Times* later put what it described as Corzine's "jaw-dropping spending spree" in perspective. He spent roughly $141.50 for each of the 251,216 primary votes he received. I spent $13.89 for each of the 182,212 votes I got.

I ran as good a race as I could on a $2.5 million budget. I have no regrets about the one last run I made at statewide elective office, and I was not at all concerned about Jon Corzine's ability to do a good job representing New Jersey in the U.S. Senate. What alarmed me—and alarms me even more today, as campaign spending continues to spiral out of control—is the increasingly influential role of money in politics. I do not begrudge a millionaire wanting to serve the public, but I do begrudge a system that makes it nearly impossible for a person of more limited means to have the same aspiration.

When Bill Clinton was elected president in November 1992, there was a brief flurry of rumors that I might resign the governorship to join the new administration in Washington, perhaps as administrator of the Environmental Protection Agency. There was no substance to the rumors. (The irony, as it turned out, is that this is precisely what Governor Whitman did eight years later.)

When I was defeated for re-election in November 1993, the rumor mill started up again, though its grist was no more substantive than it had been a year earlier. However, I was pleased to accept President Clinton's invitation to serve on the Secretary of Energy's Advisory Board and also to offer my advice and assistance in crafting federal legislation that mirrored New Jersey's successful efforts to ban assault weapons and reform welfare.

There was one federal appointment, however, that opened up a whole new world to me. In 1999, the Clinton administration appointed me chairman of the Board of Directors of the Federal Home Loan Bank of New York. This congressionally chartered bank is a major source of credit for home mortgages and neighborhood lending programs that support hous-ing opportunities and local community development initiatives in New York, New Jersey, Puerto Rico, and the Virgin Islands.

I have always had a strong interest in housing and community devel-opment, dating to my representation of Camden in both the state assem-bly and the Congress. Many of the economic development programs I championed as governor—in Newark, Atlantic City, Camden, and elsewhere—represented the kind of public-private partnerships in which the Federal Home Loan Bank is heavily involved.

One of my major interests in elective office was promoting the public policies of homeownership, neighborhood revitalization, and community development as a means of helping my constituents achieve the Ameri-can dream. What I was less familiar with, and what the chairmanship of the bank board taught me, were the intricacies of the actual financing of the mortgage and community development programs. It was the accumu-lation of this financial knowledge that set me on a path, one year later, to try my hand, for the first time in my life, at being a businessman.

The business in this case was a company that redeemed delinquent liens and then securitized them for sale to investors. Right after my unsuc-cessful U.S. Senate bid in 2000, I was approached by some Wall Street people, who asked me if I would be willing to talk to them about start-ing a new company that would specialize in buying up tax liens in New Jersey.

I hesitated. My initial reaction was that I didn't want to profit from other people's misfortune. Liens are essentially a last resort to force prop-erty owners to pay their back taxes. Buying them up struck me as the kind of thing a collection agency does.

As I learned more about the business, however, I came to understand the company's objective was not just to collect delinquent taxes. Rather, it was to buy the liens that are offered at auction by municipalities, school districts, and other public entities that are unable to collect the taxes. This provided them revenue they would otherwise have forgone, and also provided the company the opportunity to bundle the liens and sell them as a package to private sector investors.

The company was called Xspand, Inc., and it was a classic risk-reward venture. The key to success was to recognize the value of the properties on which the liens were placed and bid accordingly at auction. If the pieces of land whose liens the company bought were undervalued—if, for example, they had potential for development or redevelopment—the liens could command a higher price when they were subsequently sold to investors.

As it turned out, this was a highly profitable business. Xspand grew from a small company doing business in New Jersey to a national company with clients ranging from the City of Camden to the Los Angeles School District. We employed sixty to seventy full-time workers. And there was genuine public benefit to the work we were doing.

Camden, for example, was carrying $120 million worth of uncollected taxes, which the city had no real hope of collecting. Many of the property owners were too poor to pay the taxes they owed, and our company worked with banks to make low-interest loans available to those folks who were going through tough times. I was especially proud that Xspand was recognized and praised for initiating this humanitarian effort.

At the same time, there were a fair number of absentee landlords and out-of-state speculators who simply weren't paying what they owed the city. These delinquent taxpayers were required by law to pay 18 percent interest on the liens against their property, and we had no hesitation, after purchasing their liens, about going after these tax cheats for the money they owed.

In this respect, we actually were a collection agency—but we weren't going after poor people who couldn't afford to pay their taxes. We were going after tax cheats, unscrupulous landlords, and others who clearly could afford to pay their taxes but weren't.

The City of Camden benefited by getting its money from my company. The company benefited by securitizing the liens and selling them at a profit to Wall Street investors.

I was the chairman and CEO of Xspand from 2000 to 2006, when the company was sold to Bear Stearns—which, in turn, sold it to J. P. Morgan before Bear Stearns went belly up in 2008.

This later-in-life experience in the private sector left me with mixed impressions. On the one hand, I think I might have been a better public official if I had gotten some private sector experience before becoming involved in government. Understanding how businesses operate, how they make decisions, and how laws and rules and regulations affect them would have broadened my appreciation of the framework in which the private sector operates and of the practical impact that public policies have on private enterprises.

On the other hand, the profit motive is so strong in the private sector that it tends to dwarf any and all other considerations. There is an almost visceral reaction against government regulation of any sort, no matter how meritorious its purpose. I like to think Xspand did well by doing good—serving a worthy public purpose in addition to making a profit—but for some of its investors, the company's bottom line was the only thing that really mattered.

In any event, the experience was both fulfilling and rewarding for me. I enjoyed running a business, and I'm perfectly willing to confess, I enjoyed making money.

⚜

By the time I sold Xspand, my term on the Federal Home Loan Bank Board had expired, and President George W. Bush had found a suitable Republican to replace me as chairman. Long before that, however, I was offered another chairmanship—and this one was considerably nearer and dearer to my heart.

The New Jersey Pinelands Commission was created in 1979 to protect the Pinelands National Preserve, which was established under a law I had sponsored the previous year in Congress. Throughout the 1980s, I paid close attention to the actions taken by the commission to adopt and

implement the Comprehensive Management Plan that guided development in this environmentally sensitive region. As governor in the early
1990s, I appointed commissioners who observed both the spirit and the
letter of the state's Pinelands Protection Act.

Thereafter, I watched in some dismay as the Pinelands Commission
came under growing pressure to ease restrictions on development, roll
back drinking water quality standards, and otherwise undermine the
protections afforded by two decades of stewardship under four governors.

Shortly after he was elected in 2001, Governor Jim McGreevey contacted me and said he was concerned that the Pinelands Commission was
in disarray. In addition to the usual conflicts between developers and
environmentalists, there were internecine battles between Democratic
and Republican members of the commission, as well as administrative
tensions between commission members and staff.

Governor McGreevey urged me to accept a three-year appointment as
chairman of the Pinelands Commission. I had some trepidation about
getting so heavily involved, especially with the responsibilities of my
teaching, my law practice, and my new business venture. What's more,
Lucinda, who frets every time I get behind the wheel of a car, told me
point-blank the only way she'd let me take round trips between Metuchen
and the Pinelands was with a driver.

"You have to do this," McGreevey persisted. "You're very much identified with the Pinelands." The commission was having serious problems,
he said, and I was uniquely qualified to "go down there and pull it out." I
told him I would do it on one condition: he would authorize a State Police
car to drive me back and forth between the Pinelands and Metuchen.
"Fine," he said without hesitation.

So I spent the next three years faithfully attending and presiding over the
meetings of the Pinelands Commission. The governor was right; the commission was in disarray, and it needed both a steadying hand and an openness to a healthy exchange of ideas and philosophies. Serious differences

had developed between factions on the commission, and between the com-mission and the staff, and they were hardening into open distrust.

I made no secret of the fact that I considered myself an environmen-talist and that I believed strongly in the Pinelands Commission's mission to preserve, protect, and enhance one of New Jersey's most precious natu-ral resources. But I also understood that those who favored easing devel-opment restrictions outside the core Protection Area designated in the Comprehensive Management Plan did not think of themselves as any less devoted to preservation of the Pinelands than I was.

To be sure, there were some who, given the opportunity, would have run roughshod over our Pinelands protection measures, and neither the majority of the commission nor I had any difficulty thwarting their efforts. Many of the contentious issues that arose in the Pinelands, how-ever, were like most public policy issues—not easily categorized as black or white. Rather, they were disagreements at the margins, and as long as everyone kept an open mind and an open dialogue, there were often ways to find agreement without sacrificing principles—not always, but often enough to make the effort more than worthwhile.

This was the abiding philosophy I brought to the Pinelands Commis-sion. It was the same philosophy I employed throughout my fifteen years in Congress and tried to exercise as governor, especially in the second half of my term, when I was dealing with an overwhelmingly Republican leg-islature. Reasonable people may differ, but they can differ reasonably—and if they are willing to sit down, discuss, and analyze their differences and seek common ground, as often as not they will find it.

Some people kid me that if I were a woman I'd always be pregnant—because I say yes to everybody. They're right. But the truth is that just about everything I say yes to is something I'm interested in. At the top of that list are organizations involved in planning.

If there is one serious shortcoming I have observed about government at all levels, it is a failure to plan. Most politicians are reactive rather than proactive, and most of the governmental bodies on which they serve tend to react to crises rather than head them off before they arise.

There are many reasons for this. For starters, the immediate concern for most elective officeholders is the next election. If the unflattering acronym applied to citizens who oppose change in their neighborhoods is NIMBY (Not In My Back Yard), the counterpart for politicians who resist change is NIMTO (Not In My Term of Office). In politics, it is almost always easier to put off an issue until it's somebody else's problem than to confront it yourself.

Planning involves change—and change creates winners and losers.

Deciding where a town is going to allow single-family or multi-family housing, where it's going to permit commercial or industrial development, where it's going to set aside land for a school or a park or open space, where it's going to build a sewage treatment plant—all of these decisions raise or lower property values, creating winners and losers.

Deciding where a county or state will encourage or discourage land development, where it will build highways and extend sewer lines, where it will build a prison or a solid waste incinerator—all of these decisions create winners and losers.

Deciding whether the federal government should lower taxes to stimulate the economy or raise them to invest in infrastructure, whether health care should be considered a right or a privilege, whether the threat of climate change should shift our energy production from fossil fuels to renewables—all of these decisions create winners and losers.

And it is a sad fact of political life that some of those who are already well off will spend whatever it takes to elect the mayors and municipal council members, the county freeholders, the state legislators, and the congressional representatives who will stand in the way of change and defend the status quo.

One of my last official acts as governor was issuing an executive order that posed a direct challenge to the status quo. It required that all state agencies follow a policy that directed housing, highway, transportation, water, and sewer funds to already developed areas.

This was, in effect, an effort to implement the land-use policies spelled out in the State Development and Redevelopment Plan—a document, more commonly called the State Plan, that described in considerable detail how and where New Jersey should direct future growth and development.

At its core, the State Plan held that public sector infrastructure investment should guide private sector development, rather than vice versa. Much of New Jersey's suburban sprawl came about because investments made by the private sector (with the acquiescence of local politicians) turned farmland into housing developments, which in turn led to enormous public investment in roads, sewers, schools, and other supporting infrastructure— much of it borne by the state.

Meanwhile, the infrastructure that already existed in New Jersey's cities was being underused, neglected, and/or falling into disrepair. It made more sense, as I saw it, to encourage private investment in areas that were already developed, where infrastructure already existed, than to commit public funds to costly new infrastructure projects in support of private investment in places where the State Plan specifically called for limited growth and development.

Regrettably, my executive order was never implemented, and the State Plan has largely proved to be an exercise in futility. I continue to actively support its vision, however, by my involvement in two nonprofit organizations committed to sound state and regional planning: the Regional Plan Association and New Jersey Future.

I have also worked with a number of Rutgers-affiliated planning groups involved in transportation and environmental policy, including the Alan M. Voorhees Transportation Center and the New Jersey Climate Change Adaptation Alliance. In the field of health care, I have worked with the nonprofit New Jersey Health Care Quality Institute, whose purpose is to undertake projects that will ensure that quality, safety, accountability, and cost containment measures inform the delivery of health care in New Jersey.

And I am especially proud to serve on the board of the Fund for New Jersey, a philanthropy that works to improve the quality of public policy decision making on the most significant issues affecting our state.

In all of these areas—land use, transportation, environment, and health care—it is my view that government should be doing the planning, with the support of nonprofits. Instead, it is the nonprofit sector that is doing the planning, with little or no government support.

To quote one of those aphorisms that has been variously attributed to Benjamin Franklin, Winston Churchill, and a host of others, "Failing to plan is planning to fail."

As much as I wish government would assume the mantle of leadership in this area, I will continue to support the state and regional planning efforts being carried out by public, private, and nonprofit organizations that are committed to making New Jersey a better place to live and work.

CHAPTER 11

The Issues I Still Care About

Old policies can't solve new problems.

One thing I have learned over the course of my public, private, and academic careers is that every major issue affecting people's daily lives and the conduct of government is as relevant today as it was more than fifty years ago.

The motto of Rutgers University—"Ever-changing yet eternally the same"—reflects how I think about the issues that confront us today.

I still speak out on many of the following issues:

• The environmental crisis that lies ahead if we fail to take steps now to combat global climate change;

• The carnage we continue to inflict on ourselves as we consistently fail to take the necessary steps to control the spread of deadly weapons;

• The need to repair our crumbling infrastructure before smooth highway surfaces, structurally sound bridges and tunnels, functioning water and sewer pipes, and efficient mass transit systems become a distant memory;

• The disparity between rich and poor—between world-class suburban schools and crumbling inner-city schools, between college-bound high school graduates and dead-end high school dropouts—that can only be resolved by redirecting resources;

- The borrow-and-spend recklessness that has jeopardized our public pension systems and perpetuates structural budget deficits that now imperil the fiscal solvency of towns, cities, and states across the country; and
- The obscene sums of money that special interests contribute, and candidates for public office spend, undermining our faith in the electoral process.

While the issues may remain constant, the world is continually changing, and the challenge of meeting society's needs, in a fair and equitable way, is changing as well. It requires new ideas and forward-thinking public servants, who think more of solving their constituents' problems than of satisfying themselves. And it requires, as it always has, a citizenry that is engaged and informed in this messy process of self-government.

If I had known twenty-five years ago what I know now—from teaching, business, and other parts of my life—I would probably have been a better governor. But I am at peace with who I was—and who I am. My intense interest in public policy hasn't waned, but family and friends have become more important in my life, and for that I am enormously thankful.

⟨⟨⟨⟨⟩

The issues I still care about share many characteristics. For the most part, they pit vested interests wedded to the status quo against the broader public interest that compels change. They require long-term thinking and planning in an age of immediate gratification and increasingly short attention spans. Their resolution depends on an engaged and informed electorate at a time of growing apathy and abysmally low voter turnout.

Climate change is an issue that embodies all of these characteristics and more.

The vested interests wedded to the status quo are the industries that produce and consume fossil fuels. They are the companies that manufacture, trade in, or are dependent on oil, gas, and coal—aided and abetted, to a large extent, by the automobile industry. The short-term profit motive for the energy companies and the auto manufacturers drives them to keep producing and using fossil fuels, despite the overwhelming scientific evidence that carbon emissions from the burning of these fuels pose an existential threat to planet Earth.

The public interest demands that we reduce our dependence on fossil fuels and shift to cleaner sources of energy—solar, wind, geothermal, even nuclear. But this requires the kind of long-term thinking and planning that is very difficult for government to engage in, even on matters that have achieved a large measure of consensus.

The fossil fuel industry takes maximum advantage of government's reluctance to put long-term benefits ahead of short-term political considerations. It challenges the science. It lavishes bountiful campaign contributions on candidates who will pick up the mantle of climate change denial and vigorously defend the status quo. And it relies on the apathy of voters to ensure that industry's voice will speak louder than theirs.

The fossil fuel industry's strategy on climate policy is virtually identical to the weapons industry's strategy on gun control.

It is in the vested interest of American gun manufacturers to produce and sell as many weapons as they can, despite the fact that the United States is the undisputed world leader in gun-related deaths. More Americans have died from gunfire in the last fifty years than in all the wars in the nation's history combined.

The gun manufacturers have an enormously vocal and powerful ally in the National Rifle Association, whose members can be counted on to vigorously defend their "right to bear arms" under the Second Amendment to the U.S. Constitution whenever a reasonable gun control measure is proposed. As I noted in chapter 1, the overwhelming majority of gun owners I have met over the years are responsible people who have no interest in owning, and see no need for anyone else to own, an arsenal of high-powered semiautomatic weapons.

But as soon as the status quo is challenged, the NRA is mobilized to do the gun manufacturers' bidding. In the wake of mass shootings in Connecticut, Colorado, Florida, California, Nevada, and elsewhere, reasonable efforts to limit the sale of assault weapons went nowhere. Requiring background checks for gun purchasers with a history of mental illness went nowhere. The vast majority of Americans—including a majority of NRA members—support responsible gun control measures, but the public interest has carried little weight against the organized, battle-tested, and free-spending vested interests.

Again, an engaged and informed public could—and should—prevail over the narrow interests of a single-issue group. I firmly believe this is what we accomplished in New Jersey by adopting, and then beating back attempts to repeal, the toughest assault weapons ban in the country. I am enormously proud of the fact that this law continues in effect a quarter-century later. I am dismayed, however, that it did not become the first of many such bans around the country.

A similar effort at the national level didn't have the same staying power. The federal assault weapons ban, adopted in 1994, expired after ten years, and repeated attempts since then to reinstate it have been killed by the gun manufacturers, the NRA, and the congressional representatives whose campaigns they have so generously supported.

On both of these issues—climate change and assault weapons—cold, hard facts are apparently no match for cold, hard cash. It is a sad commentary on the state of politics in modern America that the fossil fuel industry and the gun manufacturers carry more influence in Washington than we, the people.

⟨⟨⟨⟨

Our failure to address our infrastructure needs and our chronic underfunding of public education, public pensions, and other basic functions of government stem from a much deeper problem. Ever since the days of the Boston Tea Party, we Americans have had an aversion to bearing what we perceive as an undue burden of taxation. Today, however, many of us seem to be averse to paying any taxes at all.

Years ago, we accepted our responsibility to invest in programs and services that not only provided immediate benefit to us but also improved opportunities for future generations. We built highways and bridges and tunnels to promote the efficient movement of people and goods. We built water and sewer systems that fostered growth and development and improved public health and sanitation. We built elementary and secondary schools and public colleges and universities, and provided generous subsidies so that our children would have opportunities far beyond those available to us.

Somewhere along the line—and I would trace it directly to Ronald Reagan's reckless assertion that government, rather than being the solution to problems, *is* the problem—we turned away from some of our core civic responsibilities. We stopped investing in infrastructure: we let our highways and bridges and tunnels deteriorate, and we allowed our water and sewer systems to suffer from extreme neglect. We reduced public education aid and slashed subsidies, forcing college students to incur unimaginable levels of debt.

In New Jersey, we reneged on our commitment to teachers and other public employees. While they continued to make the required annual contributions to their pensions, the state government routinely and cavalierly skipped its matching contributions, plunging the pension fund into crisis. This also happened in other states and in many cities and towns across the country.

I speak from experience when I say that I am fully aware of the political consequences of raising taxes. But I am much more compelled by the economic and social consequences of *not* raising taxes, of instead cutting them to the point where we fail to provide even the most basic services that citizens have a right to expect and demand.

In medicine, it is said that an ounce of prevention is worth a pound of cure. In government, the corollary is that dollars spent today to fix potholes or shore up bridges will save millions when the highways don't collapse and the bridges don't fall down. Tax dollars spent today on our children's education will be recouped many times over in the future productivity of a highly trained and knowledgeable workforce.

As I have often said, if you don't like the cost of education, think about the cost of ignorance.

I am concerned that today's high school students may become the first generation in American history that will not have greater opportunities than their parents had. I am concerned that today's college students will be so burdened with debt that it will take them years longer than their parents to become financially secure, buy a house, and raise a family. I am concerned that the combination of a shrinking middle class in the United States and an exploding middle class in China and India will create intense international competition for technology, goods, services, and jobs, potentially erecting even higher barriers in America to upward mobility.

In short, I believe we have sacrificed making critical investments in our future in pursuit of immediate personal gratification. Or, to put it another way, we have failed to make the necessary sacrifices today to assure our collective gratification in the future.

$\sim$

Daniel Yankelovich makes an important distinction in his book, *Coming to Public Judgment: Making Democracy Work in a Complex World.* What Yankelovich posits, and this was very meaningful to me when I first read it in graduate school, is that there is a substantial difference between public opinion and public judgment.

Public opinion is a snapshot in time of people's impressions. In contrast, public judgment is the process of taking time to evaluate, with some degree of thoughtfulness, what the options and alternatives are and then making a rational decision with all the facts one can gather.

Too often in our current political climate, we pay inordinate attention to public opinion—people's immediate and visceral reactions to issues or events—while failing to provide sufficient time, information, or context for them to arrive at public judgment.

The mass media are obsessed with poll numbers. Political consultants build their campaign strategies around poll numbers. Politicians pander to their constituents in direct response to poll numbers. This means that public opinion, rather than public judgment, is driving public policy—a condition that violates a fundamental truth about human nature: what's popular isn't always what's right.

Denying women the right to vote was once popular in America. So was child labor. Internment of Japanese Americans in camps during World War II was popular. In the South, slavery was popular. So were segregated schools and Jim Crow laws. This didn't make any of them right.

The process of arriving at public judgment is complicated and time consuming, which makes it all the more difficult in an era when the issues are increasingly complex and the political rhetoric prizes simplicity. Democracy works by achieving compromise and consensus, but consensus becomes elusive when the issues are so complex they are often difficult for people even to comprehend, much less thoughtfully analyze and evaluate.

I have always felt that politicians should think of themselves as teachers with a big classroom. They have an obligation to give people an understanding of the full dimensions of the problems we face and what the options are for resolving them. We can't fix what we don't understand— and in a participatory democracy, the need to understand ultimately rests with the body politic.

One of the biggest problems we face in our current political climate is the way we frame issues. Instead of treating them as problems to solve, too often we look at them and talk about them in stark ideological terms. Think, for example, of how we have approached the issue of the inheritance tax.

In the Middle Ages in Europe, the lords of the manor used to hand down their wealth and power to their heirs, who maintained their inheritance for generations. In the twentieth century in the more egalitarian

"Perhaps the greatest challenge we face in trying to deal with the complex and contentious issues that confront us is our adherence to the misguided belief that old policies can solve new problems. The issues we are facing today are so multifaceted and so consequential that they require much deeper thought and study than our political institutions are devoting to them." —James J. Florio

United States, we made the collective decision that some portion of the wealth a family gathered as a result of living in a land of abundant opportunity should be given back—to help pay for education, the infrastructure, public safety, health and welfare, and other government-funded functions and actions from which they benefited.

An extremely small but enormously wealthy portion of the electorate has fought back against this policy, arguing that millions of dollars in inherited wealth should be exempted from inheritance taxes. And they have found receptive audiences in Congress and state legislatures, where their campaign contributions carry considerable weight.

But it isn't only the wealthy and their money that have taken aim against the inheritance tax. It is now an accepted principle of mainstream American conservatism that the "death tax," as opponents have derided it, is an unfair penalty paid by people who have earned their wealth and that they should be under no obligation to give it back to the government. The underlying premise, carved into another pillar of popular conservatism, is that the government would only waste it anyway.

Only a tiny percentage of Americans will ever have to pay inheritance taxes. All the rest of us, including an overwhelming majority of card-carrying conservatives, will never have to pay them. But, like those Hands Across New Jersey members told me when I met them in my office all those years ago, all Americans aspire to wealth—and if they ever achieve it, they don't want to share any of it with the government.

It seems to me the public interest would dictate that some amount of money earned as a result of living in this country ought to come back to the country, rather than simply being transferred to the next magnate in the family line. But when the issue is framed differently, when opposition to the "death tax" becomes a symbol of ideological purity, the public interest has been outmaneuvered.

Perhaps the greatest challenge we face in trying to deal with the complex and contentious issues that confront us is our adherence to the misguided belief that old policies can solve new problems. The issues we are facing today—in areas ranging from the regulation of sophisticated financial instruments to the equitable and efficient delivery of health care—are so multifaceted and so consequential that they require much deeper thought and study than our political institutions are devoting to them.

It isn't enough just to think outside the box about these issues. We need to be looking at an entirely different box—because the ones we have been using do not contain the tools that are necessary to fix our most chronic problems.

Take financial regulation, for instance. Congress has spent a great deal of time and effort debating whether Wall Street should be subjected to stricter regulation in the wake of the 2008 financial meltdown. What has largely been ignored in this debate is that many of the regulations governing financial institutions grew out of policies adopted in the 1930s. The politicians and bureaucrats who wrote these regulations knew nothing about subprime mortgages or bundled loan portfolios. They had never heard of subprime credit default swaps, interest rate swaps, or other exotic derivative products.

We had a regulatory system built in the 1930s that was simply not relevant to the problems that arose seventy years later.

The current health care system is an even more glaring example of how we continue to rely on old policies to deal with new realities. This system (if it can even be called a system) evolved from World War II, when the federal government instituted both wage controls and price controls. Employers had to do something to attract employees, so many of them decided to expand benefits, including offering to pay the premiums for employees' health insurance.

Extending this benefit to employees was considered a good thing, and it made a lot of sense at the time. Insurers responded by providing lower rates for coverage purchased by large groups of policyholders. The government responded by changing the tax code, giving employers a financial incentive to provide health insurance to their employees.

For all the changes that have taken place in the last seventy years or so— including extraordinary advances in medical technology and treatment, along with ballooning costs, and the increasingly intense competition that

American businesses face from around the world—this is still the way most Americans get their health insurance. The employer still provides the insurance, although many employees have lately been required to pay a portion of their increasingly costly premiums. The company still gets a tax break for providing health insurance coverage to its employees. And the company, as it always has, rolls the cost of the health insurance it is providing into the price of its products.

For all the heat that has been generated in the debates over Medicare, Obamacare, Trumpcare, and every other health care measure that has come along since the end of World War II, very little light has been shone on how this reliance on business to be the primary provider of health insurance coverage has become unsustainable. While the insurance companies, the doctors, the hospitals, the pharmaceutical industry, and all the other parties with a stake in this debate fight over their pieces of the health care pie, and while the politicians frame the issue as a stark ideological battle between government-regulated medical care and free enterprise, the bigger picture, which is largely being ignored, is about how a public policy that was haphazardly developed seven decades ago is no longer relevant to today's world.

There is no business operating in any other industrialized nation in the world today that passes the cost of health care along to consumers in the price of its products. For much of the twentieth century, when American businesses sold all, or even most, of their products to American consumers, and when American consumers bought most, if not all, of their products from American businesses, this didn't matter very much. But in the increasingly competitive international marketplace of the twenty-first century, it matters a great deal.

Paying the health insurance premiums of millions of workers has placed American businesses today at a distinct competitive disadvantage. They are behind the curve. The cost of producing an automobile in the United States has been calculated at 10 percent higher than in other countries because of the cost to automobile manufacturers of providing health care. That is one of the reasons Ford and General Motors have shifted some of their manufacturing operations to Mexico.

We need to start framing the issue of health care in America in its broadest possible context—and raising questions about the challenges that lie ahead. Does a business-driven health insurance system that worked well after World War II still work well today? Does the current distribution of general practitioners and specialists between urban and rural areas result in the efficient delivery of health care? Will advances in sequencing the human genome change the way health care is delivered, managed, and personalized in the future? How will these changes affect insurance coverage and markets?

In the end, the debate will always come down to who pays for health care and how they pay for it. But whether you believe the answer lies in a single-payer government insurance plan, vigorous private sector competition, or some combination of the two, you can't really engage in an informed debate—and come to what Yankelovich described as public judgment—until and unless you study the issue from beginning to end, from its historical origins right through to its uncertain future.

It probably comes as a surprise to those who think of me as a doctrinaire liberal Democrat that I am sympathetic to the unfair burden our health care system has placed on the business community. It shouldn't. Like all Americans, I want our businesses to be profitable. In fact, I would argue that one of the key functions of government should be to help the private sector make profits. In return, private enterprise should contribute a reasonable share of these profits in support of public enterprise.

This is really the covenant that has held our nation together for more than two centuries. Think back to the earliest days of the republic. Farmers and frontiersmen raised and sold crops or opened up storefronts to support their families and put down roots in a community. If the farmer's barn or the frontiersman's store was destroyed in a fire, the whole community chipped in to rebuild it, contributing their time and resources for the common good. When the community grew large enough to need a sheriff, a school, a hospital, or any other public enterprise, everyone contributed a reasonable, proportional share to support it.

Capitalism in a democratic society has always meant striking a balance between the pursuit of profit and the common good, between individual liberty and the sense of community. If you have too much of one or the other, the balance is lost. Too much community and too little liberty, if carried to the extreme, is the Soviet Politburo and five-year plans. Too much liberty and too little community is Darwinian, dog-eat-dog, survival of the fittest.

There is, or should be, a comparable balance of responsibility between the public and private sectors. The private sector provides those goods and services from which it is appropriate to make a profit. The public sector provides those goods and services that are essential for the communal well-being and that do not lend themselves to profit-making enterprise.

I believe one of the ways government can help make American businesses more profitable in the twenty-first century is to make them more competitive in the international marketplace. The health insurance burden that American businesses bear is but one example of the competitive disadvantage they face. Another, equally alarming example is the declining purchasing power of the American middle class.

Henry Ford used to say he paid his employees very well so they could buy his cars. But over the last twenty years, the automobile assembly lines have been staffed by fewer workers and more robots. Technology has sharply reduced employment availability in many other industries as well. Fewer jobs mean lower wage capacity and reduced purchasing power for American workers. The domestic market is no longer robust enough to sustain many businesses, and they have to broaden their horizons to overseas markets.

China has 300 million upwardly mobile middle-class people right now, and hundreds of millions more aspiring to join them. India has a huge and growing middle class. It is not at all irrational for an American business to make the decision to hire workers in China and India and to sell its products to Chinese and Indian consumers. This will keep the business profitable by making it competitive in the world market.

And this decision will put more and more American workers out of a job.

This is where the public and private sectors must come together. European countries understand this. They provide their businesses with generous subsidies, and workers with substantial benefits. In return, the companies and workers contribute to public programs and services. More profit for businesses means more purchasing power for workers and larger contributions to the public good.

There is a social compact in which businesses should have the latitude to do what they want to do and government will provide whatever assistance it can to help ensure that their activities are profitable. In return, businesses are obliged to contribute to the government, and the government provides programs and services that make businesses more productive—health care, day care, a modern transportation system, continuing education, and training.

This is the compact I would like to see developed between the American business community and the federal government. Invest in private enterprise that generates profits and commit a significant portion of these profits to public enterprises—health care, day care, infrastructure, education—that will increase productivity and improve people's lives.

~~~~

I have a frightening vision of what may happen in New Jersey, and perhaps the whole country, in the not-too-distant future. At some point, I see the states reaching the inescapable conclusion that they cannot handle their responsibilities under existing tax systems. I see a governor—maybe New

Jersey's—going to the president and saying, "We can't do this anymore. Here are the keys to the State House."

Our federalist system regards the states as the laboratories of democracy, but they can't be good laboratories if they don't have adequate resources. The more they compete with each other for jobs and economic development, the greater the share of revenue they give away in the form of tax breaks and other financial incentives. As states keep competing with each other in this fashion, they continue stripping away the resources they need to solve their problems.

More important, if the states are in constant competition with each other, the United States becomes less competitive with the rest of the world. The competition for high-tech industry and jobs doesn't just pit California's Silicon Valley against New Jersey's Einstein Alley or North Carolina's Research Triangle. It pits all of them against Shenzhen, Seoul, and Bangalore. It is more important for the United States—emphasis on the word *united*—to attract and keep these industries and jobs than it is for any individual state to offer the most beneficent basket of tax breaks and other financial inducements.

Compounding the problem for most states is the unfortunate fact that the resources available to them are highly volatile. Alaska and Louisiana have no trouble balancing their budgets when oil prices are high, but when there's a dip in the world petroleum market, Alaskan schoolchildren and Louisiana senior citizens suffer. When the bottom drops out of the coal market, West Virginians lose their jobs—and West Virginia's state government loses a large chunk of its revenue.

Finally, more and more states—as well as cities, counties, and municipalities across the country—are burying themselves under mountains of debt. Wall Street is divided on the question of whether Illinois state bonds have already achieved "junk" status. New Jersey's bond rating isn't much better. Unlike the federal government, the annual budget of virtually every state and local government must be balanced, meaning that as bonded indebtedness eats up an ever-larger share of spending, other services and programs have to be cut.

Greater international competition. Unstable sources of revenue. Budgets constrained by debt. These are the conditions that confront the states as they seek to educate their children, care for their sick and elderly, house and feed their poor and needy, provide transportation for their commuters, supply clean water and adequate sewerage for their residents, and otherwise offer the full range of services citizens have a right to expect from their government.

It is time, in my view, for a new age of federalism that lifts the states—and, by extension, the United States—out of the self-imposed atrophy that is rooted in our insistence on treating new problems with old solutions. Issues are becoming increasingly complex. Globalization is putting greater pressure on the American economy. States are experiencing more demands on their dwindling resources. Yet we cling to an outdated jumble of fifty separate and distinct tax systems—a hodgepodge of taxes on income, sales, property, estates, corporate profits, and gross receipts; permit, license, and registration fees; highway, bridge, and tunnel tolls; and assorted forms of creative bookkeeping.

Some states, particularly those that host large military installations, receive bountiful federal subsidies to help them meet their financial obligations. They keep their taxes low, and they use their relative affordability to attract people and businesses. Other states receive far less from Washington than their citizens send there in the form of federal taxes, and the more prohibitive cost of living in these states makes it much harder to attract people and jobs.

When attention in Washington turns to tax reform, as it often does, the discussion almost always centers on how the federal tax structure should be revised and simplified. I believe it should focus on a much bigger picture: how government at all levels is raising and spending money.

A much fairer system of taxation would shift the burden of raising revenue from the states to the federal government, whether in the form of a national value-added tax, a carbon tax, or another source or combination of sources. The money would then be distributed to the states under strict guidelines ensuring that their traditional obligations—elementary, secondary, and higher education; public safety; health and social services; streets and highways; parks and recreation—are fully met.

Given the current political climate, I do not hold out much hope that this will happen in the near future. But we must not let the current climate constrain our thinking and advocacy. If nothing else, I hope the next generation of our states' and nation's leaders, the young people who have so impressed me as being more interested in civic affairs than in politics, are already thinking along these lines. I am counting on them to recognize and understand the dramatic economic and social changes that are already taking place and to frame the bigger picture of the challenges that lie ahead.

≈≈≈

More than anything else, what I hope the next generation of political leadership will achieve is the restoration of civil discourse to our public conversation.

I have fought many battles over the years—some of them bitter, intense, and protracted—in the state assembly, in Congress, and as governor of New Jersey. I have faced some pretty harsh criticism—from the insurance industry, the NRA, Hands Across New Jersey, and other groups that opposed the policy positions I took.

But within the political structure, even the bitterest opposition never turned personal. There were many Republicans in my five years in the assembly, and many more in my fifteen years in Congress, with whom I had stark disagreements. Many of them were sharply critical of bills I introduced and of statements I made supporting or opposing particular pieces of legislation.

At the end of the day, however, we shook hands and parted, perhaps not as close friends, but certainly not as mortal enemies. We recognized and acknowledged our differences, but with cordiality and respectfulness befitting our stature as representatives of the public interest. We could disagree over how we defined that interest without being disagreeable.

In Congress, some of my proudest accomplishments—the RCRA, the Superfund, the Pinelands, the Korean War Memorial—would not have been achieved without bipartisan support. Much of that support grew out of the personal relationships I developed with Republicans like Ed Madigan of Illinois and Norman Lent of New York.

It would be an understatement to observe that as governor, I was not widely liked by Republicans. In the midterm election of 1991, their legislative candidates campaigned hard, not so much against their Democratic opponents as against me. "Florio Free in '93" bumper stickers sometimes seemed ubiquitous. And after the Republicans won large majorities in both houses, they kept up a relentless attack against my administration and its policies.

The key word here, however, is *policies*. Assembly Majority Leader (and later Speaker) Chuck Haytaian was a hard-driving conservative whose mission, it seemed to me, was to be as much of a thorn in my side as Democrat Alan Karcher was to Republican governor Tom Kean a decade earlier. But Haytaian, like Karcher, drew a distinct line between policy disputes and personal attacks. In his public statements, he never questioned my sincerity, impugned my integrity, or attacked my character. In his personal dealings with me, he was always cordial and respectful.

Senate President Don DiFrancesco was, by nature, less combative than Haytaian. I believe it took considerable courage for him to stand up to the NRA when it came time for the upper house to either sustain or override my veto of the repeal of the assault weapons ban. Although this was an issue on which we happened to agree, there were many on which we did not. But we got along well personally, and we found ways—especially on economic development projects—to work through our differences and advance the public interest.

The second half of my governorship was not what I would characterize as an altogether pleasant experience. But as I think back to those days, I wonder how much more unpleasant they would have been if the political climate then had been as poisonous as it is today. I wonder, too, if we would have accomplished anything—on welfare reform, health policy, or economic development—if the public discourse had been allowed to descend to today's level.

There are any number of reasons Congress has become dysfunctional in recent years: gerrymandered districts, the outsized influence of lobbyists and special interests, the constant competition for campaign contributions, the increasing partisanship of both parties' base of voters. Still, the institution has the capacity to function as a great deliberative body, capable of turning "compromise" from a pejorative to an attribute, if its members would treat one another with civility instead of invective.

Americans take their cues from their leaders. When the political leadership of this country behaves badly, citizens behave badly. When it becomes commonplace for public figures to demean those with whom they disagree, it becomes acceptable for citizens to degrade and humiliate those who hold a different view, or speak a different language, or practice a different religion.

If, on the other hand, our leaders recognize that the challenges we face will be met only if we are united rather than divided, if our efforts are more collaborative than competitive, if our discourse is civil instead of vulgar, I am convinced that our resilient citizens will respond accordingly.

In 2017, after twenty years in Metuchen, Lucinda and I decided it was time to be nearer our grandchildren—and closer to my political roots—with a move to a lovely ranch house in Moorestown. My study looks out on a large backyard. Beyond that is a lane that is ideal for my daily four-mile walk, and a small lake that attracts a lot of geese. Our little pug, Margo, has taken on the responsibility of keeping the geese on their side of the property line.

My grandfather was a gardener. Now I'm one. My son Gregory built a couple of large flower beds, and I'm enjoying the fresh air and the peace and quiet of a pretty backyard in South Jersey. My law firm's Cherry Hill office is just a few miles away, in a region of the state I represented for so many years in Trenton and Washington. I have my card from the Moorestown Public Library. Lucinda is already getting to know everyone in the neighborhood, if not the whole town.

Life is good.

I want the life of my children and grandchildren to be just as good—even better, if that's possible. I want them to reap the benefits of living in the richest country on earth. I want them to be engaged and informed citizens, conscious of and concerned about the affairs of their community, their state, and their country.

I want them to reject simple solutions to complicated problems. I want them to tell their political leaders that they don't need to have explanations of complex issues reduced to the lowest common denominator; that they are willing to devote their time, their energy, and their intellect to gain a full understanding and appreciation of the issues facing us as a society. I want them to demand that their leaders be open and honest with them.

My hope for them, and for everyone, is that we will, as a nation, come to public judgment. We will take the time and make the effort to evaluate the issues, consider the options, and weigh the alternatives and then make rational decisions based on all the facts at our disposal.

If we can do this in a thoughtful, collaborative manner, America's best days will lie ahead. And I will have the comfort of knowing my grandchildren will reach the highest calling their "Pop Pop" could ask of them as citizens: they will truly be engaged and informed.

Acknowledgments

I am told there are authors who actually sit down and write every word that appears in a book that bears their name. I am not one of these authors.

People who know me well will attest to the fact that I enjoy talking much more than I enjoy writing. Talking is easy; writing is hard. Throughout my career—as a lawyer, congressman, governor, teacher, and businessman—I have generally set my thoughts down not on paper but on tape. Then I review the transcription and, sometimes with the help of friends and/or colleagues, edit and refine the final product.

That is how this book was written.

I am deeply grateful to Fred Hillmann and Rona Parker, who got the book started with more than a dozen interviews conducted at my dining room table over a period of nearly a year. Fred and Rona peppered me with questions about my upbringing, my formative years, my congressional and gubernatorial experiences, and the many lessons I have learned over a half-century in public life. We then had the tapes transcribed, and the editing and refining process began.

The task of turning my sometimes rambling (and often inarticulate) thoughts into coherent sentences can be arduous. Equally daunting is the responsibility for fact-checking my admittedly faulty memory. Rick Sinding did both with extraordinary skill. He reviewed all the tapes, filled in the gaps with follow-up questions, made sure my memories of events comported with factual accounts, drafted the chapters, and sat down with me for lengthy and often laborious editing sessions, all of which culminated in the completion of this book. It would not have been finished without Rick's diligence and talent.

I am thankful, too, to the Center on the American Governor at Rutgers University's Eagleton Institute of Politics. Under the able leadership of John Weingart, it has built an impressive archive of my term as governor, as well as those of Brendan Byrne, Tom Kean, and Christine Todd Whitman. These archives include extensive videotaped interviews with administration officials, legislators, and observers of the political process during our governorships, along with panel discussions focused on the major issues that we confronted during our terms in office. This book now becomes an added piece of this archive.

The project of turning this book from a collection of audiotapes into a written manuscript was helped immeasurably by the contributions of a six-member steering committee: George Zoffinger, Rick Wright, Brenda Bacon, Karen Kessler, Angelo Genova, and Harry Pozycki. They, together with my law partners—Mike Perrucci, Doug Steinhardt, and the late Paul Fader—helped generate support for the project from a wide variety of sources, including many people who have worked for me and with me in both the public and private sectors.

Brenda Bacon and Rick Wright were among those who performed another important role in the preparation of this book: ensuring the accuracy of my recollection of certain facts and events. Carl Van Horn, David Applebaum, Greg Lawler, Joe Salema, Steve Weinstein, Amy Mansue, Russ Molloy, Laura Sanders, and Jon Shure were also very helpful in reviewing portions of the book. All of them have given me valuable advice and counsel over the years—and their guidance on this project was no exception.

Keeping my life organized is a full-time job for my exceptional assistant, Susan O'Neill. Her administrative skills are exceeded only by her unfailing cheerfulness, both of which she exhibited in abundance throughout the preparation of this book.

Finally, I want to thank my wife Lucinda. As I point out in the book, meeting and marrying Lucinda changed my life. She has stood by me and supported me through good times and tough times. She has read every word of this book and has not been afraid to challenge me when she thinks I have either been too forthcoming or too reticent. I know—and Lucinda knows—that she is fervently protective of me. But neither of us would have it any other way.

Moorestown, New Jersey
December 2017

Index